Smoking in Adolescence
Images and Identities

Barbara Lloyd and Kevin Lucas

and
Janet Holland, Sheena McGrellis
and Sean Arnold

ROUTLEDGE

London and New York

First published 1998 by Routledge
11 New Fetter Lane, London EC4P 4EE

Simultaneously published in the USA and Canada
by Routledge
29 West 35th Street, New York, NY 10001

Typeset in Times by Pure Tech India Ltd, Pondicherry
Printed and bound in Great Britain by
Redwood Books, Trowbridge, Wiltshire

British Library Cataloguing in Publication Data
A catalogue record for this book is available from the British Library

Library of Congress Cataloging in Publication Data
Lloyd, Barbara B. (Barbara Bloom), 1933–
    Smoking in adolescence: images and identities/Barbara Lloyd and
Kevin Lucas, and Janet Holland, Sheena McGrellis, and Sean Arnold.
        p.   cm.
    Includes bibliographical references and index.
    1. Youth–Tobacco use–England.   2. Youth–England–Social
conditions.   3. Adolescent psychology–England.   4. Health behavior
in adolescence–England.   I. Lucas, Kevin, 1954– .   II. Holland,
Janet   III. McGrellis, Sheena.   IV. Arnold, Sean.   V. Title.
HV5745.L56   1998
362.296'0835'0941–dc21   97–37982

ISBN 0-415-17859-2 (hbk)
ISBN 0-415-17860-6 (pbk)

Dedicated to Kevin's mother and father, and to the memory of Barbara's parents

Contents

Figures

Tables

x   *Tables*

Preface

Smoking in Adolescence is the product of an intellectual collaboration which has continued for almost a decade. Originally begun in the context of doctoral supervision, it matured into a reciprocal exploration of ideas and data. Our use throughout the text of the pronoun 'we' reflects our shared perspective.

Our study of smoking prevalence among adolescent girls was part of an initiative funded by the Department of Health. The other part of this work is the London study on protective factors in adolescent smoking undertaken by Dr Janet Holland, Sheena McGrellis and Sean Arnold. The two enterprises are brought together in this book to provide an extensive contemporary view of adolescent smoking.

Much of the research on adolescent smoking has been undertaken from a medically-oriented, largely middle-aged perspective. Researchers have long used the term 'risk behaviour' to characterise those activities that pose some immediate or distant threat to adolescent health. This notion has been taken up enthusiastically by those who study aspects of young people's recreational activities. Their list of 'risk' or latterly 'problem' behaviours includes smoking, drinking, the use of illicit substances, and aspects of sexuality. Value judgements about the 'kind' of adolescents who engage in this behaviour have resulted in descriptions of a 'syndrome'. The list of behaviours associated with smoking that pose a threat to adolescents' health seems to grow and grow. This line of argument culminated in a recent claim that early tobacco and alcohol use is linked not only to the use of illicit substances and to more permissive sexual attitudes, but even to carrying weapons. This so-called 'gateway' explanation has been invoked frequently throughout the Western world, but has so far failed to provide interventions which succeed in modifying young people's recreational behaviour.

At this point, it is useful to step back from such debate and ask whether the ever-increasing list of factors that pose a risk to teenagers is getting out of hand. Is it really so surprising that adolescents who use cannabis also smoke tobacco, given that they are ordinarily smoked together? Is it completely unexpected to find that young smokers who have had unprotected intercourse may also have consumed alcohol? Can it really be inferred that a clandestine cigarette in the playground leads to the carrying of knives and guns?

There is a very real danger that the association of smoking with such widely disparate behaviours misses the real point: *that smoking actually fulfils a variety of functions in the everyday lives of many adolescents*. Moreover, the lack of successful interventions may lie in the very different views of the world held by medically oriented academics and by teenagers themselves.

Throughout the book we seek to maintain an awareness of the meaning and function of smoking in adolescent lives. In the first chapter we review more extensively the notions of risk and problem behaviours. This is followed in Chapter 2 by an examination of questions of research methodology. Two studies, in Sussex and London respectively, are introduced in Chapter 3, and smoking prevalence is considered. The social environments in which adolescent development are examined in Chapters 4 and 5. We explore psychological dimensions such as stress and coping, body image, and mood and pleasure in Chapter 6. The meanings of cigarette smoking to adolescents are considered extensively in Chapters 7 and 8. Chapter 9 is concerned with school interventions, and raises issues related to risk and protective factors. In the final chapter, we consider prospects for reducing adolescent cigarette smoking in the wider context of adolescent life.

We would like to acknowledge the contribution of Dr Liza Catán from the Department of Health, who provided inspiration, encouragement and resources. Dr Sandra Williams and our Advisory Group ensured the successful completion of our project.

A number of colleagues contributed importantly. First among these is Hugh Graham, who not only encouraged Kevin Lucas to pursue his doctorate but also gave his support at every stage of the study reported here. David Hitchin provided invaluable expertise in data analysis. The successful completion of the study owes much to Shaun Dugan's social-psychological knowledge and data-processing skills. Neil Jacobs and Helen Cramer carried out much of the qualitative analysis. Dr Rod Bond and Dr Helga Dittmar gave support in framing the project.

Throughout this book we attempt to view the issue of adolescent cigarette smoking from a new perspective. Explorations of young people's views about the *meanings* of smoking are examined in order to compensate for the judgement-laden approach of middle-aged investigators (like ourselves) that has characterised earlier research about cigarette smoking in adolescence.

Barbara Lloyd and Kevin Lucas
May 1997

Acknowledgements

The authors acknowledge the following as the sources for the quotations used at the beginning of each chapter:

F. Farley (1985) 'Stimulation seeking behaviour in adolescence'. In R. Blackman, G. Brown, D. Cox, S. Sheps and R. Tonkin (eds.) *Proceedings of a Conference on Adolescent risk-taking behaviour*. Vancouver: University of British Columbia.

Frank Zappa (1989; written with Peter Occhiogrosso) *The Real Frank Zappa Book*, ch. 17.

A. Schultz (1963) 'Concept and theory formation in the Social Sciences'. In M. A. Natanson (ed.) *Philosophy of the Social Sciences*. New York: Random House.

Katherine Whitehorn (1970) 'Suffer How Many of the Little Children?', in *Observations*.

Elizabeth Janeway (1981) 'Incest: A Rational Look at the Oldest Taboo', in *Ms*.

Oscar Wilde (1891) *The Picture of Dorian Gray*, ch. 6.

Robert Doisneau (1992) in *Weekend Guardian*, April.

Erich Fromm (1955) 'Sense of Identify' in *The Sane Society*, ch. 3.

Henri-Frédéric Amiel (1882) in *Journal Intime*.

Lewis Carroll (1865) *Alice's Adventures in Wonderland*, ch. 6.

Helene Deutsch (1944–5) *The Psychology of Women*, vol. 1.

1 'Problem behaviour', sensation seeking and the concept of risk

Telling adolescents to 'Just say no' is like telling Christopher
Columbus to stay home.

F. Farley

For more than two decades, a disparate range of activities that
become prevalent in adolescence have been brought together and
viewed collectively as 'problem behaviours'. These activities include
cigarette smoking, drinking alcohol, taking illicit drugs, early sexual
intercourse, as well as various forms of delinquency. Our opening
chapter examines the origins of this concept, describes its later formulations, notes specifically developmental aspects of the theory and
considers its role in understanding adolescent health-related behaviours.

During the late 1960s, the United States and Western Europe
witnessed the rise of a phenomenon which was soon to become
known as 'youth culture'. Unprecedentedly large numbers of young
people spoke both articulately and vociferously against many of the
institutions, traditions and values of the establishment. Within one
generation, adolescents' and young adults' styles of dress and music,
political affiliations, attitudes towards sexuality and drugs (notably
marijuana) suddenly became so radically *different* from those of their
parents that the effect on the latter was profoundly disturbing. This
effect was especially acute in the United States, where continued
American involvement with the much-resented war in Vietnam
became a focused manifestation of the new schism between parents
and their children.

The iconoclastic nature of the 1960s youth movement was worrying
for governments and for academics alike. For politicians, the promulgation of such values and an attractively persuasive advocacy of
alternative lifestyles challenged a previously unquestioned assumption: that all power was located within the confines of adulthood in
general, and material wealth in particular. Social scientists, on the
other hand, appeared impotent because no adequate contemporary
explanations were available for the phenomenon's origins, and no one

could predict how long it was going to last. The resultant tension placed considerable pressure on social psychologists and sociologists to produce theories in order to explain what many regarded as a dangerously anarchic trend.

One of the most influential approaches to the problem was developed in the United States, by Richard and Shirley Jessor. They described how

> Youthful leadership in opposing an egregiously unpopular war, in innovating alternative ways of living, and in mounting sustained criticism of established norms and institutions had not been anticipated by the larger society and constituted, for many, a disconcerting challenge.
>
> (Jessor and Jessor, 1977: 3)

To address this issue, Jessor and Jessor undertook a large-scale longitudinal study of American high school and college students. The result of this study was the development of 'problem behaviour theory', which is still used widely today. It is from this background that many studies of adolescent health-related behaviours have arisen. Such has been the power of the associations revealed by problem behaviour theory, both within the social sciences and among other professionals who work with adolescents and young adults, that it is appropriate for this book to begin with an examination of its main tenets and findings.

PROBLEM BEHAVIOUR THEORY

Problem behaviour theory considers activities such as smoking, alcohol use and sexual behaviour to be a product of three major systems, and each of these systems is in turn viewed as comprising a number of component structures.

The first of these systems is the *personality system*. According to the theory, the personality system is seen as being composed of three structures:

1 The motivational-instigation structure. This structure is concerned with both the goals towards which an individual strives, and the sources which instigate certain behaviours. Whether an individual performs certain behaviour towards a given goal is determined by the value placed upon that goal in relation to alternative goals, and by similar variation in expectation of attaining that particular goal.

2 The personal belief structure. This consists of factors which constrain an individual from engaging in problem behaviours; these are social criticism, alienation, self-esteem and locus of control. Social criticism is used in this context to mean the degree of acceptance or rejection of societal norms.[1]
3 The personal control structure. This component of the theory refers to an individual's control against 'unconventional' behaviour. While there is likely to be some overlap with parts of the motivational-instigation structure, the personal control structure is more directly related to the problem behaviour itself, and allows for a separate examination of variables in the former which may be linked only distally to the behaviour in question. The personal control structure contains three variables: attitudinal tolerance of deviance; religiosity; and the discrepancy between reasons for and against engaging in problem behaviours.

The second of the three systems which comprise problem behaviour theory is the *perceived environment system.* This is considered to be composed of a distal structure and a proximal structure.

1 The distal structure of the perceived environment system is conceptualised as being the product of an adolescent's orientation towards his/her parents and peers, and the nature of those relationships. How an adolescent relates to these is seen to be expressed by his/her perceptions of support and control from both parents and peers, and the compatibility of expectations on the adolescent from these two sources. Also included in the distal structure is the adolescent's perception of the relative influence of peers and parents on their own behaviour. The assumption is that a greater orientation towards parents compared to peers will result in an alignment with more conventional codes of behaviour and thus to a decreased likelihood of engaging in problem behaviour. Conversely, a greater orientation towards peers is expected to be associated with an increased likelihood of engaging in such activities.
2 The proximal structure of the perceived environment is primarily concerned with two factors: the prevalence of problem behaviour in the individual's environment, and the presence or absence of social support for the behaviour in question. Such social support is seen as a continuum from lack of disapproval through to active encouragement. For example, a teenager will be more likely to experiment with drugs in an area where their use is widespread than in one where drug use is rare, and is more likely to do so if encouraged to

experiment by his or her friends. Again, such factors are considered in the context of both parents and peers.

The third and final structure on which problem behaviour theory is based is the *behaviour system*. This has two main structures: problem behaviour and conventional behaviour.

1 Jessor and Jessor viewed problem behaviour in relation to activism, drug use, sexual intercourse, alcohol use and misuse, and what they term 'general deviant behaviour' – meaning stealing, lying, vandalism, disruptive behaviour and aggression.[2]
2 Conventional behaviour, on the other hand, is considered only superficially by the theory and was assessed in terms of church attendance, together with academic involvement and achievement.[3]

All these components are seen by the theory as interrelated and work with (or against) each other to produce problem (or conventional) behaviours. It is these processes that are held to account for the co-occurrence of the various 'problem' behaviours described above. The result of this work has been the notion that such behaviours form a 'syndrome', an idea that has been investigated by many social researchers.

PROBLEM BEHAVIOURS AND SENSATION SEEKING

An alternative explanation for the co-occurrence of certain behaviours in adolescence has been proposed by Zuckerman (1979). Zuckerman's concept of 'sensation seeking' has, like Jessor and Jessor's problem behaviour theory, become influential among researchers in recent years and has resulted in several hundred published studies based on its premises. The causes of sensation-seeking behaviour are thought to be very complex and multi-faceted, and to include explanations based in psychological factors such as personality and individual differences, as well as in physiology and genetics (Zuckerman, 1994). Zuckerman proposes that many behaviours such as smoking, drinking, drug use and sexual intercourse have a common feature: they are likely to be particularly attractive to individuals who are score highly on a measure known as the sensation-seeking scale (SSS). Individuals who score less highly on the SSS will be less likely, therefore, to engage in such activities. Various forms of the scale have been produced, and Zuckerman's most recent version (1994) consists of items which address four factors:

- Thrill and adventure seeking. Included in this factor is the desire to engage in sports and other physically risky activities, and a tendency to find enjoyment in experiences that are mildly frightening.
- Experience seeking. This factor describes the seeking of novel experiences such as music, art, travel and through a kind of 'bohemian' social nonconformity similar to that described by Jessor and Jessor.
- Disinhibition. These items in the scale measure a tendency towards sensation through activities which are unconventional or illegal.
- Boredom susceptibility. A low tolerance of boredom and routine is held to increase a tendency towards sensation seeking, and this tendency is measured by appropriate items in the SSS.

Early results using the SSS showed that young adults who had high scores on the scale were much more likely to be smokers compared to their contemporaries who had low scores (67 per cent against 18 per cent respectively; Zuckerman *et al.*, 1972). More than a decade later, despite a drop in the proportion of smokers overall, a sample of similar age still showed more smokers in the high sensation-seeking group with very few low sensation-seeking subjects having ever smoked (Zuckerman, 1988). The sensation-seeking explanation of smoking behaviour appears to have high cross-cultural applicability and has produced comparable results in samples of the general American population (Zuckerman and Neeb, 1980), British male adolescents (Golding *et al.*, 1983), Norwegian adolescents (Pederson *et al.*, 1989), Dutch adults (Feij and van Zuilen, 1984) and adolescents in Israel (Teichman *et al.*, 1989).

The clustering of certain behaviours seen in Jessor and Jessor's problem behaviour theory is echoed by the findings of later applications of Zuckerman's concept of sensation seeking. Since these early studies, sensation seeking has been demonstrated to be associated with adolescent alcohol use and misuse, marijuana use, with the use of amphetamines, barbiturates, cocaine and opiates, and with multiple drug usage in a number of studies, as well as with delinquency (see Zuckerman, 1994, for review).

In a similar manner, the evidence in support of problem behaviour theory has accumulated in recent years, and a high degree of co-occurrence between delinquency, school failure, substance misuse and high-risk sexual behaviour has been reported in American teenagers (Barone *et al.*, 1995).

The notion of 'high-risk' sexual behaviours has become more prevalent and prominent since the appearance of HIV/AIDS on both sides of the Atlantic, and has become the subject of a number of studies undertaken from a problem behaviour perspective. In a study of American teenagers, Biglan *et al.* (1990) investigated the relationship between problem behaviours such as academic difficulties, smoking, alcohol use, other drug use, antisocial behaviour and low levels of self-reported prosocial behaviour with engagement in a variety of high-risk sexual activities. The latter included high numbers of sexual partners, having sex with partners not well known, partners having sex with others, partners injecting drugs, the non-use of condoms and anal intercourse. He and his colleagues found clear evidence that adolescents were more likely to engage in such high-risk sexual behaviours if they were also involved in other problem behaviours. This finding is particularly important in the context of HIV prevention programmes. While early sexual intercourse has been associated with other problem behaviours since Jessor and Jessor's original work with American teenagers, it had not been shown previously that adolescents who were involved in problem behaviours were also more likely to engage in specific sexual behaviours which put them at particular risk of HIV infection. It is of note that cigarette smoking was a strong and independent predictor of high-risk sexual activity in every analysis Biglan and his co-workers undertook. A model of risky sexual behaviour was used by Metzler *et al.* (1994) in a similar investigation of adolescent sexual behaviour, but in this study a particular focus was the influence of peer and family factors which have previously been associated with problem behaviour in adolescents. Adolescents whose peers were reported to engage in diverse problem behaviours were found to be more likely to engage in risky sexual behaviours. Poor parental monitoring and lower availability of parental figures within the family were also factors.

Thus, the weight of evidence for the existence of some form of 'syndrome' of problematic behaviours in adolescence seemed to increase across twenty years of research findings, and the list of behaviours included in the problem behaviour cluster has also grown. It has now been shown to include psychopathology such as conduct disorders (Lavery and Siegel, 1993). However, Zuckerman concluded that

> Sensation seeking is a normal trait of personality. Unlike Neuroticism, there is no necessary association with behaviour disorder at either extreme of the trait.... Sensation seeking seems to be a necessary but not sufficient ingredient of an antisocial personality.
>
> (1994: 283)

Much of the work that has demonstrated links between the various forms of problem behaviours has been correlational in nature. It is also true that some factor-analytic studies (e.g. Farrell *et al.*, 1992) have found that not only are measures of problem behaviour positively correlated with each other, but these measures are negatively correlated with measures of conventional behaviour. Furthermore, Farrell and his colleagues performed confirmatory factor analyses which replicated those of previous studies; according to their data, a single common factor appeared to underlie adolescent problem behaviours such as smoking, alcohol and marijuana use, delinquency and early sexual intercourse.

However, it should be noted that not all studies wholly support the view that problem behaviour represents a single domain. By contrast, other factor-analytic studies have provided a different perspective. For example, DeCourville (1995) tested the utility of the theory in accounting for substance use in a large sample of Canadian adolescents. In her longitudinal study, she found that attempts to fit models that included variables from all the structures proposed by problem behaviour theory were unsuccessful, in that the final models varied substantially from the hypothesised model, from one data wave to another, and by gender. Using an abridged model, however, she managed to replicate Jessor and Jessor's results. Similarly, Tildesley *et al.* (1995) used a multi-trait, multi-method design to test the theory. Their findings seem to threaten the validity of problem behaviour theory. Results of their hierarchical confirmatory factor analyses indicate that the convergent and discriminant validity of the behaviour constructs was high and that method effects were low. By contrast, a two-factor, second-order model which represented general drug use and other problem behaviours accounted for a larger proportion of variance in the lower-order factors compared to the traditional single-factor model.

RECENT DEVELOPMENTS IN PROBLEM BEHAVIOUR THEORY

Problem behaviour theory has moved on since its conception as a single syndrome. The theory is no longer a direct response to behaviours which threatened the American establishment in the 1970s, and more sophisticated explanations are currently available. The most important of these conceptual developments concerns the relationships of *risk factors* and *protective factors*. Stice and Barrera (1995) used a longitudinal study to explore the *reciprocal* relationship between adolescents' perceptions of the parenting they received at home and their own substance use. They adopted a model proposed by earlier workers (Lerner and Spanier, 1978; Sameroff, 1975) in which not only does parenting affect children's behaviour, but children's behaviour also affects parenting. They also recognised that the lack of a strong parent–child bond may increase the likelihood that adolescents will affiliate with a deviant peer group (Jacob *et al.*, 1991). Half of their sample was considered at risk for problem behaviour as a result of their parents' alcohol abuse. They found full prospective reciprocal relationships between perceived parenting and adolescent substance use. Deficits in both parental support and parental control prospectively predicted adolescent substance use, and adolescent substance use was prospectively related to lower levels of parental support and parental control. Moreover, their analyses revealed that the reciprocal effects between adolescent substance use and parenting behaviours were of approximately equal magnitude. It has been suggested that parents promote problem behaviour because of inconsistent disciplinary measures and deficits in monitoring (Patterson *et al.*, 1989). Stice and Barrera's study provides strong evidence in support of this proposal. They also suggest that if adolescent problem behaviour raises parental tolerance of such behaviour, this will result in decreased attempts at parental control. In addition, if parents reject adolescents who engage in problem behaviours, the decreased quality of their relationship with their children is likely to result in further deviant behaviour, and so on.

RISK FACTORS, PROTECTIVE FACTORS AND PROBLEM BEHAVIOURS

Many factors have been examined which appear to be protective against engaging in problem behaviours. Garmezy (1985) provides a useful categorisation of these factors into three groups:

- dispositional attributes, such as high self-efficacy;
- family attributes, such as parental support and parental affection; and
- extrafamilial circumstances, such as support from other adults, or strong community integration.

Other authors have considered such factors as bonding to conventional society (Hawkins *et al.*, 1992) and high religiosity (Newcomb and Felix-Ortiz, 1992). The reciprocal nature of what may be seen to be protective factors (such as good relationships with parents) and problem behaviour has been addressed by Richard Jessor and his colleagues in more recent work (Jessor *et al.*, 1995). They conducted a study of the relation of protective factors to involvement in problem behaviour (alcohol and drug misuse, delinquency and sexual precocity). The protective factors they considered were drawn from personality, from the adolescents' perceived environment and from behaviour components of problem behaviour theory. A large number of such variables have been identified. For the purposes of the 1995 study, seven protective variables were used:

- a positive orientation towards school;
- a positive orientation towards health;
- intolerant attitudes towards deviance (and religiosity in later parts of the study);
- positive relations with adults;
- strong perceived controls;
- friends who engage in conventional behaviour; and
- involvement in prosocial behaviours (e.g. voluntary work and family activities).

By contrast, six risk variables were utilised:

- low expectations for success;
- low self-esteem;
- a general sense of hopelessness;
- friends who engage in problem behaviours;
- a greater orientation towards friends than towards parents; and
- poor school achievement.

Problem behaviour was found to show a significant inverse relationship to protective factors. There was also a significant interaction between protection and risk in the prediction of problem behaviour. Protection was shown to *moderate* the relationship of risk to problem behaviour. Protective factors were also found to be significant predictors of change in adolescent problem behaviours over time, and these direct effects of protection were found to be consistent across all the gender and racial/ethnic subgroups in the large sample of American urban teenagers studied by Jessor *et al.*

Risk factors were seen to increase problem behaviour directly in two ways. The first was direct instigation as a result of peer pressure or peer encouragement. Secondly, risk factors seem to increase an individual adolescent's vulnerability to normative transgression: for example, adolescents in lower socio-economic groups who have low self-esteem may engage in problem behaviours because they feel they have little personal value or worth.[4] Jessor *et al.* (1995: 931) concluded that

> Psychosocial protective factors appear to play an important role in the aetiology and developmental course of adolescent problem behaviour... scientific attention should be broadened beyond its traditional preoccupation with risk factors to encompass variation in protection as well. Protective factors have been shown to relate both directly and indirectly to adolescent involvement in problem behaviour – the greater the protection, the less the problem behaviour – and, in interaction with risk factors, protective factors can moderate their relation[ship] to problem behaviour.

This interaction and reciprocity of risk and protective factors is important in attempting to understand the causes of problem behaviours in general and, in this volume, adolescent cigarette smoking. However, a further principle is essential to this process. Beyth-Marom *et al.* (1993) asked a sample of both adolescents and adults to list possible consequences of either accepting or declining opportunities to engage in various potentially risky behaviours. These activities were the same as those considered in many applications of problem behaviour theory (drinking and driving, smoking marijuana, truancy from school, sexual intercourse, drinking alcohol, etc.). Adults and adolescents produced similar response patterns, suggesting that they shared similar beliefs about the possibilities involved.

However, the most important finding was that although taking and avoiding a given risk may seem to be logically complementary (or opposite) actions, *they did not prove to be psychologically complementary*. Similarly, different consequences were perceived for one-off and repeated engagement in the same risky activities. Almost all previous research has assumed (at least tacitly, if not explicitly) a symmetrical relationship between the perceived consequences of accepting and rejecting a given risky option: Beyth-Marom and her colleagues have demonstrated that this assumption is not warranted. They note that

> This explanation of the psychological difference between taking and not taking an action is supported by the observation that negated consequences were mentioned almost exclusively as results of not doing the focal action. Perhaps people sometimes find it easier to think about *in*action by focusing on the complementary action. They almost never do the opposite (talk about the good or bad consequences that they may be missing by taking an action). By

focusing on direct consequences of their actions, people may neglect the opportunity costs of actions that they have forgone. It is an open empirical question whether decisions are naturally formulated in terms of one alternative or competing ones.

(Beyth-Marom *et al.*, 1993: 560)

One of us (K.L.) has noted similar discrepancies in beliefs held by women who smoke during pregnancy regarding the consequences of stopping smoking or continuing to smoke (Lucas, 1994). In this study, quite *different* (rather than *opposite*) outcomes were envisaged as a result of stopping smoking compared to continuing to smoke. While acknowledging the most widely publicised outcomes of smoking during pregnancy (low-birthweight babies, pregnancy complications) as being the most likely outcome of continuing to smoke, the women in this study perceived other, unrelated outcomes (such as increased self-esteem) as being the most likely should they stop. It is essential, therefore, to consider that the perceived outcomes or consequences of not engaging in problem behaviours *are not simply the mirror-images of engaging in them*. Thus, 'doing' an action may be seen as having outcomes A, B, or C. However, 'not doing' the same action may be seen as having outcomes D, E or F. The important principle expounded here is that these two *sets* of outcomes can be *orthogonal* (independent of each other) rather than *opposite* to each other.

Thus, while smokers may agree that smoking can be injurious to health, their most important beliefs about stopping smoking may have nothing whatever to do with health. Many health education campaigns rely primarily on listing the risks of smoking that can be avoided (by stopping) as the major reasons for cessation. Failure to take account of the independence of the perceived consequences of stopping smoking and continuing to smoke may explain their lack of success.

DEVELOPMENTAL ASPECTS OF PROBLEM BEHAVIOUR

In this final section, adolescent problem behaviour is considered from a developmental perspective. At its simplest, this includes empirical observations about the orderly progression from one behaviour that adults label 'risky' to others that appear to involve greater risk. From there we move on to an examination of adolescents' own perceptions of risk and to consideration of two theories that seek to chart changes in the perception and willingness, during the years of adolescence, to engage in behaviour described by adults as risky. The first theory considers the nature of decision making and the acquisition of skills that enable more mature decisions. The second describes developmental changes in the personal meaning of risky behaviour and seeks to illustrate the connections between this construct and adolescents' histories of their selves and their relationships.

The most benign approach to risk taking in adolescence is the view that the period between childhood and adult life is bound to be a time of experimentation as part of a search for identity (Erickson, 1950). As we noted earlier, historical events of protest in the 1960s provoked adult concern, and social scientists began systematic study of behaviour that such people perceived to be problematic (Jessor and Jessor, 1977). Efforts to explain these 'problem behaviours' have focused variously upon a lack of information among the young, the influence of reckless peers as well as the view that such behaviours are the response to the emotional and social stresses of this period of great change.

An empirical approach to the issue of change has highlighted a progression from the use of alcohol to the smoking of marijuana and finally to the uptake of hard drugs. The *theory of statistical independence* relies upon prevalence rates and onset ages to assert that adolescents use alcohol before marijuana because they are able to gain access to alcohol before they are exposed to marijuana. The *gateway theory* accounts for the orderly progression by viewing alcohol as necessary though not sufficient to result in the use of marijuana. As we have already seen, the *problem behaviour approach* postulates that adolescents progress from health to problem behaviour through stress and lack of resources necessary to remain problem free. Although all three theories have been invoked to explain this development, only problem behaviour theory is concerned specifically with psychosocial processes.

A methodologically sophisticated test of these three theories was recently undertaken by examining the use of alcohol, marijuana and hard drugs among adolescents aged 13 to 18 in the United States (Miller, 1994). Miller used data from four large surveys and sampled White, Black and Hispanic teenagers. Although the statistical independence theory was supported by examinations of the prevalence of four conditions (no use, alcohol only, alcohol and marijuana, alcohol, marijuana and hard drugs), there was some evidence for the problem behaviour theory too. When only the two conditions (no use and use of all three substances) were examined, there was an improvement in predictive value. Miller showed that the uptake pattern he found applied across age, gender and ethnic groups. Differences in prevalence and age of onset may function as statistically independent factors influencing progression, but this effect is exaggerated by the practices of the group that never used any substance and by the behaviour of individuals in the group that used all of them.

In a paper concerned with risk taking during adolescence, Furby and Beyth-Marom (1992) adopted a decision-making perspective which enabled them to compare adolescent and adult decisions. They defined risky behaviour as an action, or indeed an inaction, that involved a possibility of loss, and risk taking as engaging in such behaviour. Furby and Beyth-Marom described decision-making theory, whether viewed normatively or behaviourally, as involving five steps. These are:

- identification of alternative courses of action or inaction;
- identification of the consequences of each alternative course of action/inaction;
- evaluation of the consequences of each alternative;
- assessment of the likelihood of each alternative;
- use of a 'decision rule', e.g. subjective expected utility (SEU), to combine the four.

While the normative model focuses on the decision process, actual decision making is the focus of the behavioural model. Whatever decision rule is invoked, the identification of alternatives and their consequences, evaluation of consequences and assessment of likelihood were shown to reflect individuals' perceptions of the situation and their values.

The example of risky adolescent behaviour that Furby and Beyth-Marom analysed to demonstrate the usefulness of a decision-making perspective was drug taking. First, they used the model to analyse adolescent decision-making processes and then compared these to adult perceptions of the same event. They proposed that a teenager at a party where marijuana was smoked had two alternatives: to smoke or not to smoke it. In describing consequences, they asserted that there were both positive and negative aspects attached to each alternative. Smoking could produce a sense of physical well-being and group solidarity, but it could also lead to fear of addiction or guilt feelings about letting parents down. On the other hand, not smoking, or inaction, could lead to a sense of increased self-worth, or to a fear of ostracism by peers. In evaluating the consequences of each alternative there were differences in the desire for pleasurable experiences and in the need to be part of the peer group, or to preserve good relations with parents. Again, there were individual differences in an assessment of the likelihood of consequences. Some adolescents may dismiss the possibility of addiction while others are deeply concerned with it. Similarly, some may view drug taking as a route to peer acceptance while others doubt its potency as a route to popularity. Finally, the rules of combination may vary such that fear of loss, for example, of peer acceptance, could override other considerations of SEU.

Adult decision-making may differ from that of adolescents on each of the five steps. Rather than two alternatives, adults (including a certain US President) have suggested that one could 'fake' smoking and not inhale. Again, in judging consequences, adults may evaluate the impact of peer rejection less harshly than do adolescents and fail to recognise that teenagers may gain a sense of self-competence from being able to handle soft drugs. Although Furby and Beyth-Marom offered no empirical evidence to support their comparisons of adolescent and adult identification of alternatives and consequences, they provide a research finding on condom use that has been viewed as analogous. It may show differences in the evaluation of consequences by adults and adolescents. Kegeles, Adler and Irwin (1988, as cited in Furby and Beyth-Marom, 1992) found that intention to use condoms was unrelated to beliefs about their effectiveness in preventing pregnancy and the spread of infection but correlated with beliefs about ease of use and acceptance by peers. This finding demonstrates that adolescents and adults attach different value to the consequences of condom use. Similarly, adolescents and adults ascribe different likelihoods of negative outcomes to the same action. Empirical evidence shows that adolescents and young adults rate nuclear power and pesticides as more risky than do adults, but conversely young people consider hunting and mountain climbing less risky than adults do (Shtarkshail, 1986, as cited in Furby and Beyth-Marom, 1992). Finally, there is little doubt that while few people examine every alternative in order to calculate SEU (that is, systematically employ SEU theory), it is equally true that adolescents and adults may invoke different decision rules. Unfortunately, there is no empirical evidence available to evaluate this hypothesis.

Furby and Beyth-Marom (1992) provide a clear description of our current understanding about the development of mature decision making while describing the limits of present knowledge. They listed four aspects of such a theory. The first aspect, discrimination of good and bad decision making, could be considered to rest upon the maximisation of SEU. A limit of this approach has been the difficulty in determining whether the failure to find a strong relationship between components of SEU and decision choices reflects adolescents' failure to maximise utilities or investigators' failure to identify adolescents' beliefs and values accurately enough to be reflected in choices. Second, in so far as decision making is viewed as skilled behaviour there is a need to specify the components of the process. In the absence of such a model, it is hardly surprising that the third aspect of a theory of the development of mature decision making, specification of the acquisition of specific skills such as estimating probabilities, is also limited. Finally, there is the ubiquitous problem of domain specificity. Do decision-making skills develop simultaneously in all areas? Perhaps risky behaviours, with their emotional components, pose a greater challenge for the maximisation of subjective utilities.

The model proposed by Levitt and Selman (1996) examines actual risk-taking behaviour using the construct personal meaning, which mediates two psychosocial factors that shape it, knowledge and management. These authors deliberately chose a wide age group to study in order to increase variability among young people themselves rather than resorting to a comparison of adolescents and adults. Their research included 9- to 10-year-old pre-adolescents through to 16-year-olds. It documented the development of understanding of risk-taking behaviour in terms of self and relationships with family and friends. The roots of the theory are in Selman's (1980) earlier work on the development of interpersonal understanding.

Just as personal meaning influences two-component factors, so knowledge and management have two aspects. Knowledge of a particular risk includes factual information and an understanding of the interpersonal consequences of a specific behaviour. Fighting is the specific behaviour presented in their analysis and its interpersonal consequences for relationships, friendship, are a major focus. Their view that risk taking is located in an interpersonal context implies that the management function also has two interpersonal dimensions: autonomy, or interpersonal negotiation, and intimacy, or the sharing of experience. Personal meaning mediates between knowledge and management and all three shape adolescents' understanding of their risk-taking behaviour, enabling them to define themselves as individuals and in relation to others.

It is the highly individualised nature of personal meaning that takes account of the values and perceptions that shape the decision-making process. Levitt and Selman's model attempts to deal with some of the issues raised by Furby and Beyth-Marom in terms of individual differences in defining alternatives and consequences, in evaluating these consequences and assessing their likelihood. The personal meaning model also breaks through the constraints of traditional structural stage formulations of psychosocial development.

Individual differences in the capacity to process risk-taking behaviour define differences in the maturity of personal meanings. The example offered to illustrate this developmental difference is drawn from the use of alcohol. People who drink to calm down in social situations are viewed as more aware of themselves and others than people who state that they drink because everyone does. Levitt and Selman maintain that their personal meaning approach documents adolescents' developing awareness of the place of risk-taking behaviour in relation to themselves and their relationships with others. The implication of their theory is that the better equipped adolescents are to understand and integrate their risk-taking behaviour into their sense of self and their relationships with others, the wiser they will be in making decisions about the behaviours in which they engage.

The psychosocial factors (personal meaning, knowledge about risk and management skills) which undergo development that may result in wiser behavioural choices in the context of risk-taking behaviour are not held to determine risk-taking behaviour exclusively. Levitt and Selman assert that both biological predispositions and sociocultural factors may operate to override them. Extreme impulsiveness or a culture in which soft drug taking has ritual importance may override or mediate the influence of psychosocial factors. Further, Allen *et al.* (1994) showed that while problem behaviours certainly seem to co-occur, they appear to result from multiple pathways of influence.

Personal meaning thus mediates between knowledge and management. All three shape adolescents' understanding of their risk-taking behaviour, enabling them to define themselves as individuals and, most importantly, in relation to others. The meaning of cigarette smoking is explored extensively in Chapters 7 and 8 in which adolescents' images and the social identities of non-smokers and smokers are explored. Chapter 9, concerned with school interventions, again raises issues related to risk and protective factors. Before reaching these chapters, the book examines questions of research methods in Chapter 2, looks at smoking prevalence in Chapter 3, considers social environments in Chapters 4 and 5, and explores psychological dimensions such as stress and coping, body image, and mood and pleasure in Chapter 6. In the last chapter (10) we consider prospects for reducing adolescent cigarette smoking in the wider context of adolescent life.

NOTES

1 It may be pertinent to note here that Jessor and Jessor (1977) include 'militarism' as an example of the 'values, norms and practices of the larger society' (p. 21). Such inclusion may be interpreted as evidence for the pressures on academics to explain the reaction of adolescents to world events in the late 1960s.

2 Again, the choice of certain variables (activism, and drug – specifically marijuana – use) in the theory can be seen to be very much a product of the time. Such a bias is recognised by Jessor and Jessor themselves (1977: 34).

3 This choice of factors may be limiting to the applicability of the theory to other populations, for example to some Afro-Caribbean cultures where in contrast to being opposing factors, religious affiliation and marijuana use may be closely linked.

4 We would speculate here that the narrowly focused monetarism and meritocratic ethos that has so characterised the UK throughout the mid-1980s and early 1990s may have served to make this social division particularly prevalent among contemporary British adolescents.

2   Studying adolescent smoking

A drug is neither moral nor immoral – it's a chemical compound. The compound itself is not a menace to society until a
human being treats it as if consumption bestowed a temporary
licence to act like an asshole.

Frank Zappa

Two recent studies of smoking among English adolescents will be
used to furnish illustrations throughout this book. They were undertaken in response to British government concern about the high prevalence of smoking among teenagers, particularly 13- to 15-year-old
girls. One of these studies was focused specifically on the higher
prevalence of smoking among young girls (Lloyd and Lucas, 1996).
The other sought to identify factors that may protect against the
uptake and maintenance of smoking among adolescents (Holland *et
al.*, 1996a).

The Lloyd and Lucas study explored the role of social identities in
adolescence in order to understand the consistently higher prevalence
of smoking among 13- to 15-year-old girls. These researchers carried
out two interlinked studies in eight secondary schools in Sussex. One
was a quantitative survey of all pupils in Years 7 to 11. These pupils
ranged in age from 11 to 17 years, and most of them completed
questionnaires at the beginning and end of the school year. These
measures yielded information on the contributions of

- age
- gender
- social environment and settings
- attitudes towards smoking
- body image
- stress and coping
- social identities

to adolescent smoking behaviour. The summer term information provided a means to explore the influence of these factors on changes in
smoking behaviour. Their second investigation was an in-depth behavioural study of girls' friendship groups using focus group methodo-

logy. It employed specially produced video materials to investigate the role of smoking in girls' social identities.

The study by Holland *et al.* explored the meanings that smoking holds for young people, and developed new hypotheses about the processes involved in adolescent smoking cessation. Two different approaches were also employed in this study. A questionnaire was completed by pupils aged 11 to 16 years in four schools in London. It examined the influence of

- social class
- gender
- health beliefs
- images and identities
- peer groups
- school environments
- families

on the smoking behaviour of young people. A second investigation was developed from information provided by questionnaire responses and employed both focus group discussions and family interviews. Topics examined in this phase included the meaning of smoking to young people, peer and family influences on smoking, and images of smokers and non-smokers. The intention of both major studies was to improve the design and implementation of future prevention and cessation interventions.

Studies of teenage smoking are complicated by the intermittent and transient nature of adolescent smoking behaviour, which renders the essential task of defining categories of smoking behaviour difficult. For example, an individual who reports having smoked a few cigarettes in the last week may be classified as a current smoker, but may be simply experimenting and may not be smoking in a week's time. Similarly, a young person who reports having smoked a month ago, but not in the last week, could be viewed as either a quitter or as an individual yet to relapse. In a 6-year longitudinal study of adolescent smokers in New Zealand, Fergusson and Horwood (1995) found that self-reported non-smokers and regular smokers were classified with better than 95 per cent accuracy. The reporting accuracy of occasional smoking, on the other hand, was poor, with 42 per cent of this group being falsely classified as non-smokers. This finding exemplifies the difficulties in categorising an individual adolescent's smoking status. In addition, most adolescents do not smoke enough cigarettes, on a regular enough basis, to develop sufficiently substantial levels of psychopharmacological dependence for it to contribute reliably to the prediction of behaviour (Regis, 1990).

The variable and transient nature of teenage smoking means that a single question is inadequate to categorise an individual adolescent's smoking status. In the Lloyd and Lucas study the categorisation of smoking behaviour was based upon three questionnaire items. The first was a self-classification of smoking behaviour; the second was a self-estimate of the number of cigarettes ever smoked; the third was a self-report of the period elapsed since the last cigarette was smoked. All three questions contributed to a composite measure which was then used to categorise the smoking behaviour of the pupils in the study.

These items were combined initially to yield five distinct smoking behaviour categories. These were:

1 never smoked
2 recent experimenter
3 old experimenter
4 regular light smoker
5 daily smoker.

These categories are similar to those of the University of Exeter's Schools Health Education Unit's Health Related Behaviour Questionnaire (Balding, 1995).

The five categories were later reduced in number to identify individual smoking status in a manner that had meaning for adolescents' day-to-day behaviour. *Never-smokers* were defined as only those adolescents who reported never smoking on both of the first two questions. The two regular smoking categories were combined to include adolescents who smoked only weekly but who nevertheless did so on a regular basis. This formed a meaningful categorisation of the *regular* smoker in terms of a social identity. The remaining pupils were labelled *occasional* smokers. This third category was later shown by the summer term information to be transient. This finding further illustrates that while it is possible to identify never-smokers and regular smokers reliably, there is a transient smoking status that is fluid and changing.

The study by Holland *et al.* also used the categories never, occasional and regular smokers. In addition, they included a category of ex-smokers. The number of adolescents found in this latter category was very small at age 11 and increased until age 16. However, like 'occasional smoker', it exhibits considerable instability and does not necessarily represent a permanent behavioural category. Yet again, this shows that categorising the smoking behaviour of adolescents is problematic. This category was important in Holland *et al.*'s study for indicating possible reasons for young people to attempt to stop, or even succeed in stopping, smoking.

The descriptions of the procedures used to identify never-, occasional and regular smokers are those of the (middle-aged) researchers in the Sussex and London studies. In focus groups in the Sussex study, a group of girls in Year 9, all of whom were smokers, described three phases in their careers as regular smokers.

The first experience

Regular smokers confirmed never-smoked groups' suspicions that there are two routes to the first instance of smoking. Some described a curiosity-based experiment (involving either just themselves, or a small group of non-smokers). Others described being pressured into smoking by a friendship group of smokers. The role of the instigator was given less emphasis in their accounts than in the reports by occasional smokers. The sense of place was strong for regular smokers, as it was for occasional smokers. The first smoking experience was not always described as unpleasant.

Hesitant smoking

There were various descriptions of this phase. One girl emphasised the difficulty in saying 'no' after she had been seen smoking. Others noted the desire to be active and out in the world with their friends rather than being bored. Smoking gave them an opportunity to go off to the woods and 'have a laugh'. Finally, one girl said that the second cigarette had been less unpleasant than she remembered the first one to have been, and this lent credence to smokers' claims that smoking is pleasant once you get used to it.

Regular smoking

Most of the girls said they just continued to smoke 'hesitantly', until one day they realised they were addicted. However, one girl, pressured into smoking by her friendship group, reported that she suddenly realised she would be a smoker:

> 'before I went round with you lot [smoking friendship group] I never smoked, and everyone's going, "You're going to smoke in a year, I bet you next year you're going to be smoking." And I never ... And then after that I thought, "I'm going to smoke", like something happened, I can't remember what.'

Apart from the above, there was no mention in this context of exclusion from non-smoking friendship groups, or of any reaction from non-smoking (ex)-friends. There was little mention of boys, except the comment that one reason younger girls smoked more than boys might be that at this age, boys were not yet in a position to take part in 'adult' pursuits, such as smoking and relationships:

> 'You do it for a laugh with your friends. It's something to do 'cos it like gets boring after a while. Before you've actually been introduced to boys and stuff, you know, like, started going out with them, not serious like, you just go out with them for a joke. But I mean when you've got something to do like smoke you just go out into the woods or something and have a fag.'

FACTORS AFFECTING ADOLESCENT SMOKING BEHAVIOUR

Factors that have been studied repeatedly in the search for explanations of adolescent smoking are reviewed below. Those topics that are considered extensively in later chapters are dealt with in a summary manner, while issues that are not explored in detail later are considered more extensively here. (An exception is gender, which *is* examined in detail later.)

Issues of gender

Defining adolescent smoking is difficult but there is clear and consistent evidence that between the ages of 13 and 16 years girls smoke more cigarettes than do boys. These differential rates of smoking prevalence for girls and boys have remained roughly constant and have shown little sign of change in recent years (Goddard, 1990; Balding, 1995). The 1994 Exeter survey reported that the average number of cigarettes smoked in a week is the same for boys and girls at age 12 but that in the later years, girls smoke more cigarettes than do boys. Reviewing the Exeter data over ten years, Balding concluded that the higher observed smoking rates for girls in older years remained constant. In addition, he noted that the decline in smoking between 1985 and 1988 – more marked for boys than for girls – was only temporary and that smoking levels have subsequently increased.

Being a girl is a significant factor in becoming a smoker. The different gender identities that boys and girls construct as they grow up are implicated clearly in differential smoking prevalence rates. There are three major psychological theories that seek to explain the development of a gendered identity. These are psychoanalytic theory, social learning theory and cognitive developmental theory. A recent survey of the empirical research related to these approaches to gender identities can be found in Golombok and Fivush (1994).

Social class

An association between social class and adult cigarette smoking is well established (Office of Population Censuses and Surveys, 1994). Conventional measures of social class have also been associated with adolescent smoking in the United States (Ashby, 1995), Canada (Millar and Hunter, 1990) and Scotland (Green *et al.*, 1991). In a major study among English secondary school pupils, Balding (1995) identified the social class position of the families of adolescents by categorising the newspapers that were read in their homes. He reported a clear inverse relationship for girls between social class and smoking behaviour, such that girls from working-class families were more likely to be smokers and girls from families in the highest category were least likely to be smokers.

In addition, DeVries (1995) has reported that among Dutch teenagers, motivation for smoking and non-smoking differs by social class. Working-class Dutch teenagers described smoking as a pleasurable experience that relieved boredom, while middle-class teenagers explained their non-smoking in terms of health and social disadvantages. These explanations are evidence of different risk and protective factors at work as perceived consequences of smoking. By contrast, smoking was more a part of the social and cultural life of working-class teenagers, and served a more important social function for them. Research does not always support a clear relationship between social class and teenage smoking. In a recent study of health beliefs and practices of English 15- to 16-year-olds and their families, Brannen *et al.* (1994) found no relationship between young people's social class (as defined by parental occupation) and their smoking behaviour. Similarly, Glendinning *et al.* (1994: 1457) concluded from a longitudinal study of adolescent socialisation, leisure and lifestyles in Scotland that "the direct transmission of smoking behaviours and attitudes between parents and their children cannot provide an adequate explanation for class-based differences in smoking [in adolescence]". However, the Scottish study did identify a relationship between smoking behaviour and the social class of middle and late

adolescents themselves, identified in terms of their current employment or education and occupational trajectory. The trajectory was
defined in terms of attitude towards school, school leaving age and
qualifications. This study suggests that a class-related pattern of differences in smoking prevalence may emerge as young people make the
transition into adulthood. The appearance of an association between
social class and smoking in late adolescence was also found in an
American study that identified this relationship in 15- to 19-year-olds
(Terre *et al.*, 1992).

Even when a relationship between social class and adolescent smoking is found, the process may not be straightforward. Studies have
shown that when the smoking behaviour of family members, parents
and siblings is taken into account, social class is not a strong predictor
of adolescent smoking (Green *et al.*, 1991; Swan *et al.*, 1991). Both
parental smoking and parental education have more influence on the
smoking behaviour of American high school students than social class
per se (Borland and Rudolf, 1975).

Ethnicity

Almost all published studies of the relationship of ethnicity to adolescent smoking have been carried out in the United States. While it may
be difficult to transfer their findings to countries that have a different
cultural background, such as the United Kingdom, consistent patterns
do emerge.

Overall, smoking prevalence has declined in all racial and ethnic
groups since 1976, with the trend continuing into the first half of the
1980s. However, the rate of decline has been greater among Black
adolescents, who by 1980 were less likely than White adolescents to
become smokers. A slight increase in smoking prevalence among
White adolescents followed throughout the 1980s. Other ethnic differences have also been reported: Native American adolescents show a
higher prevalence of smoking than do White or Hispanic adolescents
(Bachman *et al.*, 1991).

It has been suggested that there may be some under-reporting of
tobacco use among Blacks and over-reporting among Whites (Bauman and Ennett, 1994). Nevertheless, a lower prevalence of smoking
among Black teenagers has been reported consistently in large North
American samples (Wallace and Bachman, 1991; Chisick *et al.*, 1992;
Allen and Page, 1994; Biafora *et al.*, 1994; Landrine *et al.*, 1994;
Warheit *et al.*, 1995). Warheit and his colleagues also found that
ethnicity was predictive of alcohol use but not of using illicit drugs.

Nevertheless, in a large sample of American adults Parker *et al.* (1995) found that White individuals were also significantly more likely to use alcohol, marijuana and cocaine than were Black or Hispanic people. Similar findings are reported by Morgan (1995) among working-class American high-school students. It has been suggested that some of the observed differences in smoking prevalence between ethnic groups may be attributable to Blacks starting smoking later than Whites (Andreski and Breslau, 1993; Headen *et al.*, 1991), despite their being less likely to give up (Escobedo *et al.*, 1990; Hahn *et al.*, 1990).

There also appear to be ethnic differences in the effects of parental and peer smoking behaviour on an individual teenager's smoking. Feigelman and Lee (1995) examined peer and family smoking behaviour in a large sample of American Black and non-Hispanic White adolescents aged 12–17 years. They found that *peer* and *sibling* smoking were associated with smoking status in all adolescents. By contrast, *parental* smoking behaviour was associated with the smoking status of White teenagers, but *not* with that of Black adolescents. Similar findings are reported by Botvin *et al.* (1992). They found no relationship between parental smoking, own educational performance, parents' educational status, or smoking knowledge and the smoking status of Black teenagers; yet *all* these factors were related to smoking behaviour among White adolescents. Similarly, Headen *et al.* (1991) found that having a best friend who smoked was associated with a twofold increase in the likelihood of smoking initiation among White 12- to 14-year-olds, but had no effect on Black adolescents of the same age.

Among migrant adolescents, the ability to integrate aspects of different cultures may be associated with a lower likelihood of starting to smoke. For example, many Hispanic-American adolescents in the United States are first- or second-generation immigrants. The high rates of smoking and drinking observed in this group may be related to the disparity between traditional values and those of American society in general (Bettes *et al.*, 1990). It appears that the greater the degree of acculturation of migrant adolescents to the values of the dominant White society, the more likely they are to smoke (Landrine *et al.*, 1994; Deosaransingh *et al.*, 1995). On the other hand Belgrave *et al.* (1985) suggest that 'Afrocentrism' (possessing a strong Black identity) can increase self-esteem in Black adolescents, thereby decreasing the likelihood of taking up smoking. Other authors have suggested that the relationship of acculturation to smoking is a product of stress: the greater the acculturation, the greater the stress, and the higher the risk of smoking or substance misuse (Castro *et al.*, 1987; Galan, 1988).

Education

Smoking has consistently been shown to be more common among individuals with low levels of education as compared with those with higher levels of education (Bewley *et al.*, 1974; Chassin *et al.*, 1984; Skinner *et al.*, 1985; Pierce *et al.*, 1989). In addition to an increased smoking prevalence, Allison (1992) found higher levels of both alcohol and marijuana use among Canadian high-school students in basic and general academic streams when compared to advanced-level students. Several studies have found a higher smoking prevalence among adolescents whose parents have low levels of educational attainment (Bachman *et al.*, 1981; Mittelmark *et al.*, 1987; Waldron and Lye, 1990). Given that low parental educational attainment is associated with high rates of parental smoking (Oechsli and Seltzer, 1984; McNeill *et al.*, 1988), it has been suggested that the apparent association between low levels of parental attainment and adolescent smoking simply reflects an association between parental smoking and adolescent smoking (Chassin *et al.*, 1992).

The increase in mean level of education in the United States has been linked to the decline in smoking prevalence observed in recent years (Pierce *et al.*, 1989). These researchers examined US government health survey data covering the period 1974–85. They found that the proportion of those not completing high school declined steadily from 38 per cent to 26 per cent, while those reporting either graduating from college, or having had some college education, rose from 26 per cent to 37 per cent. Over the same period, smoking prevalence decreased across all groups, but the rate of decrease was found to be directly related to educational level. Smoking among college graduates decreased by over 10 per cent, while smoking among those who had some college education decreased by 8.6 per cent. High school graduate smoking rates decreased by 3.3 per cent, but smoking among high school dropouts decreased by only 2.1 per cent.

Newcomb *et al.* (1989) tested a model which related measures of emotional well-being and academic lifestyle orientation to the length of time for which an individual had smoked. They found degree of commitment to academic achievement to be a protective factor which was predictive of smoking behaviour over a long period (8 years). It also predicted greater emotional well-being, subsequent adult academic engagement and social relations with smokers. The authors conclude that future prevention policy should concentrate on methods of promoting habits conducive to the adoption of an academic lifestyle, and discouraging casual work and entertainment, and possibly subsidising higher education:

> General features of academic training such as systematically enlarging one's knowledge about a well-defined topic through reading, discussion and observation, and a willingness to invest substantial effort over long periods without immediate emotional reward are perhaps characteristics that are diametrically opposed to the impulsive practices of typical drug users and problem behaviours in general.
>
> (Newcomb *et al.*, 1989: 253)

Nutbeam and Aaro (1991) reported on the findings of a study across eleven European countries which examined the relationship between attitudes to school and smoking status. A much higher proportion of pupils who did not like school was found among self-reported smokers. A similar relationship was found between smoking and lower self-assessments of current academic performance, and with lower future academic aspiration. These investigators conclude that a supportive school environment that fosters good links with the local community may reduce feelings of alienation from school and thereby protect young people from taking up smoking.

While the rejection of school may not be causally related to smoking, it may reflect a more general rebellious attitude that is further evidenced by a poor performance at school. In these individuals, smoking may help to demonstrate rebelliousness, independence or gaining acceptance (Franzkowiak, 1987; Perry *et al.*, 1987). Eckert (1983) suggests that students who intend to attend college have more reason to engage in, and identify with, school activities. Because they are reliant on adults to achieve their educational goals, such individuals may, Eckert suggests, be more accepting of adult authority, including rules which proscribe smoking. As those who do not plan a college career have less invested in school, and consequently less need for adult approval, they are more likely to assert their adult status by taking up cigarettes. Waldron and Lye (1990) found strong support for Eckert's hypothesis in a study of American high school seniors.

Religion

There are several difficulties inherent in attempts to establish whether religious practice, belief or affiliation has any impact on young people's smoking behaviour. First, it is difficult to separate the effect of religion from other factors such as ethnic or cultural background. Second, what should be measured – attendance at services, personal beliefs, affiliation to a particular organisation, or religious knowledge? The measurement of strength of religious conviction is particularly difficult. Self-reported membership of any religion is of little more utility, as most faiths contain a spectrum of views from fundamentalist to liberal. Nevertheless, some tentative associations have been found in the United States between religious observance and low rates of smoking (Bachman *et al.*, 1981; Gottlieb and Green, 1984; Johnston *et al.*, 1984). The widely reported higher rate of smoking among teenage girls has not been found among American adolescent girls described as being 'very religious' (Waldron *et al.*, 1991). These results echo findings that have been reported from studies within the problem behaviour theory framework.

Sport

Several studies have examined the relationship between participation in sport and smoking. Swan *et al.* (1990) found that girls were less likely to take up smoking if they took part in organised sport, but significantly more likely to do so if they were involved in organised social activities. Conversely, no association was found between sporting activity and smoking among boys. However, Tucker (1985) examined a wide range of physical, psychological, social and lifestyle measures in a sample of adolescent boys, and recorded their intentions to smoke. Boys who did not intend to smoke were found to be more physically fit and more likely to participate in organised sports than those who intended to smoke. Boys who did not intend to smoke also spent less time watching television and drank less alcohol.

Vilhjalmsson and Thorlindsson (1992) examined the psychological and physiological effects of sports participation among Icelandic adolescents. They found that participating in team sports was inversely related to smoking and alcohol consumption; team sport members were less likely to smoke and drink alcohol. Participation in individual sports, by contrast, showed only a small inverse relationship to smoking and was unrelated to alcohol use. Despite the body of evidence in support of problem behaviour theory, this study showed that the antecedent of different problem behaviours (in this case smoking and drinking) may differ. In a longitudinal study of Finnish schoolchildren, Rantakallio (1983) found that a low level of participation in sports increased the likelihood of smoking in both boys and girls.

Kelder *et al.* (1994) describe similar observations among American high school students, and note that the association became stronger as the students grew older.

In an examination of the symbolic function of smoking for adolescents, Eckert (1983) identified participation in school sport as one of a range of activities by which middle-class adolescents express their transition to adulthood through officially sanctioned and approved roles. These adolescents may be contrasted with those who are likely to begin smoking at school. Such individuals are seen to be expressing their perceived adult status in ways that challenge the authority of the school. Thus, the assumption behind existing prevention programmes – that there is one homogeneous adolescent culture which all teenagers take part in or aspire to – may be viewed as fundamentally flawed. Even participation in school sport may have different meanings for adolescents with different life plans.

Social environments

Home

Much evidence exists to suggest that having parents or siblings who smoke is associated with adolescent cigarette smoking (Swan *et al.*, 1991). Parental smoking behaviour has been found to be a significant influence on adolescent smoking in a large number of cross-sectional and longitudinal studies carried out in the United Kingdom, North America and Europe (e.g. Cooreman and Perdrizet, 1980; Krosnick and Judd, 1982; Murray *et al.*, 1983; Chassin *et al.*, 1984; Gordon, 1986; Green *et al.*, 1991; Oei *et al.*, 1986; Hundleby and Mercer, 1987; Jacobs *et al.*, 1988; Goddard, 1992; Bailey *et al.*, 1993; Jackson *et al.*, 1994). Similarly, numerous studies have reported results which show that having a sibling who smokes, particularly an older sibling, is associated with teenage smoking (e.g. Cooreman and Perdrizet, 1980; Aaro *et al.*, 1981; Murray *et al.*, 1983; McCalister *et al.*, 1984; Gordon, 1986; Santi *et al.*, 1990; Fidler *et al.*, 1992; Goddard, 1992).

The large increase in the number of 'non-standard' families over the past three decades has been accompanied by concern, voiced by politicians and the media alike, that such an environment has an adverse effect upon the socialisation of children. In response, social scientists both in the United Kingdom and elsewhere have examined the impact of non-standard family structure on various adolescent 'risk' behaviours, including smoking, illicit drug use, alcohol, early sexual intercourse and delinquency (Wells and Rankin, 1991; Foxcroft and Lowe, 1991; Young *et al.*, 1991; Hoffman, 1993). Overall, studies are fairly consistent in finding an increased prevalence of such behaviours among adolescents living in non-standard families.

Peers

Peer influence is an important factor in adolescent smoking behaviour and appears repeatedly as a factor that predicts adolescent smoking in both cross-sectional studies (Aitken, 1980; Krosnick and Judd, 1982; Gordon, 1986; Hundelby and Mercer, 1987; Eiser *et al.*, 1991; Melby *et al.*, 1993), and longitudinal studies (Murray *et al.*, 1983; Chassin *et al.*, 1986). Chassin and his colleagues showed that having close friends who smoked predicted not only the transition from non-smoking to experimentation, but also from experimentation to more frequent use.

Studies of friendship groups or 'crowds' have reported that group members tend to be similar in smoking status (Ennett *et al.*, 1994). Smoking attitudes and norms vary between friendship groups depending on whether the group contains smokers or not. This in turn affects the levels of expressed disapproval or approval of smoking to which the adolescent is exposed (McNeill *et al.*, 1988; Urberg *et al.*, 1990; Eiser *et al.*, 1991). Moreover, the closer the relationship between friends, the more likely they are to influence each other. 'Best friends' are most likely to share the same smoking status category membership (Gordon, 1986; Charlton and Blair, 1989; Eiser *et al.*, 1991; Urberg, 1992).

Importantly, there is evidence that the influence of peers increases with age. For example, Krosnick and Judd (1982) found that while parents and peers are equally important to smoking among 11-year-olds, peers have a greater influence among 14-year-olds.

Body image

The relationship between cigarette smoking and *actual* body weight has been researched extensively (Klesges *et al.*, 1989). Recent evidence demonstrates that *beliefs about* weight differentiate experimental from regular smokers and suggests that girls smoke, at least in part, because they believe that smoking helps to control their weight (Camp *et al.*, 1993). Girls, in particular, are vulnerable to advertising and social pressure to lose weight (Gritz, 1986). Psychological concern with body image and smoking has received less attention. Differential satisfaction with body image has been suggested as an influence on the uptake of smoking among girls (Rauste van Wright, 1989).

Stress and coping

Change is a major source of stress in everyday life. During adolescence, individuals experience many changes including puberty, shifting relationships with parents and peers, school transitions and assessments, and the search for a secure self-identity (Frydenberg and Lewis, 1993; Seiffge-Krenke, 1993a). Adolescent stressors have commonly been analysed using distinctions drawn from adult stress research.

Adolescent girls tend to report more stressful experiences in their lives than do boys and this may be relevant to the observed higher prevalence of cigarette smoking among girls (Burke and Weir, 1978; Byrne *et al.*, 1995; Bruns and Geist, 1984; Dise-Lewis, 1988; Allgood-Merton *et al.*, 1990; Allen and Hiebert, 1991; Kearney *et al.*, 1993; Seiffge-Krenke, 1993b). Girls in early adolescence appear to be particularly vulnerable to stress (Compas *et al.*, 1993; Seiffge-Krenke, 1993a, 1993b).

Pleasure

Smoking can afford satisfactions for young people quite apart from the pharmacological effects and perceived stress reduction. It can be associated with the initiation and pursuit of relationships, particularly with the opposite sex, and the consolidation of group membership, whether or not this leads to identification as a smoker. The activity and use of the paraphernalia associated with smoking can be pleasurable: handling cigarette boxes, matches and lighter, lighting up, inhaling, exhaling and watching the smoke drift away, blowing smoke rings have all been identified by young and adult smokers alike as giving pleasure (Holland *et al.*, 1996a). One important satisfying function of cigarettes for young people is in the use and construction of time. Smoking has been referred to as a way to fill spare time, to pass time, to prevent boredom and to punctuate the day or other activities. The act of smoking can create a space for the smoker, a respite from other demands (Graham, 1993).

Social identities

The concept of social identity is useful as it helps to maintain a focus on the *sharing of significant characteristics with others*. It ensures awareness that individuals are constructed in terms of the groups of which they are members (Duveen and Lloyd, 1986). The term *social identity* reflects our interest in the social psychological theories of Moscovici (1973, 1976, 1981, 1984, 1988) and Tajfel (1981, 1982). Individuals' social identities are held to reflect the social representations of the groups in their society that are significant for them.

The nature of adolescent smoker and non-smoker identities and the smoking status of those holding these images has an influence on adolescent smoking. A number of studies using samples from distinctive cultures (England, United States, Finland) have explored adolescents' image of young smokers and non-smokers (e.g. Bewley and Bland, 1978; Barton *et al.*, 1982). A negative appraisal of teenagers who smoke has been reported to be a factor inhibiting smoking uptake (e.g. Dinh *et al.*, 1995), but teenage smokers were evaluated relatively more favourably by adolescents who were themselves smokers (Bewley and Bland, 1978; Kannas, 1985) or who intended to smoke (Barton *et al.*, 1982; Burton *et al.*, 1989).

An American study suggested that sex role identities influenced adolescent smoking frequency (Evans *et al.*, 1990). Bem (1974) proposed that sex roles be measured by requiring individuals to place themselves on both masculine and feminine scales. Masculine traits included being competitive, competent, self-confident and persistent. Feminine traits included being kind, emotional, helpful and empathetic. Persons described as having a masculine identity rated themselves significantly higher on the masculine scale than on the feminine scale. A feminine identity was achieved by scoring significantly higher on the feminine scale than on the masculine scale. Predictably, masculine identities were more prevalent among men, and feminine identities among women. Despite these stereotypes, Evans and colleagues also found that some adolescents rated themselves above average on both masculine and feminine traits; these individuals are described by psychologists as 'androgynous'. The androgynous adolescents were less likely to smoke cigarettes than were adolescents with other gender identities.

INTERVENTIONS

The recommendations for intervention presented later in this book draw primarily on recently completed research carried out in Sussex and London. Chapter 9 includes a review of published intervention studies, and the findings of this research are then utilised to develop suggestions for the personal, social and health education (PSHE) curriculum in secondary schools. The Sussex data are a source of suggestions for improving schools' antismoking programmes, and it is likely that their use will enhance previously limited success in reducing smoking prevalence among adolescents.

The Sussex study was commissioned specifically to investigate issues related to cigarette smoking among young adolescent girls. Consequently, the behavioural study was undertaken with girls alone and statements about gender differences are restricted to the quantitative findings based upon questionnaires completed by both girls and boys.

It is clear that school interventions alone will not be sufficient to eradicate smoking among adolescents, notwithstanding the recommendations for classroom-based work which flow from the studies reported in this book. In a broad-based review of teenage smoking intervention strategies, Reid *et al.* (1995) note that a range of activities are necessary to achieve substantial and lasting change. They identified the following as essential in addition to school interventions:

1 the maintenance of effective non-smoking policies which establish non-smoking as the norm in all public institutions;
2 an immediate and complete ban on all forms of tobacco promotion; and
3 fiscal measures which result in price increases on all tobacco products; these not only should be above the rate of inflation but also should outpace increases in real disposable income.

On the basis of the findings of the Sussex and London studies, we support the view that all these measures are likely to be necessary in order to make significant inroads in reducing adolescent smoking prevalence.

3 Two empirical studies of adolescent smoking

In general, it is held that the natural sciences have to deal with material objects and processes, the social sciences, however, with psychological and intellectual ones and that, therefore, the method of the former consists in explaining, and that of the latter in understanding.

Alfred Schultz

In this chapter two recent British studies that sought to explore the meanings of smoking to adolescents are described. They furnish much of the evidence to be considered in the following chapters. This chapter begins with a brief overview of the nature of the two studies. The second section contains a detailed description of the quantitative, questionnaire phase of the studies. The prevalence estimates that were derived from the questionnaire data are presented in the third section. Finally, qualitative methods of data collection are described.

OVERVIEW OF THE TWO STUDIES

The two empirical studies of adolescent cigarette smoking that furnish the evidence to be considered in the following chapters both combined quantitative, questionnaire approaches with qualitative data collection techniques. In the Sussex study the qualitative techniques included focus group discussions that were preceded by specially produced videos of a young teenage girl and her friends. The video material was used to elicit free descriptions of girl smoker and girl non-smoker identities, and set the scene for the focus group discussions. The qualitative data in the London study derived from focus group discussions and family interviews.

The Sussex study was undertaken in four phases. The first of these was an autumn term questionnaire survey in six secondary schools chosen both as representative of the county and on the basis of willingness to participate in the project. This was followed in the spring term by the collection of qualitative data in four of these schools. The third phase was a further questionnaire survey in the same six schools in the summer term. The final phase was an additional questionnaire survey in two all-girl secondary schools, one carried out during the following autumn term and the other during the following summer term.

The first of three phases in the London study was a questionnaire survey in four secondary schools in the area. These schools were selected in order to sample a range of demographic variables: gender, socio-economic class and ethnicity. Those pupils who were interested in taking part in the second phase, focus group discussions, were asked to give their names and they were contacted later through their school. In the third phase of the London study, volunteers from the focus groups and others who had taken part in the phase 1 questionnaire survey were interviewed with members of their families.

The questionnaire data from both studies are consistent in showing that young adolescent girls smoke more cigarettes than do boys. More girls are regular smokers and fewer girls than boys report being never-smokers. The Sussex study placed considerable emphasis on quant-itative findings, and that material provides the figures for the analysis of smoking prevalence described extensively in the third section of this chapter.

Although focused on related questions: 'Why do young adolescent girls, in particular, smoke?' and 'How can young adolescents be protected from cigarette smoking?', the two studies approach these issues from different perspectives. The Sussex research was guided by developmental–social psychological theory while the London work was carried out within a sociological tradition. The use of these conventional disciplinary labels does not tell the whole story and the quotation from Schultz (1963) at the beginning of the chapter only hints at the nature of these differences.

It is more than thirty years since Schultz described a fundamental schism within the social sciences between practitioners who saw their task as implementing a positivist, scientific programme, and practi-tioners trying to identify new approaches particularly suited to the study of human society. The debate about what constitutes knowledge in the social sciences and the methods to be used in acquiring such knowledge continues to the present (cf. Blaikie, 1996). The epistemo-logical argument is important but not at issue in this chapter. Our concern here is to examine the research procedures employed in the two studies that provide the majority of data to be considered in the chapters that follow.

The Sussex study sought to provide information representative of the factors that influenced young adolescent smoking. This study can be described as adopting a position of realism (cf. Bhaskar, 1986; Harré, 1986) in the contemporary debate about the nature of and the methodology appropriate to the social sciences. The London study can be viewed as interpretative. An important aspect of the realist view is the belief that the social sciences can be scientific in the same sense as the natural sciences but that social objects are of a fundamentally different nature from natural objects. The need to develop methods appropriate to the study of social objects flows from this distinction.

Both the London study and the Sussex study can be considered as examples of empirical work in Harré's sense of a critical descriptive phase even though the London study adopts an interpretative position and the Sussex study a realist perspective. They each sought to provide an account of the non-random patterns in adolescents' understanding of their smoking behaviour (Harré and Secord, 1972). Differences in emphasis follow from the greater commitment of researchers in the London study to an interpretative position through which the voice of the social actor is given a privileged position. Thus, in the London study each succeeding phase was informed by knowledge derived from the preceding phase. This strategy enabled the voice of young people actively to shape an understanding of their smoking experiences. In the Sussex study the qualitative material was used both to verify and to improve the collection of quantitative data. Improved data collection can also be viewed as strengthening the voice of social actors. In combining these two studies, with their different emphases, the limitations of each may be overcome.

QUANTITATIVE PROCEDURES

The questionnaires used in both the Sussex and the London studies measured conventional demographic factors and items about smoking attitudes and behaviour. In the Sussex study additional attention was given to satisfaction with body image, stress and coping, home environment, peer relations and, most importantly, social identities.

The questionnaire used in the London study explored young people's and their families' smoking practices, attitudes and experience, and included questions about health status, attitudes to health, and engagement in other risk-taking practices, as well as young people's social relationships, networks and activities. The primary aim of this study was to identify factors which could prevent young adolescents from taking up cigarette smoking and help them when they wished to stop smoking.

The major focus of the Sussex study was young adolescents' construction of social identities which incorporated social representations of cigarette smoking and non-smoking. Information about smoking identities was also intended to inform interventions aimed at reducing adolescent smoking, particularly that of girls.

The need to produce a questionnaire that could be completed in year groups from 7 to 11, with pupils aged from 11 years to 16 years, and by adolescents from different social backgrounds, raised four specific issues. These were:

• Readability: the range of reading ages included skills appropriate to 9-year-olds through to reading capacities equivalent to those of 18-year-olds. The material needed to be manageable by the least skilled.
• Attention span: one class period was provided in each school for questionnaire completion.
• Research focus: material dealing with smoking behaviour and social identities needed to appear early in the questionnaire.
• Response set: as a consequence of individuals' tendency to respond in the same direction, questionnaire construction often reverses the direction of items. Given the range of ability of the pupils, and with the help of advice from a statistician, all items with positive values were positioned in one direction and those with negative values in the other.

A further problem in studies that rely upon self-reports is the need to ensure the validity of responses to the questionnaire. All self-report techniques risk respondents' seeking to provide answers that will show themselves in a good light, and will give the researchers the answers that the respondents believe they want to hear. Charlton *et al.*, (1985) have argued that accurate reporting of adolescent smoking prevalence can be assured if anonymity and confidentiality are established. Effective procedures are held to produce results as valid as those from research which employs biochemical sampling of breath or saliva.

Three procedures established the anonymity and confidentiality of questionnaire replies in the Sussex study. These were:

• Presentations in year group assemblies by research staff in all schools before questionnaire administration that emphasised the anonymous and confidential nature of the study.
• Generation of a self-created personal code number based upon date of birth and first two letters of mother's first name. The code allowed matching of autumn and summer term questionnaires while maintaining anonymity.

• Provision of an unmarked sealable envelope for use after completion of the questionnaire ensured confidentiality while the questionnaires were on school premises.

In the London study anonymity and confidentiality were assured for the young people who completed the questionnaire by the following procedures:

• The researchers administered the questionnaires themselves.
• They provided envelopes in which pupils placed and sealed their completed questionnaire.
• The sealed envelopes were then removed from the school premises.

In the London study the questionnaire was administered once in each of four schools in the area.

Descriptive terms for use in measuring social identities of smokers were sought in published findings that described images of adolescent smokers and non-smokers (Bewley and Bland, 1978; Barton *et al.*, 1982; Kannas, 1985). Terms used in these studies were chosen as the descriptive terms that adolescents themselves might employ in talking and thinking about smokers and non-smokers. In the questionnaire, adolescents, both girls and boys were asked to use fourteen such terms to rate different identities: themselves as they were and as they would like to be, and girl and boy non-smokers and girl and boy smokers. Table 3.1 shows the descriptive items and six-point rating scales used in the first phase of the Sussex study.

Table 3.1   Terms used in the Sussex questionnaire to measure social identities

uncool	0	1	2	3	4	5	cool
wimpish	0	1	2	3	4	5	tough
sticks to rules	0	1	2	3	4	5	breaks rules
childish	0	1	2	3	4	5	grown-up
unhealthy	0	1	2	3	4	5	healthy
unhappy	0	1	2	3	4	5	happy
follows others	0	1	2	3	4	5	makes up own mind
dull	0	1	2	3	4	5	exciting
popular	0	1	2	3	4	5	unpopular
unattractive to opposite sex	0	1	2	3	4	5	attractive to opposite sex
thick	0	1	2	3	4	5	clever
doesn't care about environment	0	1	2	3	4	5	cares about environment
doesn't like partying	0	1	2	3	4	5	likes partying
doesn't like the opposite sex	0	1	2	3	4	5	likes the opposite sex

In the Sussex study, pupils in six schools completed the questionnaire in both the autumn and the summer terms of the same academic year. To enable comparisons across the school year only minor changes were made to the autumn questionnaire. They were as follows:

- Three questions were removed. One of these was a question about musical preferences that had failed to yield any meaningful information. Another assessed ethnicity and showed in the autumn term that only 7.4 per cent of the sample was non-Caucasian. A further item that duplicated a question already raised in another part of the questionnaire was also removed.
- Three descriptive terms were added to the identity questions. These had been used spontaneously by girls in describing the video presentations of a girl smoker and a girl non-smoker preceding the focus group discussions. These terms are shown in Table 3.2.

Table 3.2 Terms added to summer questionnaire to measure social identities

doesn't like school work	0	1	2	3	4	5	likes school work
unfriendly	0	1	2	3	4	5	friendly
boring	0	1	2	3	4	5	fun

- A space for 'any other comments' was provided at the end of the questionnaire.

Schools in the questionnaire studies

Questionnaire data were collected initially in six mixed-gender state secondary schools in Sussex, southern England. Four of these were situated in large urban locations and two in smaller towns located in more rural areas. The schools are referred to throughout as Town 1, Town 2, Town 3, Town 4, and Country 1 and Country 2. Table 3.3 shows the age of pupils in each year in the six Sussex schools during autumn term data collection.

In the fourth phase of the Sussex study a questionnaire was administered in two all-girl schools. The summer term questionnaire was administered in an all-girl state secondary school during summer term

Table 3.3 Mean age in autumn term by year in schools

Year	7	8	9	10	11
Mean age	11.7	12.7	13.5	14.7	15.7

and an autumn term questionnaire in an all-girl independent school during autumn term. The state school is designated Girls 1 (G1) and the independent school Girls 2 (G2).

The six Sussex mixed schools were selected to represent the social class distribution of families in the county. Country 1 and Country 2 were chosen as examples of country schools that have wide catchment areas which include both urban and rural families. Town 3 and Town 4 are medium-sized comprehensives (originally girls' grammar schools) located in residential areas of towns. Town 2 is a larger comprehensive school also located in an urban area. These three schools recruit children from homes of a wide range of socio-economic status. Town 1 is located in a large council estate and admits many pupils from relatively deprived backgrounds. Girls 1 is the sole girls-only state secondary school in Sussex. It is comparable in the socio-economic background of its pupils to the majority of the six mixed-gender state schools.

Examination of fathers' occupations suggests that the six mixed schools in the Sussex study were representative of the county and, broadly, of England as a whole. Table 3.4 shows fathers' occupations in the original six schools compared to figures for economically active men in the county and in England. Father's occupation by school is presented as an approximation to the social class composition of participating schools. Table 3.5 shows that the independent girls' school (G2) recruits from a different population as compared with the other schools.

Although the Sussex and London studies employed similar techniques (questionnaire data collection) in the first phase of their study, different overall methodological strategies guided the two studies. The questionnaire data in the London study were held to reflect the views

Table 3.4 Fathers' occupations in Sussex schools compared to the county* and to English men*

Occupational group	Six schools	County	England
I. Professional (%)	8	7	7
II. Managerial (%)	32	32	27
IIIn Skilled non-manual (%)	15	12	11
IIIm Skilled manual (%)	28	28	31
IV. Semi-skilled (%)	9	13	14
V. Unskilled (%)	1	5	5
Other (%)	7	3	6

* The data for the county and for England derive from the 1991 Census

Table 3.5 Fathers' occupations in the six Sussex schools as a percentage of the total by school

School	I	II	IIIn	IIIm	IV	V	Other*
C1	13	35	12	25	8	2	5
C2	12	39	10	27	7	1	4
T1	2	16	11	41	12	3	15
T2	10	31	11	25	10	2	11
T3	5	33	21	24	10	1	6
T4	4	21	28	22	9	1	15
G1	3	27	11	30	16	4	9
G2	29	47	6	10	3	0	5

* 'Other' includes fathers described as being unemployed

of young people in four London-area schools. However, as is usual in research with a primarily qualitative focus, it was not intended to be interpreted as generalisable to the population of young people as a whole. Rather this phase of the study was viewed as providing information to aid the selection of participants and methods for use in the next phase and descriptive information from the sample which could be compared with the findings from other studies.

Table 3.6 shows the number of pupils who participated in the London study according to school and year group. The choice of schools in the study was guided by the need to sample gender, social class and ethnicity rather than by a wish to collect a sample that reflected the distribution of these characteristics within the London area.

In the London questionnaire study, girls made up 46 per cent or 499 of the participants, and boys the remaining 597 participants. Fathers' occupations were used to provide an estimate of socio-economic class. In the total group of 1,096 pupils, there was a larger proportion of adolescents from the higher socio-economic classes with 16 per cent of

Table 3.6 Number of pupils participating in the London study by school and by year group

	Year 7	Year 9	Year 11	Total
School 1	166	164	132	462
School 2	171	139	158	468
School 3	19	0	0	19
School 4	86	0	61	147
Total	442	303	351	1,096

pupils' fathers placed in socio-economic class I and 24 per cent in socio-economic class II than occurs nationally (see Table 3.4). The remaining 60 per cent of fathers' occupations were distributed as follows: 17 per cent in socio-economic class IIIn and 25 per cent in socio-economic class IIIm. Eighteen per cent were labelled 'other categories'. This skewed distribution is accounted for by Schools 1 and 2, which contributed the highest numbers of respondents and which were predominantly middle class (categories I–IIIn). Schools 3 and 4 were predominantly working class (categories IIIm–V) but contributed little more than 15 per cent of pupils in the questionnaire study.

The majority of pupils (66 per cent) in the London study described themselves as White; 10 per cent described themselves as either Black African, Black Caribbean or Black Other, and 9 per cent as Indian. The 7 per cent who classified themselves as 'other' were generally of mixed race, but small numbers belonged to other ethnic groups. Schools 1 and 2 were more ethnically mixed than Schools 3 and 4.

An aim of the Sussex research strategy was to provide a representative description of the county's young adolescents' perceptions of their peers who smoked cigarettes and those who did not smoke. Different criteria apply to the London study. Here the aim was to develop knowledge that is transferable (Henwood and Pidgeon, 1992) and to provide results which can be applied to similar contexts and situations.

PREVALENCE ESTIMATES

The prevalence analyses use the categories of smoking behaviour described in Chapter 2: *never-*, *occasional* and *regular smoker*. The proportion of pupils in each of these categories in the Sussex study in both autumn and summer terms is shown by year group in Table 3.7. The percentage of *regular smokers* is highlighted.

The results shown in Table 3.7 can be summarised as follows:

- Smoking prevalence increases significantly across the academic year for every year group.
- Smoking prevalence increases across school years.

The prevalence figures from the Sussex study are similar to those found in large-sample national surveys (Balding, 1995).

A major concern of the Sussex study was the increasing rate of smoking among adolescent girls. This phenomenon is shown in Table 3.8. Ignoring Year Group 7 results, girls in the Sussex study were less likely to be *never-smokers* and more likely to describe themselves as *regular smokers* than were boys. For both girls and boys, there was a marked shift from never smoking to experimentation and an increase

Table 3.7 Smoking prevalence by school year

Year 7	Autumn term All pupils (n = 749)	Summer term All pupils (n = 749)
	%	%
Never smoked	82.9	70.2
Occasional	16.5	26.4
Regular smoker	**0.6**	**3.4**

Year 8	Autumn term All pupils (n = 809)	Summer term All pupils (n = 809)
	%	%
Never smoked	64.6	52.6
Occasional	31.1	35.2
Regular smoker	**4.3**	**12.2**

Year 9	Autumn term All pupils (n = 752)	Summer term All pupils (n = 752)
	%	%
Never smoked	53.8	41.9
Occasional	36.8	41.2
Regular smoker	**9.4**	**16.9**

Year 10	Autumn term All pupils (n = 675)	Summer term All pupils (n = 675)
	%	%
Never smoked	41.5	32.0
Occasional	39.4	40.0
Regular smoker	**19.1**	**28.0**

Year 11	Autumn term All pupils (n = 557)	Summer term All pupils (n = 675)
	%	%
Never smoked	35.2	29.3
Occasional	37.9	37.9
Regular smoker	**26.9**	**32.8**

in regular smoking during the school year. Table 3.8 shows smoking prevalence by year group as well as by gender. Again, the proportion of *regular smokers* is highlighted.

Table 3.8   Boys' and girls' smoking prevalence by year group and gender

Year 7	Boys (n = 391)		Girls (n = 358)	
	Autumn term	Summer term	Autumn term	Summer term
	%	%	%	%
Never smoked	80.3	66.8	85.8	74.0
Occasional	18.9	29.7	13.9	22.9
Regular smoker	**0.8**	**3.6**	**0.3**	**3.1**

Year 8	Boys (n = 409)		Girls (n = 400)	
	Autumn term	Summer term	Autumn term	Summer term
	%	%	%	%
Never smoked	63.3	52.8	66.0	52.5
Occasional	31.6	36.6	30.8	33.8
Regular smoker	**5.1**	**10.5**	**3.3**	**13.8**

Year 9	Boys (n = 370)		Girls (n = 382)	
	Autumn term	Summer term	Autumn term	Summer term
	%	%	%	%
Never smoked	56.2	47.3	51.6	36.4
Occasional	36.8	40.6	36.9	41.9
Regular smoker	**7.1**	**12.2**	**11.5**	**21.7**

Year 10	Boys (n = 359)		Girls (n = 316)	
	Autumn term	Summer term	Autumn term	Summer term
	%	%	%	%
Never smoked	46.8	37.0	35.4	26.3
Occasional	39.3	39.9	39.6	40.2
Regular smoker	**14.0**	**23.1**	**25.0**	**33.6**

Year 11	Boys (n = 275)		Girls (n = 282)	
	Autumn term	Summer term	Autumn term	Summer term
	%	%	%	%
Never smoked	43.3	33.8	27.3	24.8
Occasional	37.8	42.5	38.0	33.3
Regular smoker	**18.9**	**23.6**	**34.8**	**41.8**

In Year Group 7 and in the autumn term for Year Group 8 there was a higher prevalence of smoking among boys than girls. However, by the end of Year 8 more girls were regularly smoking cigarettes than were boys. By Year 11 almost twice as many girls as boys were regular cigarette smokers.

While the rate of regular smoking increased consistently from Year Group 7 to Year Group 11, the proportion of occasional smokers remained roughly constant from Year 8 onwards. *It is important to appreciate that occasional smoking represents a transitory phase through which individuals pass into regular smoking or abstinence.* Consequently, Figures 3.1 and 3.2 show only *never-smokers* and *regular smokers* by year group for boys and girls separately. Comparison of the figures shows the steeper fall in *never-smokers* and the steeper rise in *regular smokers* among girls.

The London study also reported that smoking prevalence was higher among girls (10 per cent) than boys (9 per cent) and that girls smoked more cigarettes than did boys: 8 per cent smoked more than 6 per week, compared with 5 per cent of boys who did so. Twelve per cent of *regular smokers* were aged 13 and under, 15 per cent were aged 14, and 73 per cent were in the 15–16 age group.

Smoking prevalence and other substance use

Questionnaire data were collected in the London study about the use of other substances. Adolescents categorised as *regular smokers* and

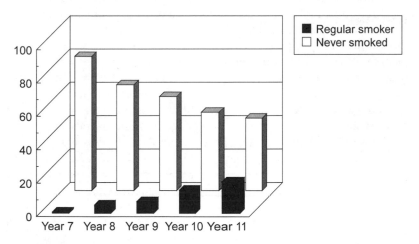

Figure 3.1 Boys: proportion of never-smokers and regular smokers in the autumn term

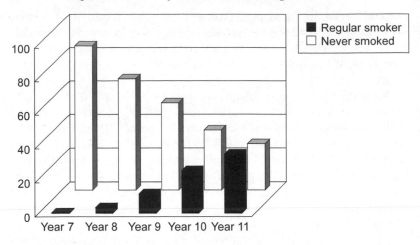

Figure 3.2 Girls: proportion of never-smokers and regular smokers in the autumn term

occasional smokers were more likely to report frequent use of alcohol. Those pupils who had identified themselves as *never-smokers* reported the lowest levels of alcohol use, across all types of alcohol. *Never-smokers* also had a much lower level of experimentation with alcohol. The differences between category of smoker and level of alcohol use were highly significant in statistical analyses.

Similar relationships were found between smoking behaviour and cannabis use. Adolescents who reported that they smoked on a regular basis were much more likely to report frequent (34 per cent) or occasional (28 per cent) use of cannabis. Over 90 per cent of the non-smokers said that they had never tried cannabis, compared with just over 16 per cent of the regular smokers. Over a third of *regular smokers* reported frequent cannabis use, compared with less than 1 per cent of non-smokers. Again, the differences between category of smoker and other drug use were statistically highly significant.

In the London study almost half the pupils who reported that they had never smoked were in Year 7. The majority of *regular smokers* were in Year Group 11, and these pupils may also have had more opportunities for experimenting with cannabis. Consequently, the analysis of the relationship between cigarette smoking and cannabis use was restricted to pupils in Year Groups 9 and 11. The association between cigarette smoking and cannabis use was stronger in Year Group 11. Although a strong relationship was found between cigarette smoking and the use of cannabis, in the United Kingdom cannabis is usually smoked mixed with tobacco. Allbutt *et al.* (1995) have made the interesting suggestion that young people may be introduced to cigarette smoking through cannabis use, and not vice versa. This challenges conventional gateway theory.

QUALITATIVE DATA PROCEDURES

Although there has been an implication in the social sciences that quantitative methods imply a positivist-scientific methodology, while qualitative methods indicate a rejection of such views, the link between method and philosophical position is not inevitable. Indeed, there has been a resurgence of interest in quantitative methods within feminist research. The London and Sussex studies illustrate this *rapprochement*.

Qualitative data in the social sciences are typically derived from interviews, observation and documentation of many types, and may take the form of written records, audio and video tapes, their written transcriptions, and artefacts. Generally qualitative data are extensive, rich and voluminous. The interpretative task is challenging, but if successful produces a product that goes beyond simple description or the confirmation of the investigators' pre-existing hypotheses. Success allows others who have not observed the phenomenon to understand it more thoroughly.

Both the social actors who are observed and the researchers themselves come to the interpretative task with their own sets of assumptions. From a positivist perspective, each can be seen as a source of bias. Other social scientists see the differing standpoints, perspectives and assumptions of researchers and the researched as inevitable, and part of the interpretive task. There are many types of qualitative analysis including ethnomethodology, discourse analysis and deconstruction. In both the London and Sussex studies a computer-assisted form of content analysis (NUD*IST – Non-numerical Unstructured Data Indexing, Searching and Theorising) was used to manage the vast amounts of material generated by focus group discussion and by family interviews. In the section that follows the use to which NUD*IST analysis is put reveals the differing strategies of the two studies.

The Sussex study

The qualitative procedures in the Sussex study comprised an impression formation task and focus group discussions. Both of these behavioural measures were undertaken only with girls in Years 7 and 9; that is, girls from 11 to almost 14 years old. Though it would have been desirable to recruit equal numbers of smoking and non-smoking groups, the low prevalence of smoking in Year Groups 7 to 9 made this strategy impossible. Instead, girls were recruited by asking friendship groups to volunteer to take part, and in the course of focus group discussion, information about their smoking behaviour was recorded.

A total of thirty-three groups were recruited from four of the six schools that participated in the questionnaire survey, namely Country 1, Town 1, Town 2 and Town 4. Each school contributed at least four groups from each of Years 7 and 9. Group size ranged from two to six girls.

The impression formation task

Two sets of video stimuli were produced for use in the impression formation task. Young adolescent actors were provided by a local drama school. Each video portrayed the same 15-year-old girl describing a typical weekend with her friends. The two videos were identical except that in one the girl was a smoker, and in the other she was a non-smoker. After viewing one of the videos girls completed a short questionnaire. They were first asked to describe the 15-year-old girl using their own words. Then they were asked to use the fourteen descriptors from the social identity items in the autumn term questionnaire (see Table 3.1, p. 38) to rate her. The video materials were piloted in the drama school that had provided actors. They were well received and considered realistic by classmates who had not taken part in the production.

Focus group discussions

The impression formation task always preceded focus group discussions. A young woman researcher conducted all the focus group discussions. She was closer in age to the girls participating than were the other researchers. The discussions were audio recorded. Another person made contextual notes during the discussion and then collaborated on further notes after the session. The groups were conducted either in free class periods or after school. The researcher used a prepared protocol to ensure that smoking behaviour, satisfaction with body image, stress and coping, home environment, peer relations, and smoking identities were discussed.

Conventional statistical methods have been employed to analyse the ratings produced by the impression formation task. Year in school has been used in place of age in most developmental analyses. This decision reflects an emphasis on social identities and social groups. Adolescents generally form friendships within their own year groups and often report not knowing pupils in other year groups.

The audio recordings of the group discussions were transcribed commercially and then computer transcriptions were corrected by one of the researchers present during the group discussion. The computer program NUD*IST was used to analyse the transcriptions. NUD*IST serves three major functions:

- It facilitates the organisation of qualitative data in a structured form.
- It enables the researcher to explore the data and to view them in many different combinations.
- It has a hypothesis-testing and theory-building function, whereby co-occurring or overlapping coding within text units, whole documents or groupings of documents may be juxtaposed according to differing logical functions.

NUD*IST also produces basic frequency statistics related to the number of documents and text units from which the references have been found.

The Sussex study focus group discussions produced almost 22,000 individual speech turns. These were coded in categories permitting entry into NUD*IST and were given a code name that represented their content. Inter-rater reliability was assessed and varied with the domain coded. For some, there was virtually 100 per cent agreement but for others agreement reached only 85 per cent. Disagreements were resolved through discussion. As evidence from the Sussex study is presented in the chapters that follow, qualitative material from the NUD*IST analyses will be presented both to verify and to elaborate the quantitative results.

Phases 2 and 3 in the London study

Each phase of the London study fed information into the selection of participants, methods and contents of discussion in the next phase in an iterative process, one of the major characteristics of qualitative research. This strategy enabled the further pursuit of themes concerning young people's understanding of their smoking experiences as they emerged in the course of the study.

The groups of adolescents investigated in the London study reflect the views of a diverse sample of young people in London, but, as is usual in qualitative research, it is not intended to be generalisable to the London population of young people as a whole. The merit of the qualitative findings should be assessed in terms of their transferability (Henwood and Pidgeon, 1992) and the extent to which the results can be applied to similar contexts and situations. In acquiring a rich and dense data set around the meanings of smoking and non-smoking for young people, pertinent issues relevant to their experience are highlighted.

Focus group discussions

For the second phase of the London study, adolescents were recruited to participate in focus group discussions. Adolescents' interactions in focus groups were valuable sources of information in describing peer group influences on smoking behaviour. In addition, focus groups allow for more rapid collection of data than do individual interviews. The interaction between participants highlighted their attitudes, priorities and language concerning cigarette smoking. It helped to identify group norms and provided insight into the operation of group and social processes in the articulation of knowledge.

As in the Sussex study, two researchers conducted the focus groups. One person acted as facilitator, leading discussion around the central themes of the study; the second observed, taking notes which included details identifying speakers, and describing non-verbal forms of communication and interactions. The sessions were audio tape-recorded and transcribed. All transcriptions (of group or individual interviews) were entered on computer and then analysed with the aid of NUD*IST.

Twenty focus groups in the London area were studied, with six to eight individuals in each (a total of 125 individuals). All-girl, all-boy and mixed groups with varying smoking characteristics were constituted. The participants in focus groups were individuals who, while completing the questionnaire phase of the study, had volunteered to take part. These volunteers were organised into all-girl, all-boy and mixed groups for focus group discussion. More non-smokers than smokers volunteered, and the large proportion of non-smokers reflected the prevalence of smoking among those pupils who completed the questionnaire. Although the 11- to 16-year-old age group is composed primarily of non-smokers, focus group participants included a higher proportion of smokers than did the original questionnaire group. Pupils who had given up smoking comprised 11 per cent of pupils participating in focus group discussions.

A focus group guide was developed to explore perceptions and experiences of smoking, the influence of peer group and family on smoking, and factors which were identified in a literature review as being relevant to protection from smoking uptake and to smoking cessation.

Family interviews

In the third phase of the study, volunteers from the focus groups and others who had completed the questionnaire were interviewed with members of their families. In order to maximise information on the themes of the study a flexible approach in selecting the specific method to be employed in each family was used. In all, twenty family interviews were carried out. Most people were interviewed in the family home, and the study included paired and group interviews. The precise composition of these groups depended on the number of family members who agreed to participate. The interviews covered smoking experience and status, and issues related to smoking which had emerged from earlier phases of the study. Factors that may significantly deter adolescents from smoking cigarettes were of particular interest.

Data analysis

Transcriptions from both the focus groups and interviews were analysed with the aid of NUD*IST. In the London study, NUD*IST was used for the systematic coding and analysis of complex categories and for retrieval of the material in long transcriptions. Systemic networks were also used to organise and analyse the data. A systemic network is an analytical device that was developed in the field of linguistics but which is suitable for the systematic organisation and categorisation of qualitative data more generally. A network is an instrument which enables theory to be tested, translating the language of the social actor into the language of the theory. It allows for the productive development of theory in the process of analysing the data.

General methodological issues

The London study was primarily a qualitative investigation. The questionnaire results were based on an availability sample of the relevant year groups in the schools which agreed to take part, and as such is not a representative sample of young people in these age groups, although the schools approached to take part in the study were chosen to provide an adequate spread of the relevant demographic variables of gender, socio-economic class and ethnicity. It was intended not that elaborate statistical analysis would be made of these data to test hypotheses, but that the material would be used as a description of the pool from which the qualitative sample was drawn, and for comparative purposes with samples in other relevant studies.

4   The social environment
Families, relationships and smoking

> Americans, indeed, often seem to be so overwhelmed by their
> children that they'll do anything for them except stay married
> to the co-producer.
>
> Katharine Whitehorn

> Growing up human is uniquely a matter of social relations
> rather than biology. What we learn from connections within
> the family takes the place of instincts that program the beha-
> viour of animals; which raises the question, how good are
> these connections?
>
> Elizabeth Janeway

Our clearest finding from investigations of the family is this: adolescents living with both parents are less likely to smoke or to take up
smoking during the school year than those living in single-parent
families or stepfamilies. These findings are independent of gender
and school year. In the first part of this chapter explanations for
these findings are sought in published reports. Two approaches to
the question are identified. The first employs a medical model which
describes the 'transmission' of smoking in the family. The second
approach examines the structure and quality of family life in order
to explain adolescent smoking. The second major section of this
chapter presents findings from the Sussex and London studies of
adolescent smoking. The issues considered here are the structure and
nature of families, smoking in the family and adolescent smoking, as
well as family smoking and adolescent smoking uptake.

PUBLISHED ACCOUNTS OF THE RELATIONSHIPS
BETWEEN ADOLESCENT SMOKING AND FAMILY LIFE

Medical models

Evidence concerning the effect of parental smoking on the smoking
behaviour of their offspring is complex and sometimes contradictory.
Many studies, some of which are strongly medically oriented, have
suggested that families exert a strong influence on young people's
smoking behaviour. Such studies have sought the existence of a direct

and causal link between parental and adolescent smoking. For example, Rowe *et al.* (1996) investigated the application of what they describe as 'epidemic' models of influence, in which smoking is spread by way of social contact. Their study of American adolescents concluded that such mechanisms result in the rate of an adolescent's transition from never-smoker to occasional smoker being more rapid in the children of parents who smoke than in children whose parents do not smoke. In a study of English children, Charlton (1996) proposed a self-perpetuating 'family circle' in which children 'inherit' smoking from their parents. She argued that having parents who smoked contributed to poor school attendance through illness. She suggested that disenchantment and lower self-esteem resulted, and that smoking uptake was more likely to occur. Other authors take this medicalised, 'social contagion' model even further: Kandel and Wu (1995) consider the 'intergenerational transmission' of cigarette smoking in adolescence and report a 'significant and dose-related association between maternal and children's smoking' (p. 225). Support for such an arguably extreme view is found in a study of Dutch adolescent twins and their parents (Boomsa *et al.*, 1994). They concluded that while 59 per cent of interindividual variation in smoking behaviour could be attributed to shared environmental influences, 31 per cent of the variation was attributable to genetic factors. Other studies are less specific about the mechanism of influence, but nevertheless have found significant associations between the smoking behaviour of parents and that of their children. Such findings are reported in samples of American adolescents (Biglan *et al.*, 1995) and among Scottish teenagers (Green *et al.*, 1991).

On the other hand, some investigators have found no direct link between parental and adolescent smoking. In a very large study of American 14- to 18-year-olds, Wang *et al.* (1995) found that parental smoking had little effect on adolescent smoking status. By contrast, peer influence (such as the smoking status of an adolescent's best friend) proved to be the most significant and consistent predictor of smoking across all ages in their study. Similarly, Flay *et al.* (1994) showed that friends' smoking had a stronger direct influence on adolescent smoking behaviour, with parental smoking having only a minor, indirect effect. Further, following an 8-year longitudinal study of Australian teenagers, Stanton and Silva (1992) concluded unequivocally that the initiation of smoking among adolescents was influenced by friends and not by parents.

The role of parental smoking behaviour is complicated further by studies which suggest that the *nature* of the influence of parents and peers on teenage smoking differs. In an investigation of Australian 14- to 16-year-olds, Webster *et al.* (1994) employed path analysis to demonstrate that peer influences to smoke cigarettes operate predominantly through modelling behaviour. By contrast, the same technique showed that parental influence over smoking was achieved through adolescent perceptions of normative standards. The notion that parental influence operates largely via normative effects is supported by Flay *et al.*'s (1994) study of American teenagers, and by a further study of seventh-grade American pupils (Bauman *et al.*, 1992).

It may be helpful at this point to move away from questions about whether smoking is directly passed from parents to children by genetic, social contagion or normative processes, and to consider some of the investigations which link the *structure and successful or unsuccessful functioning* of families to teenage smoking behaviour.

The effects of family discord

How may families influence teenage smoking? In this chapter, we suggest that adolescent smoking behaviour cannot be realistically separated from the social environment in which children are raised. Fundamental to the nature of this environment is the structure of the adolescent's family and the quality of relationships within it.

The United States has the highest divorce rate in the world, and it has been estimated that 40 per cent of children born there during the 1980s will witness their parents' divorce. But the United States is not alone in having a high divorce rate: in the 1990s each year between 90,000 and 100,000 couples with children under the age of 16 are divorced in the UK (Diamond and Goddard, 1995). As Schaffer (1990) has pointed out, not only does parental divorce result in children watching the painful disintegration of the relationship between their mother and father, but the child is likely to have strong emotional bonds with both parents. Divorce or separation also usually results in the severance, or at least radical alteration, of the child's relationship with one parent, typically the father.

For many years, much of the research concerning the effects of parental divorce on children was of variable quality and hence of limited usefulness. Participants were often obtained from clinical psychology or psychiatry referrals and were thus biased towards problem behaviour, and most lacked proper control groups. More recently, studies of much better quality have become available, and have provided a clearer, more consistent picture of the effects on children of parental divorce in particular, and of family disharmony in general.

Perhaps the most important single insight provided by the recent literature is that divorce is not a discrete, one-off event in the life of any given child. Wallerstein *et al.* (1988) emphasise that parental separation is 'not a single circumscribed event, but a multistage process of radically changing family relationships'. The implication of this observation for researchers is that the study of the effects of family disunion on children must be of a longitudinal nature. Wallerstein and her colleagues studied families near the time of parental separation, and followed up the children at 18 months, 5 years and 10 years later. They found that the way in which the children responded to the separation of their parents depended upon the age of the child concerned. Pre-school children were profoundly upset and displayed both regression and acute separation anxiety. This effect showed a marked gender difference at 18 months post-separation, with boys continuing to be severely upset while most girls appeared to have adjusted to their new circumstances fairly well. Similar patterns were found among older children, who reported feelings of powerlessness, intense anger at one or both parents, acute depression, social withdrawal and a severe drop in school performance. However, 5 years later, this gender difference had disappeared and the children's psychological adjustment was found to be closely associated with the overall quality of relationships within the post-divorce or remarried family. Nevertheless, even 10 years after parental separation, clinical assessment showed that some adolescents still had clear memories of the stressful events surrounding their parents' divorce and were apprehensive that their own adulthood might be blighted by a similarly unhappy marriage.

Among the best-known and most methodologically sound investigations available is the work of Hetherington *et al.* (1979). Their study placed particular emphasis on the effects of parental separation on children's relationships with other children at school. They found that the play of such children was less mature, both intellectually and socially, than that of children from intact families. The divorce-group children were also more anxious, guilt-ridden and apathetic than were children from two-parent families. Various immature, ineffective and negative reactions in social behaviour with other children such as dependency, attention-seeking and aggressiveness were also typical of the divorce-group children. It is clear, therefore, that the effects of family disunion extend beyond the family itself and intrude into children's behaviour at school and with their peers.

Six years later, Hetherington (1988) studied the same children. Unlike in the 10-year longitudinal study of Wallerstein *et al.* (1988)

described above, the gender variations which Hetherington *et al.* had noted at the early stages were still found at the second-wave data collection. In families where the mother had not remarried, girls were very similar in their general adjustment to girls from two-parent families. Boys, on the other hand, tended to be more aggressive and less socially competent than were those in non-divorced families. However, where the custodial parent remarried, a different picture emerged. Both boys and girls were found to have more behavioural problems than did children from non-divorced families when the remarriage was less than 2 years old. Where the remarriage had occurred more than 2 years previously, boys appeared to adjust to their new circumstances while girls were much less able to do so.

The effects of family break-up thus depend on the sequelae of the divorce and the gender of the child. In single-parent families, boys appear to fare worse than girls, but when the mother remarries, or a new partner cohabits, girls are more likely to experience behavioural problems.

Beyond these immediate outcomes, there are also long-term effects of parental separation on children which depend on the mother's own adjustment, the marital relationship in the new stepfamily, the step-father's attitude towards and treatment of the child, and the external support available. These effects include the child's relationship with siblings and other children (Hetherington, 1988).

The effect of poor marital relationships on children does not begin at the time of divorce. In an unusual and important study, Block *et al.* (1986) examined a wide range of personality, social and intellectual characteristics in a group of children both before and after their parents' divorce. They found that children from the divorce group differed in many respects from the others *well before* their parents actually separated. In some cases, these differences were apparent many years before the event. At 3 years of age, boys who would go on to experience their parents' divorce were already found to be more restless, stubborn and emotionally labile. At 7 years, they were found to be less able to cope with stress than those in the group whose parents remained together, a pattern which continued into adolescence. As Schaffer (1996: 371) notes,

> The so-called effects of parental divorce ... occurred well before the divorce, and the responsible factor [for behavioural problems] is therefore not so much the break in the relationship brought about by the dissolution of the marriage as the atmosphere of discord and tension that existed while the parents were living together.

Cummings (1994) reports a further, very important observation: when children are exposed to repeated incidents of conflict, they do not, as is popularly believed, 'get used to it'. The opposite is true: knowing what to expect makes things worse rather than better. Children become sensitised and display increasingly greater reactivity to such stimuli. Schaffer (1996) concluded that when children are repeatedly exposed to such scenes over a protracted period of time, their capacity to regulate their own emotions is reduced.

In Chapter 1 we discussed a constellation of problem behaviours in which adolescents engage, which included cigarette smoking. Studies of family life suggest that these same behaviours are also connected with family disturbances. Although we would hesitate to propose a cause-and-effect relationship in quite the cavalier manner for which we have criticised others in that chapter, it is important to be aware of this common pattern. *The quality of family life cannot be separated from a wide range of adolescent problem behaviours, of which cigarette smoking is one.*

In a large-scale study in Finland, Isohanni *et al.* (1991) examined the relationship between juvenile smoking and family background among children living with both biological (married) parents, and among children living in non-standard families (e.g. single-parent or with a stepfather/mother). They found that children from 'non-standard' families were significantly more likely to become smokers compared to those who were raised by biological parents. Similar findings are reported in a study of adolescent smoking in Scotland (Green *et al.*, 1990). While the children of single mothers were more likely to smoke, Green and her colleagues found no evidence that children who smoked did so because their mothers smoked: the children of single mothers were less likely to smoke than were those of mothers living with a partner who was not the child's biological father.

Bailey *et al.* (1993) tested a number of models for their ability to describe the relationship between parents' and their children's smoking. They found not only that teenagers' smoking was linked to that of their parents, but also that teenage smoking was *independently* associated with certain familial characteristics such as family disunion. Similarly, a 6-year prospective study of American teenagers (Doherty and Allen, 1994) has shown poorer family functioning, especially low family cohesion, to be predictive of adolescent smoking. These findings illustrate the operation of the perceived environment system within problem behaviour theory. **They are important and warrant emphasis: poor family relationships predict teenage smoking *independently* of parental smoking behaviour.**

The questionnaire data from the Sussex study which are presented below fully confirm the findings of published research. In the pages which follow, we offer evidence to support and illustrate the importance of family structure and interpersonal relationships in families on the smoking behaviour of teenagers, and present tentative explanations for the conflicting evidence of previous studies.

EVIDENCE FROM THE SUSSEX AND LONDON STUDIES

The structure and nature of families

In the Sussex questionnaire, pupils were asked to indicate whether they had a mother, father, stepmother, stepfather, and younger or older siblings, and whether these family members currently lived at home with them. This information was then used to identify types of family structure. Three-quarters of adolescents in the Sussex study lived with both their natural parents. Most of the others lived with their mother, either with a stepfather or as a single-parent family. As can be seen in Table 4.1, very few children lived alone with their fathers.

Adolescents who lived with their biological parents were much less likely to smoke than were those living in either single-parent families or stepfamilies. The Sussex study found the proportion of both occasional and regular smokers to be significantly ($p < 0.001$) higher in stepfamilies and in one-parent families, compared to those adolescents living with both parents. Contrary to findings reported by some authors (Goddard, 1990), no significant differences were found between single-parent families and stepfamilies. Table 4.2 shows autumn term smoking behaviour classified by family structure.

The clearest finding from our investigations of the family was that adolescents living with both parents were less likely to smoke or to

Table 4.1 Family structure

Family structure	%
Both parents	74.1
Mother only	13.4
Mother and stepfather	9.1
Father only	1.8
Father and stepmother	0.9
Neither parent	0.7

N = 3,529

Table 4.2   Family structure and smoking behaviour in the autumn term

Family structure	% never-smokers	% occasional smokers	% regular smokers	N
Both parents	**60.9**	29.6	**9.5**	2,616
Mother and stepfather	42.7	39.3	16.1	321
Mother only	48.5	39.9	11.6	474
Father and stepmother	53.3	30.0	16.7	30
Father only	48.4	31.3	20.3	64
Neither parent	**41.7**	29.2	**29.2**	24

take up smoking during the school year than those living in single-parent families or stepfamilies. These findings were independent of gender and of school year.

A weak relationship was found between family structure and smoking *uptake*. Of those adolescents who reported in the autumn that they had never smoked, 19.9 per cent from nuclear families reported having tried cigarettes six months later, compared with 25.1 per cent from non-nuclear families. This effect was stronger for younger adolescents.

In general, a number of studies have linked styles of parenting to adolescent smoking behaviour. For example, authoritarian parenting has been associated with adolescent smoking (Jackson *et al.*, 1994; Fletcher *et al.*, 1995). Similar associations have been reported between smoking and poor communication and discipline (Kandel and Wu, 1995), as have aspects of the mother–child relationship and the adolescent's identification with the mother (Brook *et al.*, 1989). Sweeting and West (1995) found that poor relationships and conflict, in particular, have negative effects on certain psychological and physical outcomes for adolescents aged 15 and 18. These effects were largely independent of socio-economic factors.

The London study also showed that the nature of family structure appears to influence adolescent smoking behaviour, and specifically that the quality of parent–child relationships is critical. In focus groups, an honest, open and mutually respectful relationship was often cited as an essential factor in *determining the degree of influence that parents have on their children.* With regard to smoking, as well as alcohol, drugs and sex, participants spoke of the importance of trust between parents and children. Positive relationships were seen to be based on good communication, and on an openness that encouraged an honest exchange of feelings. Both parents and adolescents felt that where such relationships existed, there was less chance of children smoking. Even a boy who admitted smoking 'occasionally' talked positively about the supportive approach his father had taken with him:

'My dad's really quite understanding, so I think he understood that I was curious and all that, and he was really surprised that I had left it [trying cigarettes] this late, so I think he really understood about it. He just warned me away from it, that if I would do it how it would affect my life and all that....I think that's the best way, because if you tell your children in a way sort of other than shouting – 'cos if you shout you don't really make many points – you show them that you're angry and that may not always come across.'

(Joe, Year 11, smoker)

Adolescents talked about having a good relationship with their parents, of having parents who were 'cool' and who talked to them openly about all matters in a balanced way. Others talked about the importance of trust. One girl felt that trust was *the* crucial element in her relationship with her parents and the reason why she had no desire to smoke:

'Yeah, but I also think my parents they trust me and my brother and they should do 'cos I just wouldn't, a lot of people say they wouldn't but I just wouldn't, I think it's to do with your parents trusting you, and stuff like that.'

(Collette, Year 7, non-smoker)

The nature of their relationships and degree of communication between parents and children is important in adolescent smoking behaviour. An openness which allows and encourages them to seek help and support from their parents if they were smoking was positively valued by both adolescents and parents. For example, one boy talked about the open relationship he shared with his father:

''Cos I tell my dad everything what happens at school, after I come back from school if there's a fight I'll tell my dad what happened and everything, if I started smoking I would tell my dad and ask him to help me stop.'

(Tom, Year 10, non-smoker)

While some teenagers acknowledged a fear of being punished for smoking, this was more often talked about as a reason why *other* people might not smoke. One girl described how a friend of hers was grounded for smoking:

'Some parents are really strict, like I know this girl and she was
caught smoking and she got grounded for three months or something.... 'Cos like some people's parents are like "Oh you
shouldn't do it" and that's like the end of it really.'

(Carol, Year 11, non-smoker)

On the other hand, an overly authoritarian approach to parenting
may cause resentment, leading to secrecy and habitual non-com-
munication between child and parents. One boy spoke of his cousins,
who both smoked and occasionally took drugs, despite having very
strict parents:

'It's 'cos their parents don't let them be independent...their parents don't let them out so they're angry at their parents so they
want to do something against them.'

(Rajan, Year 11, non-smoker)

Rajan contrasted this relationship to his own with his father, suggesting that respect for parents is dependent on parents having respect for
their children, and on trusting them:

'No, he's not really close with his parents, he doesn't respect them,
'cos he thinks that they don't respect him, 'cos they won't let him
go out; they don't trust him, that's what he thinks, but like, my dad
trusts me, he'll let me go out, so we've become closer together.'

How well, then, do parents communicate with their children about
health matters? As a part of the family interview procedure, an instrument developed to assess levels of communication in the family was
adapted from that of Noller and Bagi (1985). It was used to assess
perceptions of the frequency and quality of family discussions (Holland *et al.*, 1996b). The content of the inventory included items concerning health behaviours, school work and future career plans. With
minor adjustments, this inventory was used to assess parents' and
children's perceptions of the frequency and quality of family discussions.

The communication inventory was completed by thirty-one children
and twenty parents. The major discrepancies between children's and
parents' perceptions of the talk within the family related to smoking,
drinking, drug use, sex and relationships. For each of these health-
related behaviours, teenagers were much more likely than were their
parents to believe that talking about an issue would *never* or *rarely*
have an effect on their behaviour. For example, 22 per cent of adolescents felt that talking about alcohol use would *rarely* or *never* have an

effect on their drinking, compared to 5 per cent of parents; similarly, 39 per cent of adolescents compared to 10 per cent of parents believed such discussions would *never* or only *rarely* affect their smoking behaviour.

On the other hand, 60 per cent of adults thought that talking about smoking would *often* or *very often* have an effect on behaviour, compared to only 22 per cent of children. In the case of illicit drug use, over half of all children believed that talking would *rarely* or *never* have an effect on their behaviour, an opinion shared by just 10 per cent of parents. In addition, parents also gave higher estimates of how often any given subject was talked about in the home. For example, 35 per cent of parents felt that they talked about sex with their children *often* or *very often*, while only 16 per cent of the adolescents felt this to be the case. Forty-five per cent of adolescents thought that sex was *never* or *rarely* discussed at home, compared to only 10 per cent of adults. Similar, though smaller, differences were observed in parents' and their offspring's estimates of time spent discussing school and career issues. Parents were consistently more likely to be satisfied with the current amount of discussion of such areas than were their children. Parent–offspring differences were largest in relation to discussions about sex and substance use.

Parents were also much more likely to say that they were happy with the quality of such discussions than were their children. Specifically, children were much more likely than their parents to say that they never discussed their *own* views about these issues. These differences were most pronounced in relation to smoking, alcohol, drugs and sex. Girls and their mothers were more likely to discuss their feelings than were boys or their fathers.

Results from the inventory can be summarised as follows. Children perceive fewer and less satisfactory discussions with their parents about smoking, alcohol, drugs and sex than do their parents. In addition, parents are more likely than are their children to believe that talking about a given issue will affect their children's subsequent behaviour.

In some of the family interviews there were lengthy discussions regarding the overall influence of the family culture. One mother lamented the demise of traditional family life:

'It's very difficult, isn't it. But I'm not blaming them, I'm not saying it's the single mums or the single dads or whatever. But I do feel that children need a balance. I did; although my dad was always working, he was still there, you know. We had holidays together, or whatever it is; I feel that's very important, you know, I feel getting back to the old-fashioned values, family life I think. I think there's too much of this, divorce seems so easy, doesn't it. You know what I mean, "oh, we'll have a row, let's get a divorce next week" and the children are pushed. I mean it's happened to so many of our friends, hasn't it, after twenty, thirty years of marriage, they suddenly decided that's it.'

Smoking in the family and adolescent smoking

In the Sussex questionnaire study adolescents were asked to indicate whether their parents and siblings were current smokers, had never smoked, or used to smoke. In the autumn term, one-third of fathers and older siblings were described as smokers. Only a quarter of mothers were reported to smoke regularly. Table 4.3 shows the smoking behaviour of family members in the Sussex study.

Table 4.3 Smoking behaviour of family members

Family member	% never smoked	% used to smoke	% current smokers	N
Father	32.4	34.4	33.2	3,210
Mother	44.9	29.0	26.1	3,381
Older brother	53.1	13.5	33.4	1,127
Older sister	51.6	14.5	33.9	1,060
Stepfather	26.3	26.9	46.8	331

We found a strong association between the smoking behaviour of most family members and adolescents' smoking behaviour in the autumn term. A similar relationship was found with step-parents, though this was less strong. Half of the adolescents who reported that a parent smoked had at least tried a cigarette. Two-thirds of pupils who had an older sibling who currently smoked had tried a cigarette themselves. However, it should not be concluded from these findings that older siblings are more influential on adolescent smoking patterns than are parents. Parents influence their children's smoking both directly, and indirectly through their influence on older siblings.

The relationships between smoking patterns of family members and adolescents who have never smoked are displayed in Table 4.4.

When a family member was reported to have never smoked, it was much more likely that the adolescent reported that they had never smoked either.

Table 4.4 Smoking behaviour of family members and never-smokers

Family member	% never smoked	% used to smoke	% current smokers
Father	67.9	53.8	47.6
Mother	64.1	51.7	44.1
Older brother	65.5	35.2	28.9
Older sister	67.8	33.2	28.6
Stepmother	52.3	42.5	42.4
Stepfather	44.4	39.9	42.2

In the London study, findings from the questionnaire showed only a relationship between mother's smoking and that of their sons and daughters. Nevertheless, there was a relationship between fathers' and sons' smoking behaviour, but not between that of fathers and daughters. There was also a relationship between mothers' and daughters' smoking behaviour. The smoking status of brothers was found to be more influential than that of sisters, although girls' smoking behaviour was related to that of older sisters. In general, those with an older sibling who smoked were more likely to be either occasional or regular smokers, or to be ex-smokers, than were teenagers with older siblings who did not smoke. In the London study, adolescents observed that being brought up in a non-smoking environment could preclude any thought of smoking at an early age. For Rawi (a non-smoker in Year 7), the fact that no one in his household smoked was important for him:

'Like my parents don't smoke, no one in my family smokes, I never think about it.'

In an individual interview, another boy simply reported that he usually did what his parents did. Since his parents did not smoke, neither did he. While this type of response was more common in the younger age group, older adolescents recalled being more directly influenced by their parents when they were younger. Pauline (a non-smoker in Year 11), commented:

'I think at 11 or 12 my interest didn't really lie in smoking, it didn't bother me, my parents don't smoke so I wasn't really used to it.'

Parents also talked about their own upbringing in relation to smoking. For example, one woman reported how impressed she was when her father gave up smoking, and how this encouraged her to stop as well. Other parents talked about family culture in broader terms, and its effects on their own smoking behaviour:

'Well, I think the environment I grew up in was a lot more stricter... the discipline at home was very strict; mum and dad's words were like God's words. You didn't question elders and you didn't question teachers, and I think because the family views were no smoking – my father was also a non-drinker – that probably was another influence.'

(Father, non-smoker)

By contrast, there was also evidence that other adolescents were discouraged from smoking as a result of living with parents or other family members who smoked. One boy commented:

'I think the fact that if your parents do smoke can also put you off 'cos you can see what it's done to them over the years and you can see that they're like dying.'

(David, Year 11)

Further, some adults recalled being put off smoking by the exposure they had to it while they were growing up, and reported how they tried to persuade their parents to give up the habit:

'My parents smoked.... My dad smoked and I couldn't stand the smell. I used to say to my dad, "Oh dad, stop smoking, you smoke too much" – so that just put me off anyway.'

(Mother, non-smoker)

Parental attitudes may not always need to be verbalised to influence smoking behaviour. Two brothers, 12 and 15 years old, described how their parents had never discussed smoking with them or given any advice or warnings, but they felt that their parents would be very surprised if they found that either of them smoked, and neither anticipated doing so. Similar sentiments were expressed by a parent when she was asked if she had ever talked to her son about smoking:

'Well I mean we haven't sort of sat down and said, "Let's have a discussion about smoking now." ... I think it's more that he probably knows, you know, sort of over the years that I don't [smoke] and that it's not something that I'm particularly happy about.'

(Mother, non-smoker)

Nevertheless, there was also a belief among some parents that the giving of anti-smoking advice by grandparents was important as, if not more important, than their smoking behaviour. One woman said that her own father smoked but the fact that he told her not to smoke constituted a more powerful message:

'My Dad...I think he encouraged us not to smoke, 'cos he was a smoker, he said, "Don't ever smoke 'cos it's not good." I suppose I stuck to that.'

(Mother, non-smoker)

In relation to her own children, she felt reassured by the fact that despite their father's smoking, the children are *told* that smoking is harmful and that she and her husband actively discouraged them from doing so.

Family smoking behaviour and adolescent smoking uptake

Table 4.5 shows the proportion of adolescents in the Sussex study who reported having changed from never having smoked to having tried cigarettes during the course of the school year. The effect of family smoking on adolescents' experimentation with cigarettes was substantial. *Where family members (father, mother, older brother, older sister) were current smokers, adolescents were twice as likely to have smoked, compared to those whose family members had never smoked. This effect was cumulative: adolescents whose parents and an older brother and sister both smoke (or have smoked in the past) were four times as likely to try cigarettes.*

By contrast, the transition from occasional smoking to regular smoking appears to be less strongly influenced by family smoking patterns. Nevertheless, when taken together, both parental and sibling smoking models *do* influence the transition to regular smoking.

Participants in both the focus groups and family interviews suggested that having parents who smoked could encourage children to smoke. There was discussion about *inveterate smoking*, where children grew up in a family environment where smoking was the norm. Parents and other family members smoked; smoking was an acceptable behaviour, was not actively discouraged and in some cases was encouraged. One girl commented:

Table 4.5 Smoking behaviour of family members and smoking uptake

Family member	% never smoked	% used to smoke	% current smokers
Father	13.7	23.1	27.0
Mother	15.4	25.9	28.4
Older brother	18.5	30.9	36.6
Older sister	15.7	27.1	29.1
Stepmother	28.6	30.4	32.4
Stepfather	21.3	36.4	30.3

'Yeah, my parents have been letting me smoke ever since I was 12, so in a way they have kind of encouraged me, 'cos I could have given up in that time but they were like "Oh if you haven't got any cigarettes just ask me, I've got some."...It's not exactly what you expect from parents when you're 12 years old, but they did it.'

(Rosie, Year 11, smoker)

Conflict, however, may arise outside the home environment when young smokers find themselves in a position where friends do not sanction their smoking behaviour. Rosie went on to describe her ambivalence:

'Well I don't think they should have let me smoke in the house when I was 12 years old, which was really taking things too far, and buying me cigarettes as well. I don't think they really should have done that 'cos I was too young.'

Adolescents described the changing influence of parents on smoking in terms of their development:

'I suppose if you were little, like a little child, and your parents smoke, you see them doing it, like, you're too young to understand why they're doing it, like you get to an age where it hasn't really been discussed, and like you see the opportunity and you wonder yourself what it's like so you do it yourself to find out why your parents do it.'

(John, Year 11, non-smoker)

The desire to imitate parents is seen to diminish in later adolescence:

'I just don't think that it really bothers them what their parents are doing. Like you don't want to copy your parents or anything anyway.'

(Sharon, Year 11, smoker)

The waning of parental influence coincides with other life changes, such as a move to secondary school, increased freedom and changes in social activities:

'It's not so much what your parents are doing at this age, it's more...you go out with your friends, you do this with your friends, and your friends do this and I think you're going to do what your friends do.'

(Pauline, Year 11, non-smoker)

Gary (Year 11) saw his smoking as his own responsibility:

'I'd say I've got a pretty open relationship with my mum, talk to her about anything really, and you know, we always discuss, she never raises her voice really. But still, you know, I managed to find a way to smoke, and like she knew about it and everything, but you know, so it's not her fault really, it's nothing she's [done] wrong, you know. It's the way I am.'

The view that adolescents can take responsibility for their own behaviour was also voiced by two parents from different families. One father talked about his own childhood, which he felt was much stricter than that of his own children. He came to England when he was 16 and his adolescent environment was one where parents commanded the highest respect. A mother talked about the importance of exercising discipline within the home so that 'when they grow up they'll set an example as well'.

Parents, like adolescents, identified the fact that parents who smoked could either discourage or encourage smoking:

'No, probably not at all, I mean my parents, well my mother never smoked and my father smoked a pipe and maybe if they had smoked I wouldn't have thought it was interesting, but I always wanted to try it because I thought it was something that naughty, because we weren't allowed to do it, you know anything naughty must be fun, whereas my husband, his parents smoked and he was always violently against it 'cos he didn't like the smell around the house, and I don't think it works necessarily that way.'

(Mother, non-smoker)

It can go either way I think, because there's no doubt it my brother and myself decided it wasn't for us.'

(Mother, non-smoker)

SUMMARY

Adolescents who are brought up by both biological parents are far less likely to start smoking than are children who are raised in reconstituted families. The quality of relationships within a family also influences the likelihood of an adolescent becoming a smoker. Adolescents value open, communicative relationships with their parents. For some, such relationships obviated the need to use smoking as a symbol of rebellion.

There was an acknowledgement from both adolescents and their parents that being brought up in a non-smoking family results in a reduced likelihood of smoking in the teenage years. Occasionally, parental smoking resulted in a rejection of smoking by their children, either as a part of establishing an individuated identity, or as a result of forming negative views about smoking through exposure to it. More usually, however, exposure to parental smoking was seen *by adolescents themselves* as a factor contributing to their smoking uptake. From the perspective of problem behaviour theory this contribution to smoking uptake may be viewed as the establishment of normative expectation about adult behaviour operating within the perceived environment system.

5 Social environments
Parenting, peers and school culture

> Few parents nowadays pay any regard to what their children
> say to them. The old-fashioned respect for the young is fast
> dying out.
>
> Oscar Wilde

In this chapter, three major sources of influence on adolescent smoking behaviour are considered. The influence of parenting styles on the social skills and capacity of children to interact successfully with their peers is considered in the first section. In the second section, both quantitative and behavioural data on adolescents' own and peer group smoking behaviour are presented, from both the Sussex and the London studies. In the third section, the culture of specific schools is examined in order to determine whether there are institutional influences above and beyond those of parents and peers.

PARENTING AND PEER RELATIONSHIPS

Sources of parental influence on adolescent smoking behaviour were discussed in Chapter 4. However, recent studies of adolescent development have been characterised by a shift in emphasis away from what has been described as 'matriarchic thinking' (Lamb, 1978). This movement has been partly in response to the observed failure of parental behaviour to account for differences in children's personality development. More importantly, there has been an increasing recognition of the changing nature of most children's upbringing in recent years. The marked increase of mothers in paid employment has made it necessary for children to be cared for outside the home by a range of individuals including relatives, friends and day care staff. To this list of outside influences must be added the systems found in schools and the pervasiveness of mass media, particularly television. The result has been that from an early age, young people are now brought into contact – directly or indirectly – with more people than ever before. Such influences do not operate in isolation from each other, nor do they combine in a simple, additive fashion. Rather, they blend to form complex, integrated influences which contribute to children's and adolescents' social skills and capacities to interact successfully with their peers.

Schaffer (1996) summarises research into the nature of this process, and suggests that there are four characteristics of parenting that develop children's competence in peer interactions:

- parental warmth, which contributes to how children interact with each other;
- parental control, neither excessive nor inadequate, since both been demonstrated to promote aggressiveness and thus rejection;
- parental involvement, which promotes inner security which in turn assists in social acceptance; and
- a democratic attitude, which fosters necessary skills for the egalitarian relationships found within peer groups.

Peer groups are perhaps the most important of all extrafamilial influences. Because they are composed of individuals of equal status to the child, they are able to provide an arena in which to learn about issues such as taking turns, sharing, leadership and how to cope with hostility. As Schaffer (1996: 312) notes:

> The peer group is . . . a miniature society in its own right, seen most clearly in the gangs that adolescents form and that exert great power over their individual members. These are subcultures, each characterised by its own set of rules . . . while some of them may adopt sets of values deviant from those of society as a whole, they do at least fulfil the function of enabling their members to acquire skills of conformity, loyalty and co-operation.

The relationships which young people form with each other during adolescence are thus of critical importance. Peers provide more than support and identity in a time of uncertainty. The way in which an individual adolescent learns to relate to his or her peers may also lay the foundations for adult relationships, and for adult life in general. It is not surprising that peer groups and their shared social representations exert such a powerful influence on adolescent smoking behaviour.

It has been known for many years that failure to be accepted into chosen peer groups during childhood may have a lasting effect on those unfortunate individuals who suffer this experience. Such rejection has been associated with a number of negative consequences, including low academic achievement (Buswell, 1953; Ullman, 1957; Bonney, 1971). In addition, childhood unpopularity has been found to predict delinquency (Roff *et al.*, 1972) and emotional problems in adulthood (Cowen *et al.*, 1973).

More recently, Kupersmidt and Coie (1990) reported on a 7-year longitudinal study of children initially aged 11 years. They compared *popular*, *average*, *neglected* and *rejected* children and subsequently examined a number of outcome measures in late adolescence. Compared to the other groups, *rejected* children were twice as likely to become truant, were more likely to have dropped out of school, or to have been suspended or given detention. In late adolescence, the *rejected* children were three times more likely than were *average* children to have been in contact with the police, while none of the *popular* children had been. In general, the likelihood of *rejected* children developing some kind of problem was far greater than that for any of the other groups. By contrast, the *neglected* children showed few problems in social adjustment.

PEER INFLUENCES ON SMOKING

A 7-year longitudinal study of American teenagers has demonstrated that ineffective parental monitoring is associated with their children's involvement in deviant peer networks (Dishion *et al.*, 1995), thus confirming the link posited by problem behaviour theory between the parenting skills of individual parents and their children's social competence. The researchers also explored the relationship between failure to meet with the social acceptance of peers and the onset of cigarette smoking in adolescence. They found a rapid increase in smoking during the transition from middle to high school (13 to 16 years of age) among adolescents with a prior history of low sociometric status (low popularity). More directly, Biglan *et al.* (1995) showed an association with inadequate parental monitoring and adolescent tobacco use in a longitudinal study of American 14- to 17-year-olds.

The more general effects of peers on adolescent smoking behaviour are well known and extensively documented. Moreover, such influences have been demonstrated in a wide range of cultural settings. For example, in a very large sample of both Black and White American adolescents aged 12 to 17 years, Feigelman and Lee (1995) found smoking to be strongly associated with having best friends and siblings who smoke. Similar findings are reported among Norwegian adolescents (Oygard *et al.*, 1995), among teenagers in New Zealand

(Fergusson *et al.*, 1995), among adolescents in Jamaica (Aloise-Young *et al.*, 1994), and among British schoolchildren (Charlton and Blair, 1989).

Peer encouragement has been shown to be predictive both of initial smoking uptake (Presti *et al.*, 1992) and of initial and subsequent use of tobacco, alcohol and marijuana (Duncan, *et al.*, 1995). Importantly, several other studies suggest that peer influence is the most important and consistent of several likely factors, including parental smoking and stress at school (Stanton and Silva, 1992; Dusenbury *et al.*, 1992; Juon *et al.*, 1995; Wang *et al.*, 1995). Further, best friends seem to be particularly influential (Urberg, 1992).

Once an individual has started smoking, the strength of the bond of friendship with smoking peers influences decisions and expectations about continuing to smoke or to quit (Van Roosmalen and McDaniel, 1989). Moreover, attitudes towards a range of measures have shown clear covariances within groups of British adolescents (Eiser *et al.*, 1991). These measures include alcohol use, health locus of control, school performance and spending habits.

It is unsurprising, therefore, that conventional notions of peer influences on smoking, alcohol and drug use have tended to focus on the risks presented by the peer group. However, peer norms can also have an protective effect on these behaviours, depending on the shared social representations of the group. The representations of a friendship group may in fact provide elements of both 'risk' towards and 'protection' from such behaviours. In the London study, both risk-taking and risk-aversive identities were explored through interviews to assess the extent to which they had an effect on smoking behaviour, and how they might influence other aspects of adolescent development. A shared social identity may also discourage smoking. If the identity includes a competitive dimension, for example in sports, it can have an inhibiting effect on smoking uptake:

> 'Me and my friends, none of us smoke, but it's like we're into sports and football.... 'Cos, like everyone's in competition to like, be the best, and be fit, fast and that stuff.'
>
> (Stephen, Year 11, non-smoker)

Peer influences and smoking behaviour

In order to assess the influence of best friends' smoking behaviour, the Sussex questionnaire asked pupils to describe their best friend's smoking behaviour: whether that person was a never-smoker, an occasional

Table 5.1 Best friend's smoking and autumn term smoking group membership

Best friend's smoking status in autumn term	Non-smoker (n = 2,531) %	Occasional smoker (n = 1,431) %	Regular smoker (n = 667) %
Best friend has not smoked	83.7	42.6	9.9
Best friend used to smoke	10.7	30.8	13.0
Best friend smokes	5.6	26.6	77.1

Chi-square for table = 2,028.0, $p < 0.000005$

smoker, or currently a regular smoker. Strong associations between best friend's smoking behaviour and adolescents' own smoking status are shown in Table 5.1. Only a small minority of non-smokers (5.6 per cent) reported a best friend who was currently a regular smoker. The proportion of occasional smokers whose best friends were regular smokers was nearly five times greater (26.6 per cent). More than three-quarters (77.1 per cent) of regular smokers' friends were themselves regular smokers. It is clear that regular smokers were nearly fourteen times more likely than non-smokers to report that their best friend was currently a smoker. Within each year group there was a consistently strong and significant ($p < 0.000005$) association between the smoking status of adolescents and that of their best friends.

In the London study, the nature of friendships was also shown to be very important in determining smoking behaviour. The distinction between 'real' friendships and those based on smoking was a consistent theme in all the age groups interviewed. Since all adolescents have knowledge of the harmful effects of smoking, a 'real' friend who smoked would not try to pressure his/her non-smoking friends into taking up cigarettes. By the same token, a 'real' friend who did not smoke would try to dissuade his/her friends from smoking, or try to help them stop.

'If your friends are really good friends they'll try to stop you to try to get you off smoking, because they won't want to see you get hurt by smoking; if they just sort of hang around with you..."If you want to get yourself hooked you can, we're not going to help you."'

(Jim, Year 7, non-smoker)

'If they're your friends they won't offer you any, they won't pressure you.'

(Finbar, Year 7, non-smoker)

'They respect you, if you didn't do it and they did it, they wouldn't expect you to do it.'

(Maureen, year 7, non-smoker)

In the Sussex study, girls who belonged to never-smoked groups construed the onset of smoking largely in terms of *group* identity and behaviour. Their understanding of their present and future resistance to smoking was both *group*-oriented and *individual*-oriented. Never-smoked group members easily identified groups of smokers. The smokers were described as *active, predatory* and *demanding conformity to their smoking behaviour*. These attributes were seen as leading to the onset of smoking in erstwhile non-smokers.

Members of the never-smoked groups described smoking groups as predatory, seeking to adopt new members on the groups' terms. Among these terms is the necessity to smoke:

'These other people are quite wimps and they [smokers] actually get them and like [say]: "Oh come on, come and join us", and you can try it [smoking] and all that and they make you like it.'

Aggressive behaviour also contributed to a predatory image.

Tactics employed by smoking group members to ensure conformity

In the Sussex study, girls in the never-smoked groups believed that smoking groups did not tolerate non-smoking members for long, even when they initially accepted them as new members. Smoking groups were reputed to adopt three methods to encourage eventual compliance among potential and new members:

- Persuasion: there was some belief that good friends would not try to encourage one to smoke, but there was rather more reporting of strong and deceitful persuasion. Smokers were reported to deny the addictive potential of cigarettes when offering them to non-smokers (although the regular smoking group freely admitted that they were addicted).
- Physical intimidation: the never-smoked groups told of friends who said they were in fear of future beatings for not smoking:

'There's one girl, she hangs round with one of my friends, and he's in another form, and my friend doesn't smoke but she says she doesn't actually like being with the others that smoke because she feels that one day she's going to actually start smoking. And she also says, "What if I don't smoke? I'm going to get beaten up when I'm older."'

- Social ostracism: continual non-smoking is seen as likely to lead to being removed from the smoking friendship group:

  'I think they'd be really sly about it and they would get you thinking that you're their friend and if you don't smoke later on they'll chuck you out their group.'

Never-smokers' descriptions of these tactics suggested that they viewed smoking groups as uncompromising in their attachment to the smoking aspect of their group identity. The sole regular smoking group denied, however, that such relentless conformity formed a part of their friendships, and this attitude was also apparent among smokers in the London study. The predatory smoker was absent from the London study as well. Adolescents in the London study recognised both normative and direct pressure from the peer group to smoke.

Never-smoked individuals and the onset of smoking

Despite strong evidence in the Sussex study of a group-oriented understanding of the consequences of smoking status and group membership, there was consistent affirmation of the individual's freedom of choice or right to make a decision. Personal choice was always invoked in the context of a new smoker deciding to ignore his/her friends' advice and to continue to smoke. The never-smoked friends would affirm the right of the new smoker to make his/her choice, but this affirmation served as a boundary point in several senses:

- as the point in time at which the new smoker ceased to be a concern of the never-smoked friendship group;
- as the boundary in social space between the friendship group and its environment;
- as a marker within the friendship group, delimiting acceptable behaviours and marking off the unacceptable.

The demand for conformity that the never-smoked group attributed to smoking groups was also a feature of their own groups. The role played by the affirmation of personal choice in their groups was, in practice, a demand for conformity to their never-smoked status. An understanding of the dangers to their group identity of the change in smoking status of their group members probably led them to demand this conformity. This distinction between 'real' friends and 'smoking' friends was particularly marked among younger adolescents in the London study. It was implied that 'real' friends would respect personal decisions that went against the norms of the group, whereas friends that were only smoking friends would not:

> 'If your friends were smoking and they tried to pressure you and you didn't want to smoke, they wouldn't really be being a friend to you, 'cos they're just trying to pressure you into something that you don't really want to do; that's not really being a friend to someone.'
>
> (Barry, Year 7, non-smoker)

> 'It does form friendships, but not like real friendships, just friendships where you say "Have you got a cigarette?" or "No" and you go "All right then" but it's not like ... you don't ... I don't think it can form real friendships, just people to talk to.'
>
> (Roma, Year 11, smoker)

In addition to the theme of friendship, some adolescents felt that smoking was a personal issue, and that a true friend should neither try to persuade someone to smoke, nor to give up. Friends should respect each other's decisions, and not fall out over such an unimportant matter. Friendships should not be made or broken on the issue of smoking:

> 'But you shouldn't lose friends over smoking though, 'cos it's not worth it.'
>
> (Alison, Year 7, non-smoker)

> 'I had a group of friends and there was about eight of us, and about three of us smoked regularly, three of us didn't really smoke, and the other two smoked on and off really, so it was like a mixture, but it never really changed anything 'cos smoking wasn't really the main subject. I don't think that friendships are really based on whether or not you smoke.'
>
> (Joe, Year 11, non-smoker)

> 'If they're real friends they're not really going to care. ... I think it just boils down to, if you're with a group of friends that you feel comfortable with and you're all equal in that group, then it just basically boils down to, "I like smoking, I don't like smoking".'
>
> (Keith, Year 11, smoker)

'Real' (non-smoking) friends were seen as more likely to facilitate and support cessation:

'You could try and get one of your friends to stop, and if they do, they can stick up for you, and you can hang around together.'

(Lorna, Year 7, non-smoker)

'It depends on your friends as well if they can help you. If you say to them, that's if you've giving up smoking they can help you or if they see you with a cigarette they might take it off you.'

(Patti, Year 11, smoker)

One group of girls found the problem of what to do when a friend began smoking less clear cut, and anticipated misunderstandings:

'What I think is difficult is if you have friends who smoke, 'cos you don't know whether to leave them or to help them stop.'

(Susan, Year 7, non-smoker)

'You usually just leave them, 'cos you don't want to get involved.'

(Charlotte, Year 7, non-smoker)

' 'Cos they get sick of you trying to tell them.'

(Teresa, Year 7, non-smoker)

'They think you're jealous or that you're going around telling them ... they just say stay out of their life; it's their life, they can do what they want, you just say, "fine, it's your life no problem." '

(Maureen, Year 7, non-smoker)

These quotations illustrate the very sensitive nature of smoking as a topic of discussion and a factor in maintaining friendships. Both smokers and non-smokers may feel embarrassed and defensive about their smoking status when they perceive themselves to be in a minority. Smokers often reported refraining from smoking while in the company of non-smokers:

'You're not really looking to smoke with non-smokers because it is antisocial, and you know, you don't feel right if you're the only person smoking.'

(Gary, Year 11, ex-smoker)

Normative pressure to not smoke is strong among adolescents, and influences smokers' behaviour in specific contexts:

'Because no one else is doing it, you tend not to smoke as much; even if they don't mind you smoking you tend not to smoke at all.'

(Patti, Year 11, smoker)

'Kind of it makes you look stupid if you're the only one there.'

(Neil, Year 11, smoker)

'You just wouldn't do it, I think.'

(Andy, Year 11, smoker)

Non-smokers experienced normative pressure to smoke. They talked about their feelings of exclusion from the group, resulting in a temptation to smoke in order to fit in:

'You feel left out. You want to try it out.'

(Noel, Year 7, non-smoker)

'You don't want to be different, you don't want to be different from everyone else, if all your friends are smoking, you're at that age when you don't want to stick out and you just want to blend in.'

(Michelle, Year 11, non-smoker)

Some of the participants saw normative pressure as the only real reason for people to want to try smoking:

'Well, it doesn't encourage you, because if no one is smoking you don't think "I'll try it" because if there is no one around [smoking] you don't really think about it. None of us think about smoking because no one is smoking around us.'

(Carol, Year 11, non-smoker)

Almost all the participants acknowledged the existence of peer pressure in one form or another. When asked specifically about pressure to smoke, most adolescents reported that they had not felt such pressure directly. However, they described wanting to feel part of a group, or at least not wanting to feel excluded from a group. Adolescents of all ages identified such pressure as being particularly acute at 'our age'; that is, the age that they happened to be themselves:

'They're not like telling you to smoke, it's just like because they're doing it you feel you want to do it.'

(Declan, Year 7, non-smoker)

'It's not like they're doing it to get you to smoke. . . . it's just the fact that they're doing it. It's not that they're sitting there saying, "Go on, have a cigarette" or anything at all like that. It's just because they're doing it.'

(Patti, Year 11, smoker)

Peer influences and smoking uptake

Further strong evidence for the influence of friendship on smoking behaviour is available in the longitudinal data from the Sussex study (see Table 5.2). Among never smokers in the autumn term, those with best friends who had smoked were almost twice as likely to have tried cigarettes by the summer term as were those with best friends who were not smokers. Statistical analysis showed that the influence on the never-smoker of having a best friend who is a smoker diminishes with age. This reflects the changing composition of the group of never-smokers with increasing age. With increasing age, the never-smokers will have resisted smoking for longer. It would appear that the longer adolescents have resisted smoking, the more resistant to peer influence they become. This finding is important but is not frequently reported.

Table 5.2 Best friend's smoking status in autumn term and smoking uptake

	Adolescent smoking	
Best friend's smoking status in autumn	*% of autumn never-smokers who had smoked by the summer*	*% of autumn occasional smokers who had become regular smokers by the summer*
Never smoked	18.1	16.4
Occasional smoker	34.1	22.5
Regular smoker	35.6	35.1

Chi-square for transition from never smoking to occasional smoking = 43.4, 2 df, $p < 0.000005$; chi-square for transition from occasional smoking to regular smoking = 35.2, 2 df, $p < 0.000005$

Adolescents who were classified as occasional smokers from their responses in the autumn questionnaire, and who reported that their best friend smoked, were about twice as likely to have become regular smokers by the summer, when compared with adolescents with never-smoking best friends. The strong link between adolescents' and best friends' smoking was apparent within each year group, and in each case was highly significant ($p < 0.00005$).

While peer pressure to act in certain ways was something all adolescents seemed to have heard about *as a concept*, it was generally held to be something that happened to other people. The following exchange between adolescents in Year 11 illustrates this distinction well:

HELEN: I don't actually think there is much peer pressure put onto you about smoking.

KELLY: Not intentionally but it's there.

ROMA: No one EVER pressured me into it.

KELLY: But did your friends start smoking before?

ROMA: Yeah, but...

KELLY: Well there you are then.

ROMA: But they didn't ever offer me a cigarette ever, nobody ever did, and then it was because I got curious, because no one ever said to me, 'Do you want one?'

HELEN: Yeah, it's not peer pressure at all, it's curiosity.

Nevertheless, there was evidence of direct pressure to smoke. Several participants talked of risking being labelled a 'wimp' or 'chicken' if they refused to smoke:

'[They say] "Go on, try it." You haven't got much of a choice, have you, when they're sticking it right in front of you. And everyone else can like, spread the word that you're a chicken 'cos you didn't try it.'

(Alison, Year 7, non-smoker)

'If your friends are doing it as well, that's even more pressure 'cos say you wanted to give up, but you can't because if you do, like your friends would say "ah wimp and chicken" and that.'

(Luke, Year 7, non-smoker)

Some participants believed that peer influence was moderated by other factors, such as personality:

'It depends what kind of person you are; some people will change the kind of music they like, and they'll change everything to try and fit in with a group, and some people will stay how they are and find a group of people who accept them for who they are. It depends what kind of person you are.'

(Andy, Year 11, smoker)

One 11-year-old girl made an interesting connection between direct peer pressure to smoke and the stress this induced:

'Sometimes, if you're in a gang and all your friends smoke and you're under loads of pressure to smoke and you think, "Oh well, I might as well try it", and you smoke and then they all stop pressuring you. It feels like the smoking stopped the pressure because it made you feel better. But it's only because they've stopped nagging you because you have smoked.'

(Maureen, Year 7, non-smoker)

There was a general view that the influence of peers is very strong during adolescence, and that this influence is very hard to resist. During adolescence there is a move away from dependence on parents, and an increased emphasis on life outside the family home. Relationships with peers are critical to this process:

'At our age you always want to be like your friends, or you want to fit in or be better than your friends. If your friends... are doing one thing you're not going to totally rebel against it, because your friends are like, who you look up to... yeah, it's not so much your parents at this age, it's more... you go out with your friends, you do this with your friends and your friends do this... you're going to do what your friends do.'

(Monique, Year 11, non-smoker)

One of the girls in the Sussex study (who had never smoked) noticed that a change of schools was related to previously non-smoking girls taking up smoking for the first time:

'She... seems to have gone that one step further now we're at secondary school.'

A change of schools is recognised by girls as an opportunity to choose new behaviours, new friends and possibly a new social identity. It is also likely to have disrupted friendship groups established during primary/other school, and to have placed the identities of such groups in a new and challenging environment.

SCHOOL CULTURE

Neither the influence of peers nor smoking education can be viewed in isolation from the specific social characteristics of individual schools. In this section three dimensions that define the social settings of the eight schools that participated in the Sussex study are compared. Each of these variables has been identified in research on smoking prevalence in secondary schools. These dimensions are:

• fathers' occupation or social class
• examination results
• school smoking policy.

The occupations of pupils' fathers, the GCSE results for each school, and school rules about smoking give an indication of the cultures of the eight schools participating in the quantitative studies.

Fathers' occupations

In Chapter 3 we showed that fathers' occupations in the six schools in the Sussex study were representative of the county and broadly comparable to those for England as whole. Fathers' occupations for all eight schools are presented as an approximation to the social class composition of participating schools. Table 5.3 shows that Girls 2 recruits from a different population as compared with the other schools.

Table 5.3   Fathers' occupations by school as a percentage of the total by school

School	I	II	IIIn	IIIm	IV	V	Other
C1	13	35	12	25	8	2	5
C2	12	39	10	27	7	1	4
T1	2	16	11	41	12	3	15
T2	10	31	11	25	10	2	11
T3	5	33	21	24	10	1	6
T4	4	21	28	22	9	1	15
G1	3	27	11	30	16	4	9
G2	29	47	6	10	3	0	5

Note: 'Other' includes fathers described as being unemployed. C indicates a rural, 'country' school, T an urban, 'town' school and G an all-girls school, as explained in Chapter 3

GCSE results

A further indication of the characteristics of these schools is provided by statistics for examination results published in Department of Education and Employment league tables at the time of data collection (Table 5.4).

The social problems of families in the Town 1 catchment area are reflected in these examination results. The privileged economic position of Girls 2 families is also evidenced.

School rules about smoking

The culture of smoking within a school is defined in terms of the stance taken by the management in regard to cigarette smoking by

Table 5.4   Examination results of the schools studied (1995)

School	5+ A*–C	5+ A*–G	1+ A*–G
C1	59	99	99
C2	45	97	99
T1	25	79	90
T2	44	91	97
T3	62	94	98
T4	52	94	97
G1	40	84	92
G2	100	100	100

GCSE: Percentage of 15-year-old pupils achieving 5+ A*–C means 5 or more grades A*–C; 5+ A*–G means 5 or more grades A*–G; 1+ A*–G means 1 or more grades A*–G

pupils and by all others on school premises. The descriptions presented below derive from material provided by schools about their explicit policies, guidelines and rules about smoking and from observations undertaken during visits to the school by research staff.

Country 1

A decision in 1990 that the campus be totally smoke-free was modified in 1992 to recognise the loss of income that resulted from imposing this restriction on external lettings. Pupils found smoking have a four-hour detention with their year head and their parents are informed. From October 1996 there will be a positive, after-school course to which 'offenders' will automatically be referred and which pupils wishing to stop smoking may join. During an initial visit to the school in July 1994 a senior teacher explained that on a Duke of Edinburgh Award trip a smoking area in the woods was designated in order to ensure safety.

Country 2

The campus is a non-smoking environment and no one is permitted to smoke within the premises. This is a condition of service for staff. These rules apply to students on school trips and journeys to and from school. 'Offenders' initially receive break or lunchtime detention and parents are informed. Persistent offenders might be excluded for a fixed term but this circumstance has not yet arisen. The aim of the policy is to ensure that the playground is not a recruiting ground for smoking.

Town 1

Town 1 was the only one of the original six schools that failed to reply to a request for information on its smoking policy. The school has undergone a number of changes following a recent inspection by OFSTED (the national schools inspection agency), including the appointment of a new headteacher. It is difficult, therefore, to comment on smoking policies retrospectively.

Town 2

From 1 September 1993 the school has operated a no-smoking policy which applies to everyone on the entire site. The no-smoking rule applies to pupils travelling to and from school. First-time 'offenders' receive detention and their parents are sent a letter. On a second occasion smokers are excluded from school. Documentation for a school trip overseas made clear that the school would not punish smoking by 18-year-olds, but requested them not to smoke within sight of younger pupils.

Town 3

Pupils, parents, staff and new staff are informed that the school is a smoke-free environment. Smoking is not allowed on the premises even if parental consent is forthcoming. Persistent 'offenders' are not allowed to remain on the premises at lunchtime and a standard letter warns of a one-day suspension for persistent smoking on the premises.

Town 4

A policy of no indoor smoking was introduced on 1 January 1995. Teachers continued the practice of not smoking within sight of pupils, and advice and counselling is offered to teachers wishing to stop smoking. Visitors and other users are informed of the new policy.

All schools in Sussex have been moving towards the implementation of no-smoking policies. Nonetheless, there are differences between schools in the speed with which such policies have been implemented. In addition, there are differences in attitudes towards regular smokers. Town 4 stands out in trying to assist established staff who may experience difficulty in stopping, and Country 1 plans to assist pupils who wish to give up smoking.

Smoking prevalence

In the Sussex study, self-reports of smoking behaviour in the two all-girl schools were compared with the rates reported by girls from the six mixed schools. The relevant smoking behaviour for the six mixed schools is presented in Table 3.8 (p. 44). Data from Girls 2 were compared with data from the six schools in the autumn term survey. Data from Girls 1 were compared with those for girls in Years 7 to 10 from the summer term survey in the mixed schools. The unadjusted prevalence rates for the two all-girl schools are shown in Table 5.5.

Table 5.5 Percentage of girl never-smokers, occasional smokers and regular smokers from all-girls and mixed secondary schools

	Autumn term		*Summer term* *(Years 7, 8, 9, and 10)*	
	G1 %	*G2* %	*G1* %	*G2* %
Never smokers	53.2	62.2	47.8	40.8
Occasional smokers	30.2	27.1	34.7	38.6
Regular smokers	16.7	10.7	17.5	20.6

Note: Autumn term comparison, chi-square = 13.4, 2 df, $p < 0.01$; summer term comparison, chi-square = 8.9, 2 df, $p < 0.05$

From the autumn term comparison, it is clear that girls from the private school (Girls 2) were more likely to have never smoked a cigarette than were girls from the mixed state school. The difference (62.2 per cent v. 53.2 per cent) is statistically significant. However, the summer term comparison shows that girls from the girls' state school were less likely to have never smoked a cigarette than girls from the mixed-sex schools (40.8 per cent v. 47.8 per cent), a difference which is also statistically significant.

The lower rates of smoking in Girls 2 compared with Girls 1 implies that the smoking behaviour of girls in all-girl schools cannot be described simply as involving more, or less, smoking than that of girls from mixed schools. There are, however, indications that the raw estimates of smoking prevalence require closer scrutiny before conclusions are drawn about the impact of single-sex education on smoking behaviour. An examination of the culture of the two all-girl schools presented above is revealing. Table 5.3 shows that the occupations of the fathers of girls from Girls 2 differ substantially from those of pupils in state schools. Girls 2 pupils tend to have fathers who are

disproportionately drawn from professional and managerial occupations. Social class is inversely related to smoking among adults
and two American studies have reported an inverse relationship
between socio-economic status and smoking prevalence for teenagers
(Ashby, 1995; Dent *et al.*, 1993). The occupational data suggest that
social class may be a factor influencing rates of smoking found in
Girls 2.

In order to assess the influence of fathers' occupation on smoking
prevalence among girls two statistical analyses were undertaken.
These procedures needed to control for age, since smoking increases
directly with age. The aim of the analyses was to determine whether
significant differences in the smoking patterns of girls from all-girl and
mixed schools remained after age and father's occupation were statistically controlled. These analyses yielded several clear results.

Overall the data were consistent with the pattern that has previously
been observed among adults and for American teenagers. Children
with fathers in high-status occupations were more likely never to have
smoked, and were correspondingly less likely to be regular smokers,
than were children whose parents were manual workers. The smoking
behaviour of girls from Girls 1 followed the pattern of girls in mixed
state schools. By contrast, pupils in Girls 2 whose fathers were classified as clerical or manual workers were no more likely to be regular
smokers than girls with fathers in professional or managerial occupations. This finding suggests that the particular culture of a school
contributes something beyond the social background factors that
pupils bring with them to school. Both the American studies identified
academic expectation/achievement as another major factor predicting
smoking prevalence (Ashby, 1995; Dent *et al.*, 1993).

The emphasis on academic achievement in Girls 2 is reflected in the
examination results reported in Table 5.4 and in the aspirations for
further education reported by the girls themselves. When asked to
indicate whether they intended to leave school as soon as possible, to
stay for A-level or to attend university, a highly significant difference
was found. Eighty-one per cent of Girls 2 pupils reported that they
planned to attend university but only 45 per cent of Girls 1 pupils
indicated such intentions. It is probably a combination of social background factors and specific school culture that accounts for this
difference.

In Chapter 4 we have already shown the influence of family and
family smoking on adolescent smoking behaviour. Further statistically
significant differences were revealed in the family background and
smoking histories of girls from the two schools. Living in a nuclear

family with one's natural mother and father was reported by 78 per cent of Girls 2 pupils but by 68 per cent of Girls 1 pupils. These girls reported that 68 per cent of their fathers were currently, or had been, cigarette smokers compared to 50 per cent of the fathers of Girls 2 pupils. Current or past cigarette smoking was reported for 45 per cent of Girls 2 pupils' mothers but for 59 per cent of mothers of Girls 1 pupils. In a consistent manner, the parents of Girls 2 pupils were reported to be more likely than the parents of Girls 1 pupils to mind if their daughters smoked.

Overall it is clear that attendance at an all-girl school *per se* is not a major determinant of smoking prevalence. Although both the girls' schools studied are single sex, they differed along many dimensions. As a consequence of the state/private distinction, they draw girls from different social backgrounds. The difference in socio-economic status was reflected in family structure, smoking behaviour of family members and family attitudes towards girls' smoking. In addition, the two schools provide very different school cultures: Girls 2 is characterised by particularly high academic expectations.

SUMMARY

- Peer influences were important in influencing patterns of smoking among teenagers. Having a best friend who smoked was a significant risk factor for starting to smoke, and for increasing smoking.
- Both family members and peers were important in predicting the transition from never smoking to regular smoking. However, while the progression to regular smoking was less clearly predicted by family smoking, it was substantially affected by the smoking behaviour of best friends. This provides support for the findings of a similar American study (Chassin *et al.*, 1986).
- Children with fathers in high-status occupations were more likely to have never smoked, and were correspondingly less likely to be regular smokers, than children whose parents were manual workers.
- Schools' public statements of their smoking policies were relatively consistent, although there were differences in the dates from which these policies had been implemented.
- The particular culture of a school influences smoking prevalence in addition to the particular social background factors pupils bring with them to school.

Fathers' occupations, family structure and school culture differed widely between the two single-sex girls' schools. Consequently, the belief that single-sex education *per se* is meaningful in predicting smoking prevalence is seriously questioned.

Data from the London study illustrate aspects of how adolescents interact with their peers. This is a complex process and peer pressure is multi-faceted: adolescents described how peer pressures could be an influence both for and against smoking cigarettes. Others felt that smoking was a matter of individual choice. While adolescents understood the term 'peer pressure', they did not usually consider themselves to be subject to such pressure either in terms of behaviour generally, or specifically in relation to smoking. Instead, powerful normative and behavioural pressures *not* to smoke are found within adolescent friendship groups.

6 Smoking and mood
The control of stress, the pursuit of pleasure and concerns about the body

One half of the world cannot understand the pleasures of the other.

Jane Austen

A cigarette is the perfect type of pleasure. It is exquisite, and leaves one unsatisfied. What more can one ask?

Oscar Wilde

Adults use food, alcohol and drugs, including cigarettes, to alter their mood states. It is hardly surprising that adolescents follow a similar course. Adolescents' use of cigarettes to moderate affect is explored in this chapter. The first section examines questionnaire results from the Sussex study in the context of published accounts of stress, coping and smoking. These studies raise the possibility that smokers perceive more stress in their lives and use different coping strategies as compared with non-smokers. The questionnaire results indicate that despite the belief that adolescent girls experience greater stress than do teenage boys, the gender differences in smoking prevalence considered in Chapter 3 cannot be attributed directly to differences either in perceived stress or in coping strategies.

In the second section of this chapter, data from the London study indicate the functions that adolescents ascribe to their use of cigarettes. These include reports of finding pleasure in the physical act of smoking, the use of smoking to control stress and alter affect, the use of cigarettes to establish a rebellious identity, the use of smoking in peer group relationships and the use of cigarettes in the construction of personal time. In the final section beliefs about smoking and weight control are explored in the context of young adolescents' views about their bodies.

STRESS, COPING AND ADOLESCENT SMOKING

Stress and coping in adolescence

Change is a major source of stress in everyday life. During adolescence, individuals experience many changes including puberty, shifting relationships with parents and peers, school transitions and assessments, and the search for a secure self-identity (Frydenberg and Lewis, 1993; Seiffge-Krenke, 1993a, 1993b). In studies of adolescents, stress has been viewed as a significant cause of physical and mental health problems (see Seiffge-Krenke, 1993a, for an overview of historical trends in such research).

Adolescent stressors have commonly been analysed using distinctions that were initially developed during research about stress among adults. Three related components of adult stress have been identified. These are major life events, minor life events (so-called 'hassles') and chronic difficulties (Compas *et al.*, 1993; Rice *et al.*, 1993).

Within the past fifteen years research with adults has addressed the issue of individual differences in reactivity to stress (Krause, 1990). Longitudinal studies have shown that current symptoms and stress are related even when account is taken of earlier symptoms (e.g. Siegal and Brown, 1988; Allgood-Merton *et al.*, 1990; DuBois *et al.*, 1994; Ge *et al.*, 1994).

The view that coping resources may function as potential moderators of the stress–illness relationship has been a major focus of research in this area (Carver *et al.*, 1989; Folkman and Lazarus, 1985). More recently, this approach has been adopted in studies of stress in adolescence, and inventories of adolescent stress and coping have been developed (e.g. Dise-Lewis, 1988; Frydenberg and Lewis, 1991; Seiffge-Krenke, 1993b).

Results showing that adolescent girls tend to report more stressful experiences in their lives than do boys might be relevant to the observed higher prevalence of cigarette smoking among girls (Burke and Weir, 1978; Bruns and Geist, 1984; Dise-Lewis, 1988; Allgood-Merton *et al.*, 1990; Allen and Hiebert, 1991; Kearney *et al.*, 1993; Seiffge-Krenke, 1993b; Byrne *et al.*, 1995). Girls in early adolescence appear to be particularly vulnerable to stress (Compas *et al.*, 1993; Seiffge-Krenke, 1993a, 1993b). Girls also report more depressive symptoms (Ge *et al.*, 1994).

Measuring stress and coping among adolescents

In the Sussex study, stress was assessed by self-reports of stress experiences in connection with school work, and interaction with teachers, parents and/or step-parents, siblings, boys and girls. Pupils were also asked how well they got on with parents, step-parents and siblings.

Coping has been defined in terms of attitudes and behaviours that attempt to control demanding external circumstances or unwanted intrapsychic states. Two broad ways of coping with stress have been identified (Lazarus and Folkman, 1984). *Problem-focused* coping deals with the problem causing the stress, while *emotion-focused* coping seeks to regulate the associated emotional distress that follows stress. Statistical analyses of adolescent data provide only partial support for this classification when attempting to order adolescent strategies for coping with stress (e.g. Dise-Lewis, 1988; Frydenberg and Lewis, 1990; Seiffge-Krenke, 1993b).

Girls' reports of higher levels of stress than those of boys may be partially explained by gender differences in coping strategies. Dise-Lewis (1988) found that girls were more likely to ventilate negative affect through crying and screaming. In a later study Frydenberg and Lewis (1993) observed that girls were more likely to utilise non-productive coping styles such as 'wishful thinking' and 'tension reduction' (involving cathartic expression of negative emotions) than were boys. Girls are also more likely to seek out both instrumental and emotional social support than are boys (Patterson and McCubbin, 1987; Frydenberg and Lewis, 1993; Seiffge-Krenke, 1993b; Shulman, 1993; Copeland and Hess, 1995).

In order to improve upon the adult classification of coping strategies, the Sussex study employed measures derived from Seiffge-Krenke's research on stress and coping among German teenagers (1993a, 1993b). She distinguished three broad coping strategies: *internal coping* (e.g. reflection on possible solutions to a problem), *active coping* by means of social resources (e.g. advice seeking), and *withdrawal* (e.g. defences such as denial and repression). Seiffge-Krenke reported that withdrawal coping is associated with psychopathology.

In the Sussex study, pupils were asked to indicate how they most often try to cope with problems. Two dimensions of adolescent coping strategies were defined from a statistical analysis of eight 6-point scale items based on the coping measure developed by Seiffge-Krenke (1989). The first scale was labelled *problem-focused coping*, and consisted of five items (Cronbach alpha = 0.60). The items were:

- I try to tackle the problem directly by talking to the people involved.
- I look for support and sympathy from a friend.
- I look for information from books and magazines.
- I think about the problem and run different solutions through in my mind.
- I turn to my family for help.

The second scale was labelled *cathartic coping*, and consisted of three items that have emotional discharge as their common theme (Cronbach alpha = 0.50). The items were:

- I try to get it out of my system through loud music, dancing, sports.
- I get rid of my anger and frustration through screaming, crying, slamming doors, etc.
- I try to make myself feel better through eating, drinking alcohol or taking drugs.

Stress, coping and smoking

There are several pathways through which stress and coping may influence adolescent smoking behaviour. The widespread belief that smoking alleviates stress may contribute to initial experimentation with cigarettes by adolescents.

Stress may be a factor in smoking maintenance and relapse. A field study by Lotecka and Lassleben (1981, cited in Mitic *et al.*, 1985) supports this view. Lotecka and Lassleben found that negative affect was the most common reason given by adolescents for restarting smoking after a period of abstinence.

Stress has been implicated as a determinant of conduct disorders and delinquency. A suggested pathway involves chronic parent–child conflict that may lead adolescents to spend more time away from the family home in situations where parental control cannot be exercised. Such associations are consistent with the way in which the distal structure of the perceived environment system is thought to operate within problem behaviour theory (Chapter 1). Numerous studies that have found positive associations between conduct disorders/delinquency and smoking have implicated family tension as well (e.g. Jessor and Jessor, 1977; Bell and Champion, 1979; Oei *et al.*, 1986; Hundleby, 1987; Welte and Barnes, 1987; Gerber and Newman, 1989; Farrell *et al.*, 1992; Henry *et al.*, 1993).

Smoking as a coping resource

Four behavioural beliefs were used to assess adolescents' perception of smoking as a coping resource (Cronbach alpha = 0.88). These were:

- Smoking would calm me down
- Smoking would help me to be in a good mood
- Smoking would help me to cope with my problem
- Smoking would help me concentrate on my homework

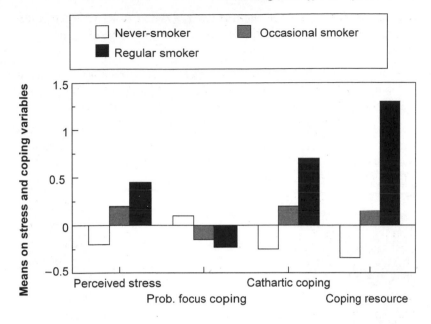

Figure 6.1 Stress and coping variables for never-, occasional and regular smokers in the autumn term

Note: Stress and coping variables were standardised (mean = 0, standard deviation =1) prior to graphing to aid graphical presentation

Autumn term analysis

Statistical analysis showed that when age and gender were controlled, adolescents who smoke:

- perceive more stress in their lives;
- report making less use of problem–focused coping and more use of cathartic coping strategies;
- perceive smoking as a coping resource.

These differences are shown in Figure 6.1. They are greatest when *never-smokers* are contrasted with *regular smokers*, but are also significant when *never-smokers* are contrasted with *occasional smokers*.

Combined autumn and summer term results: longitudinal analysis

With age controlled, the longitudinal analysis showed that stress and coping measures were highly predictive of changes in smoking status.

Adolescents who described themselves as never having smoked in the autumn term, but who had become smokers by the summer term:

- reported more stress in the autumn term;
- responded to stress in their lives more often by means of cathartic coping strategies;
- reported that smoking may have some coping benefits.

Adolescents who shifted from being occasional to being regular smokers over the school year were compared to adolescents who remained occasional smokers (Figure 6.2). The increasers were more likely to:

- report using a cathartic coping style;
- view smoking as a coping resource.

Multivariate analyses indicated relationships between increases in reported stress and cathartic coping over the school year and increases in smoking, but the direction of causality cannot be established from these analyses.

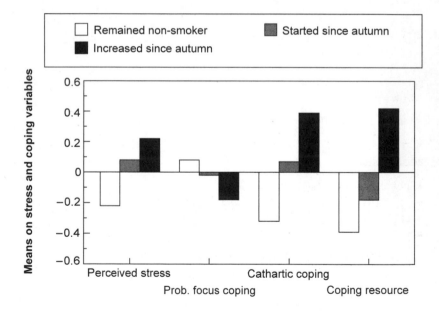

Figure 6.2 Autumn term stress and coping variables and smoking uptake
Note: Stress and coping variables were standardised (mean = 0, standard deviation = 1) prior to graphing to aid graphical presentation

Stress, coping and gender differences in smoking behaviour

In Chapter 3 smoking prevalence was shown to be higher among girls than boys. This finding replicates those of well-known studies (Goddard, 1990; Balding, 1995). Explanations for this gender difference are still incomplete. Girls experience greater stress and employ different coping strategies as compared with boys, and these factors may account for the gender difference in prevalence.

Results from the Sussex study do not support the widely held belief that adolescent girls are more likely to smoke because they experience more stress in their lives or because they cope with stress differently as compared with boys. A logistic regression analysis showed that the gender difference in smoking prevalence is still maintained when perceived stress, problem-focused coping and cathartic coping are statistically controlled. It should be noted that controlling for these variables does not reduce the association between gender and smoking at all.

On the basis of these results, the simplest conclusion is that gender differences in adolescent smoking behaviour cannot be attributed directly to differences in perceived stress, or in coping strategies. We have shown that stress and coping variables are predictive of changes in smoking behaviour for girls and boys, and *may* be causally related to smoking uptake among adolescents. These data do not allow a more precise statement about gender, stress, coping and smoking.

Moreover, variables that were not measured directly in the Sussex study may also contribute to the stress, coping and smoking relationship. These include the personality traits of neuroticism and rebelliousness, and a constellation of problem behaviours. For example, perceived stress and cathartic coping may both be evidence for the personality trait of neuroticism (or negative affectivity). The self-report measure of stress may be influenced by an individual's negative affect. An independent measure of recent life events would be necessary to differentiate this source of confound. Similarly, negative affectivity may contribute to cathartic coping. The correlation between perceived stress and cathartic coping is moderate, but statistically significant ($r = 0.41$, $p < 0.001$), and consistent with the view that both variables are indicators of a fundamental personality construct, such as neuroticism.

A further variable that may have produced the association between the perceived stress measure and smoking uptake is rebelliousness, which has been reliably related to smoking uptake and other forms of drug use (Konrad *et al.*, 1992). High rebelliousness may have produced high scores on the perceived stress measure (which includes 'getting on' with parents and teachers as components) even in the absence of conventional life stress events. Together or separately, these factors may influence adolescents' experience of stress.

Summary of the Sussex study findings

In the autumn term, when age and gender were controlled, adolescents who smoked:

- perceived more stress in their lives;
- reported using cathartic coping strategies more, and problem-focused coping strategies less;
- perceived smoking as a coping resource.

With age controlled, the longitudinal analysis showed that stress and coping measures were highly predictive of changes in smoking status.

- Initiators reported more stress in the autumn term than did never-smokers, and they used cathartic coping strategies more often.
- Increasers also reported coping benefits from smoking.
- Increasers viewed smoking as a coping resource and reported using a cathartic coping style.
- Gender differences in adolescent smoking behaviour cannot be attributed directly to differences in perceived stress, or in coping strategies.

THE FUNCTIONS THAT ADOLESCENTS ASCRIBE TO CIGARETTE USE

Pleasure and paraphernalia

The *pleasure* that adolescents gained from the use of cigarettes and the various *functions* that smoking served were distinctive themes that emerged from focus group discussions and family interviews in the London area study. Two aspects of smoking which provided pleasure and positive reinforcement for many were the activities and paraphernalia associated with smoking cigarettes. Adolescents and their parents talked about the enjoyment and pleasure gained from action involved in smoking: handling cigarette packets, matches and lighters, lighting up, inhaling, exhaling, watching the smoke drift away and blowing smoke circles:

'And once you ... once you start smoking you're going to try loads of different techniques out, like lighting your fag off someone else or starting chain smoking.'

(Jeff, Year 9, smoker)

'And some people, they can do tricks with smoking, like blow bubbles out and things like that.'

(Charles, Year 7, non-smoker)

There was a general feeling among the groups that this fascination with the tricks of smoking was most prevalent among boys, although girls also talked about the act of smoking in a positive, sometimes wistful, way:

'I think it's sometimes like just having it in your hand and some-times just ... actually the way you breathe, you know, the way you can blow it out, it's just so ... [addressed to others in the group] I can't explain, do you know what I'm talking about?'

(Roma, Year 11, smoker)

The release of stress and mood control

The release of stress was identified by both smokers and non-smokers as an important function of cigarette smoking. Non-smokers were less convinced about the efficacy of cigarettes in reducing stress, and commonly suggested a placebo effect: '*they think it calms them down so therefore it does*'.

Smokers were more sure of, and more likely to talk positively about, the calming effects of cigarette smoking. Those who were aware of the calming functions of smoking saw such properties as important in maintaining smoking among older adolescents, and associated these effects with dependence. They were also more likely to describe the smoking behaviour of adults in these terms. One boy described his mother unwinding with a cigarette after a hard day's work:

'Well, like, sometimes when my mum's at home, she might be tired or come home from a hard day's work and I see her sit down and she'll spark up a cigarette and she'll smoke it and she'll just go "ahhh", and like, she'll just relax and have a cigarette, and like, it just looks like it gives her some relief or something.'

(Ray, Year 9, smoker)

The potential of cigarette smoking to relieve anxiety clearly impressed young people. The London pupils' responses supported the notion of a link between cigarette smoking and stress relief. Pupils as young as 11 made a link between smoking and relaxation, and offered stress, feeling sad or feeling depressed as reasons why they were either tempted or had decided to smoke.

While the capacity of cigarettes to alter emotional states and moods was a commonly held belief, some adolescents were reluctant to acknowledge the existence of levels of stress in the lives of teenagers comparable to those of adults. They therefore dismissed stress as a viable or acceptable reason for adolescent smoking. The discussion below was recorded from Year 11 pupils. Ann and Kelly have given up cigarettes; Roma and Helen are regular smokers. Between them, they present the arguments for both sides:

> 'I don't think that stress really – it's not aimed at our generation, I don't think that we really think that about smoking – that it relieves your nerves. Maybe older people.'
>
> (Ann, ex-smoker)

> 'No, when you're upset and that, it takes your mind off it.'
>
> (Helen, smoker)

> 'No, I don't think so.'

> [addressed to Roma] 'It does, doesn't it?'

> 'If you're stressed that's a way out of it but it does not exactly work.'
>
> (Kelly, ex-smoker)

> 'It's psychological, it's not meant to work.'
>
> (Helen, smoker)

Helen is left defending her argument alone when Roma and Kelly agree with Ann's stance that stress is the preserve of adults:

> 'I just think adults smoke mostly for stress. . . . [addressed to group]: I don't think teenagers think about stress, do they?'
>
> (Roma, smoker)

> 'No.'
>
> (Ann, ex-smoker)

> 'Except at exams.'
>
> (Roma, smoker)

Feeling isolated in her position, Helen compromises her argument but is clearly annoyed by what she regards as the dismissive tone adopted by the others, and by Kelly (an ex-smoker) in particular:

> 'Well, I agree with Kelly that we don't actually get stressed but we have a high emotional level, and at this age at the minute we do break down a lot.'

> [Kelly giggles dismissively]

> [loudly]: 'Well maybe you've got a nice settled life, Kelly.'
>
> (Helen, smoker)

Despite non-smokers' scepticism concerning the reality of stress in young smokers, both smokers and non-smokers offered a number of stressful situations for which smoking is a useful antidote. These included arguments with parents, exams, relationship problems, bullying, and other problems at school. In the face of such problems, some likened the role of the cigarette to that of a listening friend who

> '...wouldn't argue with you or tell you anything'.
>
> (Polly, Year 11, regular smoker)

For some smokers, the association between cigarettes and stress release was that smoking shifts attention away from the stressor, albeit temporarily, to the activity of smoking, thereby enabling the smoker to lose themselves in the activity:

> 'You just relax.... 'Cos you're concentrating on your cigarette, having a cigarette.'
>
> (Audrey, Year 9, smoker)

Risk and rebellion

There is little doubt that teenagers, both smokers and non-smokers, are well informed of the health risks involved in smoking, but these are not seen as personally salient. By contrast, some other risks associated with smoking provide excitement. It is the very chance of being caught doing something of which authority disapproves that may lead to the adoption of a smoking identity. This function is often associated with other risky behaviours.

> 'If I wanted to smoke and I did it behind my mum's back, I'd find it more fun, you know, just imagine if my mum found out,

but then when the time does come close, just say some part of your family found out, you'd think, "Oh my God, that's it – I'm dead." '

(Josie, Year 9, non-smoker)

Social life

The association with a smoking group is an important step in becoming a regular smoker. In this instance smoking is something that happens when (or is the reason why) a particular group get together in a certain place. Some people smoke in a group where it is the norm to smoke, but do not smoke in other situations. Young smokers are less likely to smoke alone, while older, more serious smokers are more likely to do so. The relationship between a smoker and the group can also define the smoker's identity as either that of a serious, '*deep*' smoker who does not need the support of a group to smoke, or someone whose smoking behaviour is largely dependent on its being part of a group activity.

'They don't do it when they're on their own. Only the old ones maybe, but not our age, they only do it with their friends.'

(Collette, Year 7, non-smoker)

Adolescents talked about the camaraderie associated with sharing the same behaviour with others, and there was a suggestion of a degree of security to be gained from this.

'Sometimes when you're with your friends, and everyone's smoking, you feel like you've all got something in common, and that, it's a group thing.'

(Marvin, Year 9, ex-smoker)

Smoking was also regarded as a way to establish relationships or initiate contact:

'A girl can start smoking if maybe there's a boy she quite likes but he smokes and he's in a big crowd and she might start to smoke and when she sees him she might light up and think, "Oh, look, take notice of me. I can do it as well." '

(Fay, Year 9, smoker)

In terms of relationships and intimacy, smoking was seen to help to bolster confidence in a group or one-to-one situation. It was valued for its capacity to initiate social contact and to facilitate bonding with both boys and girls.

The use and construction of time

Themes related to time were raised as reasons for smoking by both smokers and non-smokers. One of the themes relating to time was the identification of 'vacant' time as opposed to leisure time that was occupied with structured or regular activity. Smoking was often referred to as a way of filling in small parcels of 'vacant' time, or of avoiding the feeling of having nothing whatsoever to do. Perhaps the most commonly used phrase was 'to pass time'. Smoking was seen as an antidote for boredom:

> 'I know some people that just do it to pass time really, like if you're waiting for a bus or whatever.... Yeah, it's just something to do.'
>
> (Joe, Year 11, non-smoker)

> 'If you're not married, or if you're bored or unemployed then it's something to do, if you've got nothing to do.'
>
> (Luke, Year 7, non-smoker)

> 'It's just something to do really, like if you're bored, and you're sitting waiting for something, light a cigarette, and it's something to do.'
>
> (Gemma, Year 7, ex-smoker)

For Gary, this filling in of time was very precise, with an exact timing of how long a cigarette lasts:

> 'I think a main reason is, you know, to pass the time as I said; you know it takes... it took me seven minutes to finish a cigarette; yeah, so if I've got seven minutes, or you know, fourteen minutes, I'd smoke two, you know, and it's just, while you're smoking it, you're not really thinking of, you know, you're not bored, you know, you've actually got something to do.'
>
> (Gary, Year 11, ex-smoker)

Someone with 'vacant' time to fill is more likely to smoke:

> '...if you're a busy person, you know, involved in sports activities, or, you know, you've got some things to do, then you won't have time to smoke really, and then, you know, you can like have a cigarette in your free time, and you know, go and, go along with your course, but if you haven't got anything to do, you're bored, you'll be wondering, you know, "Oh, might as well have a cigarette."'
>
> (Gary, Year 11, ex-smoker)

'Because smoking could have filled up time, or just time that they [smokers] had on their hands, gaps that they had between activities, and to have nothing to do in those times might lead them to smoke again.'

(Monique, Year 11, non-smoker)

The habitual nature of smoking means that cigarettes at particular times become scheduled parts of smokers' daily routines. At these times, smokers feel unfulfilled without a cigarette:

'I just do it, it's the first thing I do when I get up in the morning, have a cigarette.'

(Rosie, Year 11, smoker)

'And when you eat as well, after you've eaten.'

(Angie, Year 11, non-smoker)

'And it makes you feel like "Yeah, I'm totally full now, and I can face the next stage of the day."'

(Tracey, Year 11, smoker)

The notion that cigarettes are useful in helping to fill up otherwise vacant time, with the implication that each segment of time must be filled, is continued in Brian's speculations about smokers' reasons for giving up smoking:

'I s'pose it's hard to give up smoking because like, if you do want to get off it, you want to find something that'll take up that time. You know, so instead of having a cigarette you'll have to find an alternative that you can do within that short period of time.'

(Brian, Year 11, non-smoker)

Smokers reported that anticipation of a cigarette contributed to and enhanced the enjoyment of actually smoking it.

'Like, if you're at school, and you want a cigarette... and then when you do have it, it's enjoyable, isn't it?'

(Elizabeth, Year 11, smoker)

One of the attractions of smoking is that it provides a time when the smoker is not doing, or expected to be doing, anything except smoking. In describing the daily routine of young working-class women confined to home with very young children, Graham (1993) has identified smoking as the way these mothers claim a few moments of time for themselves. This capacity of cigarettes to delineate personal space and time is so widely accepted that it was cited by an adolescent girl who was herself a non-smoker:

"Cos when you smoke you're not doing anything, are you, except perhaps standing or sitting smoking, or watching television. You're not like working, or cooking, or something like that, so it's just like time for yourself.'

(Samantha, Year 11, non-smoker)

Smoking can also be used to relax, unwind and think things through:

'It sometimes just helps someone to clear their head, 'cos if they're sitting down, oh for five minutes and having a cigarette... it just sort of clears everything from their head if you see what I mean. They've got that five minutes to sit down and relax, whereas if they weren't having a cigarette they'd probably just carry on and do something else.'

(David, Year 11, smoker)

'Well I don't know. I s'pose, as they said like, if you've had a hard day, people make it out to be like, an antidepressant because, like whenever you're just relaxing, people just say, "okay", when they've got the habit of having a cigarette, they want it when they're actually relaxing, not while doing something. I s'pose while you're relaxing you can just say that it's an antidepressant or something.'

(Brian, Year 11, non-smoker)

Smoking and the control of weight

Adults often explain cigarette smoking in terms of weight control, claiming that smoking is an appetite suppressant. Body image is a highly salient aspect of adolescent identity especially as adolescence is a time of dramatic bodily changes. Relatively little is known about boys' body image concerns, but for girls, fears about gaining weight and striving towards the cultural ideal of a thin body shape become increasingly important. This raises the question of whether girls, in particular, may view smoking cigarettes as a strategy for avoiding weight gain in the same way as adults do.

Dimensions of body image: thinness and attractiveness

In the Sussex study questionnaire, adolescents were asked to rate a number of statements about fear of weight gain (e.g. 'I think a lot about being thinner' or 'If I gain a bit of weight I worry that I will keep gaining') and about their sense of physical attractiveness (e.g. 'I usually feel physically attractive' or 'The opposite sex finds me attractive'). Ratings of these statements yielded two dimensions of body image – thinness and attractiveness – that were distinct, and were not substantially related to each other for either boys or girls. This means that for Sussex pupils wanting to be thinner was largely independent of one's sense of attractiveness.

The finding that feeling thin and feeling attractive were not related was surprising, as it failed to support the popular belief that the motivation to be thin is causally related to feelings of being unattractive. However, a relationship between being fat and feeling attractive may hold for the proportion of the adolescent population who are overweight. This hypothesis could not be tested since height and weight data were not collected.

The thinness and weight items did not receive high ratings generally when measured using 6-point ratings from 0 to 5. There were no statistically significant relationships with year group either. However, there was a highly significant ($p < 0.0001$) linear relationship between feelings of physical attractiveness and age. Both boys and girls reported feeling less physically attractive as they grew older.

Gender differences in body image

There were differences between girls' and boys' ratings along both dimensions of adolescent body image. Figure 6.3 shows that there is a

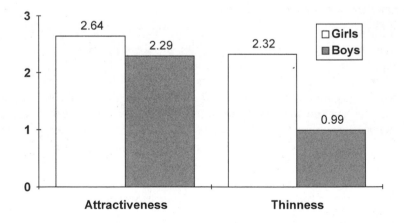

Figure 6.3 Girls' and boys' feelings of attractiveness and concern with thinness (mean ratings)

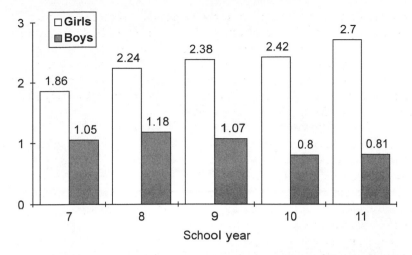

Figure 6.4 Girls' and boys' concern with thinness by school year (mean ratings)

larger gap between boys and girls on the concerns with thinness and weight dimension than on the feelings of physical attractiveness scale. Girls were concerned about having a thin body shape and avoiding weight gain; this was of little importance to boys. Girls felt slightly more physically attractive than did boys.

Not only were boys less concerned with weight and thinness than were girls overall, but for girls, concern with being thin increased with age, measured in terms of year in school. The significant interaction between gender and year in relation to concerns about body shape and thinness is shown in Figure 6.4. The low ratings of boys in Years 10 and 11 on the concern with being thinner dimension allows speculation that they may be aspiring to a heavier and more muscular body shape.

Body image and smoking behaviour

Both the autumn term and longitudinal data were used to determine whether there was a relationship between body image concerns and adolescent smoking behaviour.

Autumn term data

Each individual was classified as either a never-smoker, an occasional smoker, or a regular smoker on the basis of the classification

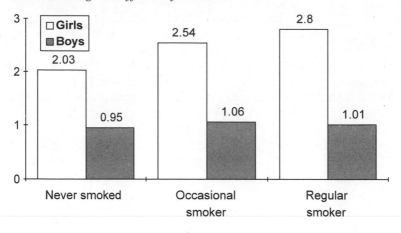

Figure 6.5 Concern with thinness by smoking behaviour and gender in the autumn term

described in Chapter 2. The relationship between body image and smoking behaviour was examined separately for boys and girls. Figures 6.5 and 6.6 show the relationship between smoking, gender and the body image variables.

Figure 6.5 shows a gender difference in the relationship between body image and smoking behaviour. For boys, concern with thinness and weight was essentially unrelated to their smoking behaviour.

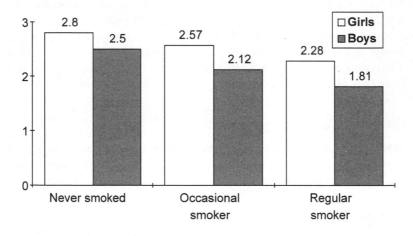

Figure 6.6 Perceptions of attrativeness by smoking behaviour and gender in the autumn term

However, for girls, there was a highly significant linear trend ($p < 0.00001$) such that weight concerns increased with increasing levels of smoking behaviour.

Figure 6.6 shows the relationship between smoking behaviour, gender, and perceptions of self as attractive. The relationships do not vary by gender but there was a highly significant linear trend ($p < 0.0001$) between smoking and feelings of being attractive that applies to both girls and boys.

These findings appear to suggest that smoking behaviour may be influenced by a concern with avoiding weight gain and desiring a thinner body shape among girls, and that self-perceptions of attractiveness may affect smoking both for girls and boys. However, there are several reasons for caution.

First, *the magnitude of the relationships described is very small.* The concern with thinness and perception of attractiveness variables share less than 2 per cent and 4 per cent of their variance with the smoking measure. Thus the association is quite marginal, and unlikely to be of any practical consequence with regard to smoking intervention strategies.

Second, *the relationship between the smoking variable and the body image variables may depend upon a third variable that determines both.* Age and trait neuroticism are plausible candidates. For example, smoking and concern with weight could be associated for girls because both smoking and concern with weight are associated with age, and age is an important determinant of smoking behaviour. There is a further possibility: that both smoking behaviour and concern with weight are 'determined' in part by a common personality disposition, for example trait neuroticism (e.g. McCrae and Costa, 1990). Neuroticism, also known as negative affectivity, refers to a tendency to experience negative emotional states. People high in trait neuroticism tend to be dissatisfied with life, worry, experience more life problems, and cope less well with stress (McCrae, 1990; and see below). It is likely that neuroticism is related to concerns about body image among adolescents. Furthermore, several studies have shown that adolescents and young adults high in neuroticism (Breslau *et al.*, 1993; Byrne *et al.*, 1995) and related constructs such as self-esteem (Simon *et al.*, 1995) are more likely to be smokers. This is a relationship that has also been recorded among adults (e.g. Costa and McCrae, 1981; Forgays *et al.*, 1993).

Finally, the existence of a causal relationship between weight concern and adolescent smoking uptake was questioned further when other relevant factors such as age and trait neuroticism were controlled. Further statistical analysis revealed that controlling for these factors reduced the association between smoking and body image to an almost negligible level. The analysis provided evidence that some of the association between body image and smoking was in fact due to other variables.

Longitudinal analysis

The longitudinal analyses of the body image scales aimed to identify variables that successfully predicted transitions to higher levels of smoking between the autumn and the summer terms. Three logistic regression analyses were computed to determine whether the two body image dimensions (1) concern with thinness and (2) self-perception of attractiveness could predict subsequent changes in smoking behaviour. The first analysis assessed the ability to predict shifts from non-smoking to smoking, the second looked at shifts from occasional smoking to regular smoking, and the third examined the possibility that adolescent regular smokers who are more concerned with body image would be less likely to reduce smoking once they have started smoking on a regular basis. The negative affectivity (neuroticism) variable used in the autumn term analysis was also used as a covariate in these analyses.

Transition from never having smoked to having smoked

The logistic regression model did not predict smoking uptake very well, but there was a substantial significant effect for the negative affectivity variable ($p < 0.00005$). The significance of negative affectivity also appears in the results described in the first part of this chapter in relation to stress and coping. After controlling for year group, puberty and negative affectivity, small and marginally significant effects were obtained for the body image by gender interactions. Girls, but not boys, who were concerned with being thin were slightly more likely to report having taken up smoking in the time between the two administrations of the questionnaire ($p < 0.05$). Boys, but not girls, who rated themselves low in physical attractiveness were slightly more likely to have taken up smoking.

Both body image variables were predictors of smoking uptake for both boys and girls, though their effects are different. For girls, concerns with thinness were more important whereas for boys, concerns about physical attractiveness were more important. It must be remembered that these effects are very small.

Transition from occasional to regular smoking

The model predicting transitions from occasional to regular smoking was even less successful than that predicting the transition from never to occasional smoking. The only significant effect was obtained for the negative affectivity measure. The body image variables do not significantly predict transition to regular smoking.

Transition from regular smoking to occasional smoking

The model was unsuccessful in predicting a transition from regular smoking to occasional smoking. None of the variables in the model – concern with being thin, with attractiveness, negative affectivity – was a significant predictor of decreases in smoking, after controlling for the effects of the other variables. The interaction of gender by concern with thinness was nearly significant ($p < 0.06$). There was a non-significant trend for girls who reported being concerned with being thin and dieting to have reduced their level of smoking between the two test administrations.

The London data support this conclusion. Adolescents' views of the relationship between smoking and weight control, and the importance of body image for girls is illustrated by this comment:

> 'But boys don't get pressured so much by how they look, and in girls' magazines you get bombarded with pictures of skinny models. Boys don't get that.'
>
> (Emma, Year 11, smoker)

This theme ran through all the London interviews, and was offered by both girls and boys. Rather than from peers, they saw pressure coming from media representations of women, particularly 'supermodels', who were believed to have a double impact in that they were both very thin and often seen smoking.

The connection between smoking and weight control rarely arose spontaneously in focus group discussions. When it appeared, it was introduced primarily by boys in relation to girls. Many girls reacted strongly and with hostility to the suggestion that girls might smoke to keep their weight down. This response to a question about smoking and weight control was typical of that of many other girls:

> 'Rubbish. Doesn't make you lose weight – eating, stop eating so much would help you lose weight but not smoking.'
>
> (Alison, Year 7, non-smoker)

A typical comment from boys was:

> 'If you're fat, then to become thin [you smoke]. Although it's more in girls, I'm not sure, but I think so. Maybe.'
>
> (Peter, Year 11, non-smoker)

This hesitant approach was shared by girls who thought there might be a connection:

> 'No, I was going to say something, but it's not really true – I don't know, girls seem more concerned with their weight than boys do, but then that's probably not true, but it just appears that way to me.'
>
> (Samantha, Year 11, non-smoker)

There was disagreement about how smoking might have an effect on weight. Some pupils suggested that no one would start smoking to lose weight, and that smoking in itself would not have any effect. Conversely, adolescents thought that stopping smoking might lead to an increase in weight as a result of eating more. Others maintained that some (younger) girls might start smoking with weight loss in mind, and pointed out that cigarettes could be used to stave off feelings of hunger:

> 'Yeah, and girls are trying to, young girls, like 12 or 13, think that "Oh yeah, smoke and we'll lose weight." '
>
> (Polly, Year 11, smoker)

The firm conclusion to emerge from all these analyses is that body image concerns are unlikely to be of major importance in explaining the smoking behaviour of adolescents.

Summary

- As expected, adolescent girls were much more concerned with thinness and weight than were adolescent boys.
- There were small but statistically significant associations between smoking and body image concerns. The statistical analyses suggest that concerns about thinness and weight are only minor factors influencing the smoking uptake of girls, and a concern with physical attractiveness can be detected by statistical analysis but is even less predictive of boys' smoking behaviour.
- *These findings challenge one of the widely held adult beliefs about the function of cigarette smoking by suggesting that concerns about weight are of little practical importance in influencing adolescent smoking behaviour.*

The failure to find strong statistical relationships between the body image ratings and adolescent smoking behaviour found support in adolescents' responses to a direct belief statement in the questionnaire about the function of smoking and slimness. In the autumn survey, 69 per cent of pupils strongly disagreed, and 91 per cent of pupils disagreed to varying degrees, with the statement '*Smoking cigarettes would help me to stay slim.*'

In the Sussex study focus groups, girls who were both occasional smokers and regular smokers talked about smoking and slimness more than twice as much as did girls who had never smoked. ($N = 2.4\%$; $O = 5.5\%$; $R = 5.4\%$).

Slimness was an issue for girls, in relation to whether boys will find them attractive:

'They [boys] think that if you look good then you're okay but if you're fat and tall then they don't like you.'

Although girls understood the link between smoking and weight/size issues it was considered primarily relevant to the adult smokers that the girls knew, mostly their parents. Mothers were reported as being perhaps too much concerned with their *weight/size*, and fathers too little concerned with their *fitness*. Although not seeing themselves as unduly fat, the girls recognised fatness as a *potential* problem via their awareness of adults' 'problems'.

There are two ways in which smoking and weight/size issues were linked at a peer level within the regular smokers' group:

1 Regular smokers say they did not smoke to stay slim, but there was discussion of the associated concept of 'fitness' in this context. Unfit or fat or 'slobby' peers are not respected, and unfit or fat or 'slobby' parents are embarrassing. It seems to be better to be thin, fit and a smoker rather than fat, unfit and a non-smoker.

   Smokers admitted that it is best to do sports and not smoke, but it is better to be a fit smoker than an unfit non-smoker. Among regular smokers, doing sports was considered some compensation for smoking. Indeed, continuing to smoke could be seen as ensuring slimness, it being an essential prerequisite to sporting activity. Smoking does not preclude regular smokers from sport, should they wish to engage in it.

2 Limited finances meant that there is often a choice between sweets or chocolate and cigarettes. Choosing cigarettes prevented some sweet consumption:

*'I wouldn't say it makes you more fat because if I have a fag then I
either have a fag or a chocolate bar, and it'll normally be a fag.'*

Both the quantitative Sussex questionnaire data and the free-dialogue
focus group material indicate that the appetite control function of
cigarette smoking is understood by these adolescents, but that it is not
an important function of smoking for them at present.

7   Smoking and image formation

Nowadays people's visual image is so much more sophisticated, so much more developed – particularly in young people
– that now you can make an image which just slightly suggests
something, they can make of it what they will.

Robert Doisneau

In this chapter, adolescent images of smoking and of smokers are
explored using a qualitative technique. Conceptual mapping and subsequent content analysis enabled researchers to map the factors which
constituted adolescent images related to smoking. This technique is
described in the first section. The intrapersonal dimensions of smoking images are described in the second section. Interpersonal dimensions related to social status, social desirability and sophistication are
considered in the third section. A network of interpersonal images is
then discussed in terms of sociability, social inclusion and related
behaviours. Finally, the physical attributes of smokers and non-
smokers are presented.

CONCEPTUAL MAPPING

Conceptual mapping, otherwise known as cognitive mapping, is a
standardised research method used both in the social sciences (Axelrod, 1976) and in market research (Krueger, 1994). In the London
study, a conceptual mapping exercise was employed in focus groups in
order to generate discussion about the images that adolescents held of
smokers and of non-smokers. The first purpose of this procedure was
to encourage the participants to describe such images. Second, the
exercise was designed to elicit those factors which, in the participants'
views, characterised different types of smoker, or different types of
people who smoked.

Group participants were each given a grid with six boxes printed on
an A4 sheet of paper. They were then asked to list all the different
images they had of a smoker, placing those they considered to be
related to each other in the same box. The pupils were told that they

did not need to use all boxes, could add extra ones, and could use the same words in more than one box. Participants were also told that they could draw pictures instead of, or as well as, words if they so preferred, and were asked to work individually for a 5- to 10-minute period. Content analyses were then undertaken both of the resulting maps and of the groups' associated discussions. Each image within the six-box grid was treated as a separate unit of analysis. Theoretically derived coding frames were generated and each image was categorised within the different coding frames. The results of these analyses are presented in the chapter that follows.

The adolescents in the study produced a wide and vivid range of images of smokers. Their sometimes contradictory attributions suggest that rather than making unequivocal judgements about cigarette smoking, teenagers hold ambivalent attitudes to tobacco use.

The images derived from the mapping exercise and the discussions that ensued suggest that adolescents have images of smokers which may be classified broadly into three categories characterised by psychological (intrapersonal), social (interpersonal) or physical attributes. Many of the images described were contradictory and illustrated adolescents' capacity to accept dimensions of themselves and of others which represent apparently conflicting views. This capacity may help teenagers simultaneously to hold negative images of both smoking and of smokers, while being smokers themselves.

The fact that adolescents who smoke are able efficiently to dissociate from attributes they consider unpalatable in other smokers may represent a defence mechanism with which to deal with their own ambivalence. In any event, such processes underline the important role smoking plays for many teenagers. By the same token, non-smokers were equally ready to present positive attributes of smoking and of smokers, without expressing any desire to smoke. Non-smokers identified positive aspects of smoking, but other considerations may prevent them from taking up cigarettes themselves.

Adolescents' images of smokers can be simultaneously positive and negative, and are often dependent on the age and gender of the smoker in question. The discussion that follows illustrates the complex nature of these images, and suggests how they are constructed. A network analysis expands this discussion so that the diversity, range of and relationships between such images can be seen more clearly. The analysis demonstrates how smoking is perceived as a multi-functional, multi-faceted, behaviour which also carries powerful messages, both positive and negative, to the observer. Gender differences are described where appropriate.

INTRAPERSONAL DIMENSIONS AND IMAGES OF SMOKING

For some adolescents, smoking was regarded as an expression of certain well-defined personal characteristics, notably as a sign of strength or weakness. More associations were made between smoking and character strength than with weakness of character (83 compared to 16). Specifically, a 'strong' character was usually described in terms of 'hardness' or toughness. This image was described more often in relation to boys than girls (23 times compared to 9 times), and was verbalised almost three times more often by boys than by girls. The image of a boy who smoked was generally described as tough and 'hard'. These terms were not employed by participants when describing adult smokers.

Similarly, one boy (Year 7) described his view of girls who smoked as being those who wanted to portray a 'sense of more strength'. For others, the adoption of a tough image by girls represented a move away from the traditionally feminine:

> 'Other girls who smoke . . . are tomboys who hang around with boys who want to look tough.'
>
> (Ann, Year 11, non-smoker)

Character weakness was exemplified by the description of smokers as having '*low self-esteem*', lacking in confidence, or, as one boy put it, as having a '*nervous and shaky*' disposition. Of the references of this nature, nine were about girls or women and six were not specifically ascribed to either boys or girls. Only one individual described a male smoker in such terms.

The second type of intrapersonal characteristic to be associated with smoking concerned personal control. Smokers described in these terms were seen as 'in control' emotionally and 'reasoned' in their use of cigarettes. Many adolescents perceived the use of cigarettes as indicative either of a sense of personal control or, conversely, of a lack of it. Girls were more likely to make associations between smoking and control than were boys (21 compared to 13). These individuals described smokers as portraying a cool, relaxed image. For two girls in particular, this was associated with the 1960s when smoking was a relatively uncontroversial habit.

By contrast, others presented smoking as indicative of a lack of control and a product of unmanageable stress. Addiction was cited as an explanation for an uncontrollable use of cigarettes. Of the 44 references made to this aspect of the smoker, 30 were made by boys and 14 were made by girls. Addiction was largely attributed to adults, rather than adolescents. Although most of the 44 references to addiction were not gender-specific as to persons seen as being addicted, more boys than girls made such observations (30 compared to 11).

The third category of intrapersonal characteristics employed in describing images of smokers related to intelligence. Non-smokers were particularly keen to describe an image of smokers as '*stupid*', '*silly*', '*not doing well at school*', '*not too clever*' or '*not very intelligent*'. Smokers described similar images, although they were likely to be referring to smokers younger than themselves. The theme of negative evaluations of smokers is pursued systematically in Chapter 8.

One teenager talked about adolescents who smoked looking '*as stupid as a man with a rattle*'. Those who made an association between smoking and intellect generally saw smoking as a reflection of low intelligence. By contrast, a small number of adolescents described the smoker as belonging to a select group of intelligent people, who were '*upper class*', '*went to private school*', were '*educated*' or '*stuffy*'. Some girls specifically identified as clever were alleged to smoke in order to disclaim this otherwise conservative image:

> 'Girls who are clever may smoke so that they can be accepted into other social groups and not be put into a social group they don't want to be in.'
>
> (Kelly, Year 11, non-smoker)

The images described above may be categorised according to the attitudes and emotional dispositions perceived to accompany smoking. Smoking was regarded as either an extension of an existing, well-defined profile, or a deliberate attempt to enhance or create a particular image. Positive statements about the image of smokers tended to reflect images in the mass media to which adolescents are regularly exposed. There were those images which teenagers desired for themselves, and those which they rated positively in themselves and in others. Conversely, negative images (which are uncommon in the media or youth-orientated advertising) were vividly expressed and negatively appraised. An important example of this type was that of the somewhat menacing, threatening and '*tarty*' female smoker.

A number of adolescents associated smoking with relaxation and the reduction of stress. Some saw this association in a positive way: smokers were seen as relaxed and assured, projecting their self-control and social competence. More commonly, however, smokers were seen as emotionally frayed, agitated individuals with low self-esteem. For some of the adolescents who held this view, smoking emphasised these characteristics and emotional states. In this way, a smoker was held to be undisciplined or an individual whose smoking reflected a weak and vulnerable personality.

INTERPERSONAL DIMENSIONS AND IMAGES OF SMOKING

Social aspects of smoking were of key significance for the adolescents in the London study. This importance was highlighted by the way in which the image of the smoker *was defined by the social group to which the smoker belonged* or by the group to which she or he aspired. The dimensions by which these definitions were made encompassed social class, age and gender. At a general level, such definitions may be viewed as 'in-groups' and 'out-groups'; that is, as either socially acceptable to the viewer or socially deviant.

Social status

Smoking was often identified with the business person, usually the businessman, whose smoking was connected with the stress and pressure of high-powered work. This image was presented more often by boys than by girls (15 times compared to 6 times) and was used to describe business*men* specifically 5 times, and business*women* once. Cigarettes were seen as a way to alleviate stress and tiredness, as a way to 'show off' to colleagues, or to mark the completion of a successful business deal.

Adolescents also described their images of poor smokers. These smokers were seen as destitute, unemployed or working in low-paid jobs, or as bringing up large families on small incomes. All references made to the 'poor smoker' were made by girls, and were used almost exclusively to describe women.

Social desirability

In addition to the contrasting images related to occupation or income, others commented on the degree to which individuals were included within the social system. There were many descriptions of marginalised smokers, depicted as '*drop outs*', '*homeless*', '*nutters*' and '*street kids*'. Specifically referring to boys in this category, the terms '*rebels*', '*bikers*' and '*punks*' were used, and socially deviant girls who smoked were also described as 'rebels' or as leading a '*wild lifestyle*'.

In contrast to this group were those whose image was described as '*normal*'. In particular, this category included '*married couples*', people in friendly social groups who smoked in pubs and restaurants, and at parties. This image of the sociable, affable and homely smoker was presented more often by boys than by girls.

In this context, the social desirability of the smoker was considered. For some, the image of the smoker was one which depicted a gregarious sociable person, fun-loving and happy, who was '*bubbly and loud*'. This image was described **by** boys, but was applied by them **to** girls. By marked contrast, others described the smoker as a '*sad, unhappy, bored and depressed person*' and as someone who was '*lonely*' and who '*didn't get around much*'. This image was described in relation to both adult and teenage smokers, and was applied more by girls than by boys.

Sophistication

The image of the sophisticated, fashionable smoker was described by the teenagers in the London study, and was much more commonly applied to girls and women than to boys and men (28 references compared to 5). Such descriptions of female smokers included the terms '*stylish*', '*classy*', '*elegant*' and '*fashionable*'. One boy described an attractive woman who smoked as having '*long red fingernails*', and as one who '*wore fur coats*'. This link between feminine glamour and smoking was also readily made by girls (15 of 28 such references were by girls).

By contrast, other teenagers described the image of the unsophisticated, crass smoker. These terms were applied only to female smokers, and, though less commonplace than those of the glamorous smoker, were primarily given by girls. Here the descriptions used included '*tarty*', '*slapperish*', a person who wore '*loads of make-up*' and '*real tarty clothes*'.

A NETWORK OF INTERPERSONAL IMAGES

The images presented by adolescents in the London study may be considered under four headings: *sociability*, *social inclusion*, *social compliance* and *related behaviour*. Although there is some overlap between these categories, it is evident that smoking is seen by adolescents as serving a social function and not solely associated with intrapersonal attributes. Smoking in this context is seen as a product of an individual's social circumstances, social acceptability, group involvement, and is associated with a range of other behaviours.

Sociability

The images of smokers which concerned an individual's sociability included both being *sociable* and being *withdrawn*. Some teenagers depicted the smoker as one who is socially skilled, and who belongs to a number of small and/or large social groups. For the older smoker, such groups were perceived to be located at pubs, restaurants, football matches, or in the home. The image of the younger smoker was of a person who belonged to either a large friendship group (girls were considered to smoke in, and belong to, larger groups than were boys) or a smaller but purposeful and cohesive group. The most common image cited in this category was that of the affable, friendly and gregarious smoker.

By contrast, others described the 'withdrawn' smoker, a person who is on the fringe of, or who is excluded from, social groups, and as a result of which is perceived to be socially withdrawn or reserved. Single parents and people who were not married were included in this category.

Social inclusion

A further category of the images adolescents described in discussions of smokers concerned a person's social standing and the extent to which they may be included or excluded from mainstream society. For example, the poet or artist who smoked was considered to have 'character', and was thereby accorded social acceptability as a smoker. The images of models, film stars and successful professionals who smoked shared similar status. These images may be contrasted with those which may be described as characterising an *out-group*. Members of this group were not regarded as positive role models, and their smoking serves to emphasise their disadvantage and exclusion from that which is considered socially desirable. One of the most richly and consistently described images in this category was that of financially disadvantaged and socially dysfunctional smokers. The following excerpt from a focus group of non-smokers describes a view of an inadequate mother who has no control over her many children, and who cannot manage her life. Such a person is viewed as selfishly wasting money she can ill afford on cigarettes, yet as blaming her plight on others:

> 'Yeah, some women they've got little children and they sit there with their friends and they're smoking and it just looks really horrible, and their children are just running around squealing out of control and really dirty and grubby.'
>
> (Teresa, Year 7, non-smoker)

'Well...you see these women and they've got about six kids and they're about 23 or whatever and their clothes are all....'

(Collette, Year 7, non-smoker)

'They're living in poverty but they still smoke.'

(Maureen, Year 7, non-smoker)

'They complain about how little money they've got but they've always got a fag in their mouth...'

(Teresa)

'They could save that money.'

(Maureen)

This theme was repeated in several of the focus groups, and women were almost always the subject of such images. Women who smoked were often depicted as being in low-paid jobs, unemployed, or as being 'stuck' at home with children. The common theme in all such exchanges was one of exclusion from society.

Related behaviours

Some of the images of smokers were presented in the context of related behaviours or what smokers were thought to be interested or involved in. For the teenagers in this study, smoking has meanings which extend beyond the behaviour itself, and which are strongly associated with other well-defined activities and interests and tastes. These behaviours included taking illicit drugs, drinking alcohol, sex, gambling and biking. An interest in certain types of music was also associated with smoking.

PHYSICAL ATTRIBUTES AND IMAGES OF SMOKING

The clearest theme to emerge in this category was that of the outward appearance and physical attractiveness of smokers. Most of the images described concerned adult smokers, and most were evaluated negatively. Images of adolescent smokers were also generally negative. The adolescent images described girls almost exclusively, and more than half of the images were also provided *by* girls. These included persons who were considered to be '*ugly, fat, and pimply*', individuals who had '*greasy hair, yellow teeth, bad breath and bloodshot eyes*'. One boy also described his image of a young male smoker as '*scruffy*'. Adult smokers were also described as being '*scruffy, repulsive, drunken, smelly, with dirty teeth*', and as having '*black circles under the eyes*'.

Adult smokers were not generally differentiated by gender. A smaller number of adolescents described smokers whom they considered to be physically attractive. These images were either of girls or of adults. Five teenagers, three of them boys, described girls who smoked as '*attractive*', '*good looking*', '*sophisticated*', a '*model type*', or '*skinny and pretty*'. Girls also described an image of the adult smoker which made them '*look good*', and '*almost healthy*'.

For many adolescents, smoking was associated with specific fashions and dress styles. Depending on the participant giving the description, smoking was regarded either as an accessory which confirmed a positively rated personal image, or conversely as a habit which emphasised an individual's lack of style or fashion sense. Positive images of smokers included being '*good looking*', '*glamorous*' as well as being '*thin and wearing designer clothes*'.

Fashionable boys who smoked wore '*straight jeans, designer clothes, and Armani sweaters*'. The comparable young female smoker was described as being likely to wear '*knee-high boots and A-line skirts*'. By contrast, a small number of teenagers described smokers as '*scruffy*' and '*wearing really tartish clothes – small skirts and little jackets*'. Negative images of smokers more commonly concerned bodily characteristics, and included being '*ugly and scruffy*', and having '*greasy hair*'.

Although there was some evidence that cigarettes were used by boys to project their masculinity, smoking was much more commonly perceived by adolescents as enhancing a 'feminine' attractiveness among girls. Such attributions were as frequently made by girls as by boys. A distinction was made, however, between women and girls. Women, not young girls, were able to carry off this image successfully, as shown in a discussion between Helen and Roma, both in Year 11 and smokers:

HELEN: I'm thinking more of tall women, more elegant, do you know what I mean, mature women...'

ROMA: It does look elegant in film stars...but women who smoke do look elegant, but *women*, not girls.

HELEN: Mature women...

ROMA: Mature women don't look so stupid...I don't know why.

HELEN: It's the way...it's the way they are.

ROMA: If they had red nails and red lipstick it wouldn't look terrible, do you know what I mean, if she's wearing a nice dress and sitting at a desk [laughs].

HELEN: And they're holding it like this... [demonstrates holding a cigarette 'elegantly'].
ROMA: It's just a stylish woman.
HELEN: 'Sophisticated – mature women, mature sophisticated red-nailed women.'

The image of the glamorous, 'classy' woman is an image which is commonly portrayed in popular culture and is assimilated by both young men and young women into their interactions and social displays. It was used by adolescents in the London study as a means of reinforcing their own smoking behaviour. Both boys and girls referred to this stylish image of the female smoker and were insistent about its reality.

Less conviction was expressed concerning the ability of cigarettes to reinforce a 'masculine' image, although a few girls mentioned the fact that some boys smoked because they (the boys) thought it made them look mature or masculine. Helen, however, described how a boy she knew used cigarettes to portray what she termed masculinity:

'But boys *do*. The only person I know... is Luke, and he stands there with his pint glass, the only reason... he's got it like this... [mimics holding a pint glass in one hand and a cigarette turned into the palm of the other]... you see what I mean, that's a more masculine way.'

Similarly, Kelly believed that boys use cigarettes to make them more attractive to girls:

'I've got that boys who tend to smoke usually do it to make themselves look more masculine and more attractive to women.'

Images of non-smokers

Adolescents in the London study were also asked to describe images they had of non-smokers. These images were less colourful than those of the smoker, and were generally less contradictory. One of the most frequently cited images of a non-smoker was that of a sensible, studious and obedient teenager, who was very involved in school work, was family- and parent-oriented. Such an image was commonly described by Year 7 and Year 9 groups, and was usually derogatory:

'... a boffin, like someone who's really good at their school work and worships their parents and everything... because their friends –

they're normally in with a group of – a crowd of – other boffins
who won't smoke either'.

(Nicky, Year 9, non-smoker)

For boys, non-smoking was associated with high parental and
school involvement, and with an unwillingness to take risks. For
girls, non-smoking was associated with *'primness'*. A distinction was
made by some of the older girls between girl smokers and non-
smokers on the basis of their relationships with boys. A group of
15- to 16-year-old girls described girl non-smokers as being *'girlfriends
for the boys'*, while the smokers were *'mates'* with the boys.

This image of a *'prim'* girl was not a positive evaluation, and may be
compared to the way boys (and some girls) described non-smokers as
'nerds' or *'boffins'*:

'I think that sometimes people who smoke...like they think you're
a wimp or you're a boffin or whatever if you don't smoke. I don't
know why.'

(Eileen, Year 7, non-smoker)

Nevertheless, many positive images of non-smokers were provided.
This theme is repeated in Chapter 8, where the questionnaire results
indicated that non-smokers are rated more positively overall than are
smokers. The positive images of smokers included teenagers who were
involved in sports and out-of-school activities, who were *'normal'* and
had a *'clean'* image. Such non-smokers were described as being *'happy'*
and *'mature'*. Older adolescents spoke of the changing social climate
in which smoking is deemed less socially acceptable, while others
described non-smokers as more mature, stronger and more self-
contained:

'I think like if someone said, "do you smoke?" and they said, "No,
I've given up", it's like they're trying to...show a harder image
than if they did smoke, 'cos like they've got the power to give up.'

(Thomas, Year 11, non-smoker)

SUMMARY

The creation of an image is a central component in adolescent development and identity formation. Within the process of identity construction, cigarettes are a tool with which teenagers may create and
manage such images. Adolescents hold many and varied images of
smoking in relation to themselves and to other people. These images
are often contradictory and internally inconsistent.

In the London study, images of girls who smoked were described more frequently than were those of boys who smoked. This observation was found to be true among boys and girls. Overall, more negative images of smokers were described than were positive images. Images of smokers encompassed an individual's physical appearance, psychological factors and social standing. Smoking was seen at once to be an individual act or statement, and a symbol of group membership and belonging.

8 Social identities of adolescent smokers

> Man may be defined as the animal that can say 'I', that can be
> aware of himself as a separate entity.
>
> Erich Fromm

In this chapter, cigarette smoking is considered in terms of the social
identities which adolescents adopt by choosing either to be a non-
smoker or a smoker. In the first section, we examine the concept of
adolescent identity by reviewing its history within the social sciences
and by considering its usefulness in understanding adolescent smoking
behaviour. In the second section, quantitative questionnaire results
measuring six aspects of adolescent social identities are reviewed, and
in the third section social identities are explored using qualitative
approaches.

In the final section, a different approach to identities is described,
and we compare the results of an American study that linked gender
identities to smoking with findings from the Sussex questionnaire
study.

THE CONCEPT OF SOCIAL IDENTITY

The concept of identity was originally introduced into the social
sciences by Erickson (1946, 1950), who used the psychoanalytic term
ego identity. Two themes have been distinguished in Erickson's original
formulation (Gurin and Markus, 1990). The first is the individual's
persistent sense of an enduring self across the life span. The second is
the continuous sense of sharing significant characteristics with others.
The sharing of significant characteristics with others is the focus of our
research on adolescent cigarette smoking. This social-psychological
approach maintains an awareness of individuals as constituted in
terms of the groups of which they are members (Duveen and Lloyd,
1986). Other aspects of adolescent identity development are considered
in another book in this series, that of Jane Kroger (1996).

The use of the term 'social identity' in the Sussex study reflected a
theoretical interest in the social-psychological theories of Moscovici

(1973, 1976, 1981, 1984, 1988) and Tajfel (1981, 1982). We believe that individuals' social identities are constructed from the social representations of the significant groups in the society to which they belong. The development of social identities depends upon the internalisation of the social representations of these groups.

Moscovici introduced the term 'social representation' into social psychology. Social representations are the products or features of social groups and form organised systems of 'values, ideas and practices' (Moscovici, 1973: xiii). It is through access to shared social representations that individuals are able to understand the structure of social life and to communicate with others. The interdependence between social representations and the collectives for which they function means that social life is always viewed as a construction, rather than being taken as a given.

Unlike the scientific knowledge of the natural world that was the starting-point of Piaget's (1971) studies, Moscovici (1976), in his initial investigations of social representations, observed the transformation of psychoanalytic theory. He described the reconstitution of social representations of psychoanalysis by different groups in French society. In this chapter we investigate the social representations of smoking as our reference point for analysing the social identities of young adolescent smokers and non-smokers.

The influence on individuals exercised by social representations takes different forms (Duveen and Lloyd, 1990). Some social representations impose an imperative obligation on individuals to adopt a particular social identity. This is the case, for example, with representations of age, gender or ethnicity, where individuals are generally constrained to construct prescribed social identities. In other instances, the influence of social representations is exercised through a contractual obligation rather than an imperative one. In these cases an individual joining a social group contracts to adopt a particular social identity. Social representations of the medical profession provide an example of a contractual obligation. A person need not train as a doctor, but should they choose to do so in the United Kingdom they must abide by the regulations of the General Medical Council. In a less formal but no less restrictive manner, adolescent peer groups shape the behaviour of their members. Tajfel's stress on the emotional and evaluative significance of group membership is particularly important when considering smoking in adolescence. In the second and third sections of this chapter we explore the nature of adolescent social representations of smoking and their impact on young adolescents' construction of their social identities.

Relatively few studies have examined adolescents' social identities as young cigarette smokers and non-smokers, or the social representations from which they are constructed. This is surprising, given that a prestigious review of smoking interventions (Leventhal and Cleary, 1980) suggested that the potential adolescent smoker passes through a preparatory period prior to smoking initiation in which the social image associated with smoking is evaluated. If this social image is evaluated positively, adolescents may begin smoking to become more like this desired image (Barton *et al.*, 1982). Conversely, a negative appraisal of teenagers who smoke should be a factor inhibiting smoking uptake. The review clearly identified the importance of image or identity in smoking uptake.

Adolescents' images of young smokers and non-smokers have been explored in several studies using samples from the United Kingdom (McKennell and Bynner, 1969; Bland *et al.*, 1975; Bewley and Bland, 1978), the United States (Chassin *et al.*, 1981; Barton *et al.*, 1982; Burton *et al.*, 1989; Bowen *et al.*, 1991) and Finland (Kannas, 1985). Two quite clear findings emerge from these studies.

First, the overall ratings of smokers were more negative on socially desirable traits such as cleverness, foolishness, friendliness, laziness and being a 'troublemaker' than those of non-smokers or of the self (Bewley and Bland, 1978; Chassin *et al.*, 1981; Barton *et al.*, 1982; Burton *et al.*, 1989). These psychological traits may be viewed as the social representations which comprise the image or social identity of smokers, non-smokers and the self.

Second, smokers were described more favourably by adolescents who smoked (McKennell and Bynner, 1969; Zagona and Babor, 1969; Bewley and Bland, 1978; Chassin *et al.*, 1981; Kannas, 1985; Bowen *et al.*, 1991) or who intend to smoke (Barton *et al.*, 1982; Burton *et al.*, 1989). For example, Bewley and Bland (1978) found that English non-smokers were less likely than adolescent smokers to view the young smoker as 'clever', 'friendly', 'good at sport', 'good-looking', and more likely to view the smoker as 'big-headed', 'foolish', 'lazy', someone who 'likes to do forbidden things', and 'troublemaker'. These findings echo Tajfel's description of in-group bias.

The convergence of these findings is impressive given that the studies span more than twenty-five years, and were often based on small samples drawn from different cultures. Additional aspects of the social representation of the smoker identity are revealed in published reports. Among the findings of Bewley and Bland (1978), for example, as noted above, are that an adolescent smoker was more likely to be described as a 'troublemaker' and as someone who 'likes to do forbidden things'.

Similarly, both McKennell and Bynner (1969) and Barton *et al.* (1982) found that smokers were rated as tougher, more disobedient, and more interested in the opposite sex than non-smokers. Bowen *et al.* (1991) found high rates of endorsement for the descriptors 'try to act cool' and 'try to act older' applied to smokers. This constellation of traits, or social representations, suggests that an aspect of the social identity of adolescent smokers is of a social actor who is delinquent and non-conformist. These traits are not necessarily undesirable from the point of view of adolescents. Certainly, they are more ambiguous in social desirability than other descriptors attributed to smokers in these studies such as unhealthy, foolish, weak, weird, dumb, dirty, and bad at sport. These can be labelled 'negative' with a degree of certainty.

A significant limitation of existing research is that social representations of smokers and non-smokers have not been linked to subsequent changes in smoking status over time. As Tajfel's theory would suggest, smokers and non-smokers have been shown to hold different images of smokers and non-smokers. However, published reports fail to make clear whether differences emerge before and/or after smoking uptake. The longitudinal design of the Sussex study enables us to examine this issue in the next section of this chapter. The Sussex questionnaire data also allow us to test four hypotheses derived from previously published research. These are:

1 Smokers will be evaluated less favourably than non-smokers.
2 Smokers will be viewed as less conforming/more rule breaking.
3 The smoking status of adolescents will moderate these evaluations so that smokers provide more favourable evaluations of adolescents who smoke.
4 Increases in smoking behaviour will be less likely among adolescents who evaluate smokers more negatively relative to non-smokers.

A QUESTIONNAIRE APPROACH TO SOCIAL IDENTITIES

The hypotheses listed above were all tested using data from the questionnaire surveys in the Sussex schools during the autumn and summer terms. The presentation of these quantitative results has three components. Adolescents' self-perceptions of what they are currently like form the first analysis that is presented. It is followed by a similar analysis of adolescents' descriptions of their ideal selves. The final analyses focus on the social identities of girl and boy smokers and non-smokers. All these results are based upon adolescents' ratings of identities using the fourteen identity descriptors discussed in Chapter 2. The perceived self, ideal self and four smoking identities are examined in relation to changes in smoking behaviour during the school year.

Self-perceptions using identity descriptors

Self-perception scales

Data from the autumn term questionnaire were used to assess adolescent self-perceptions. Pupils were required to rate themselves on the fourteen descriptors using 6-point scales. From principal components analysis, scales were formed representing three distinguishable aspects of adolescents' identities:

1 The first scale represented a general positive versus negative self-evaluation. This scale differentiated boys and girls who tended to rate themselves positively (*exciting, happy, popular, healthy, clever* and *makes up own mind*) from those with a less favourable self-image (*dull, unhappy, unpopular, unhealthy, thick* and *follows others*).
2 The second scale constructed from self-perception analyses was labelled fun loving. This scale distinguished adolescents who reported that they *liked partying, liked the opposite sex, were attractive to the opposite sex* and *cool* from others not rating themselves in this way. This dimension reflects adolescent sexuality. The descriptors *exciting* and *popular* were associated with this scale as well as with the first scale. There was a small positive association between positive self-evaluation and perception of self as fun loving. Despite this, these have been treated as two distinct scales.
3 The third scale was labelled conforming–nonconforming. It distinguished boys and girls who reported that they *cared about the environment* from those who viewed themselves as *rule breakers*. This scale was not as well defined as the first two. However, an interpretation of this scale as representing conformity was enhanced by the finding that an additional descriptor added to the summer questionnaire (*doesn't like school work–likes school work*) was strongly related to this scale.

Gender and school year differences on the three self-perception scales

There were statistically significant differences between boys and girls and between year groups on all three scales:

- positive evaluation
- fun loving
- conforming.

The absolute magnitudes of the gender and year group differences were small, but the gender difference on the conforming scale was highly significant statistically. Girls rated themselves as more *conforming* than did boys.

In addition there were two important year group differences.

- Girls' and boys' descriptions of themselves across school years showed increases on the *fun loving* scale. Again this difference was highly significant statistically; see Figure 8.1.
- Girls' and boys' ratings of themselves across school years showed decreases on the less *conforming* scale. This difference was also highly significant statistically; see Figure 8.1.

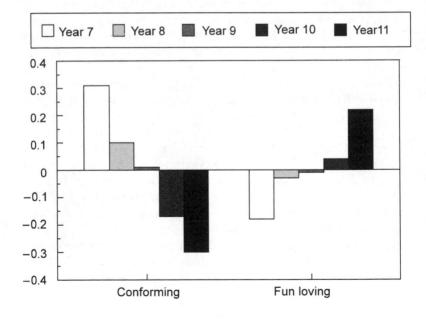

Figure 8.1 School year means on the fun-loving and conforming scales

Note: The fun-loving and conforming–nonconforming variables are expressed as *Z* scores with a mean of 0 and standard deviation of 1

Self-perception and smoking status

The three identity scales constructed from the autumn term data were examined for gender and smoking status differences. Since year group was an important determinant of ratings on the fun-loving and conforming scales it was used as a control in the analyses that follow.

Smoking status was associated with all three identity scales for boys and girls. There were significant differences in the strengths of the relationships between smoking status and the three scales. The positive versus negative self-evaluation scale was only weakly related to smoking status but there was a ten times stronger relationship between the fun-loving and conformity scales and smoking status. The strong links between smoking and adolescent self-identity are shown in Figure 8.2.

In summary, the autumn term data show that smokers regard themselves as more fun loving and less conforming than non-smokers. Occasional smokers occupy an intermediate position.

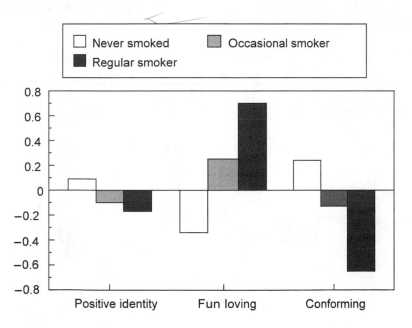

Figure 8.2 Average scores on the three self-identity scales for never-, occasional and regular smokers

Note: The fun-loving and conforming–nonconforming variables are expressed as Z scores with a mean of 0 and standard deviation of 1

Self-perception and changes in smoking behaviour

The three self-perception identity scales developed from the autumn data were used to predict changes in smoking status during the course of the school year. Adolescents who remained non-smokers were compared with those who shifted to having smoked one or more cigarettes and individuals who remained occasional smokers were compared with those who became regular smokers. The autumn term results of the analysis of self-perception and smoking status suggest two predictions:

- Adolescent non-smokers who rated them as more fun loving and less conforming were more likely to become occasional smokers
- Adolescent occasional smokers who rated themselves as more fun loving and less conforming were more likely to become regular smokers.

Results based on analyses of variance were consistent with these predictions. There were strong effects for the fun-loving and conforming identity scales for both boys and girls. Figure 8.3 shows that adolescents who remained non-smokers rated themselves the least

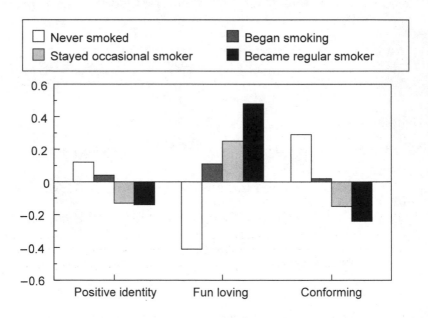

Figure 8.3 Average identity scale scores and changes in smoking status
Note: The fun-loving and conforming–nonconforming variables are expressed as *Z* scores with a mean of 0 and standard deviation of 1

fun loving and the most conforming of the four smoking status groups.

If we compare non-smokers with those who started smoking, it is clear that adolescents who were initially non-smokers but who had smoked by the summer term rated themselves as considerably more fun loving and less conforming in the autumn than did adolescents who remained non-smokers. The comparisons between adolescents who remained occasional smokers and those who became regular smokers yielded only one significant effect, that on the fun-loving scale. Adolescents who became regular smokers tended to obtain higher scores on the fun-loving scale.

In summary, regular smokers, and occasional smokers about to become regular smokers, describe themselves as more fun loving.

Ideal self

We turn now to adolescents' ratings of how they would like to be at the end of the school year. These ratings are described as ideal self identities. Statistical examination revealed three scales similar to those derived from the self-perception analysis. By and large, pupils maintained the same relative positions on the three scales.

Ideal self identity scales

There were differences in average ratings of self and ideal self on all three scales:

- Ideal self ratings on the positive versus negative self-evaluation scale were substantially higher than the self-perception ratings. The descriptors along which this desire yielded significant results were *healthy*, *happy* and *popular*.
- Adolescents described their ideal selves as more fun loving than they currently perceived themselves to be.
- Differences between ideal self and perceived self on the conformity scale were smaller than ideal self–perceived self differences on the positive–negative and the fun-loving identity scales. Nonetheless, all pupils wanted to be less conforming than they had reported themselves as being.

Ideal self identity and smoking status

The relationships between the ideal self identity scales and smoking status were similar to those for self-perception and smoking status

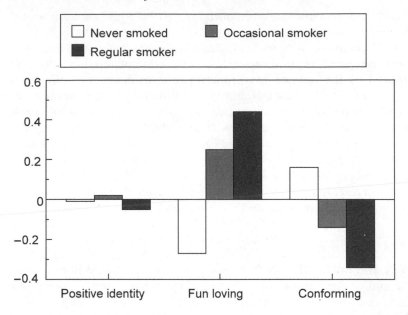

Figure 8.4 Average scores on the three ideal self-identity scales for never-, occasional and regular smokers

Note: The fun-loving and conforming–nonconforming variables are expressed as *Z* scores with a mean of 0 and standard deviation of 1

relationships. There was a substantial association between wanting to be fun loving and smoking, and between the desire to be nonconforming and smoking. These relationships were found in both the autumn term and longitudinal data but were not as strong statistically as were those for self-perception. The autumn term averages are shown in Figure 8.4.

In summary, both the autumn term and longitudinal analyses of the perceived self identity data showed that regular smokers described themselves as more fun loving and less conforming than their non-smoking peers. The ideal self identity ratings for both the autumn term and the longitudinal data yielded results in relation to smoking status that were similar to those for self-perception, but the relationships were weaker.

Social representations of smoker and non-smoker identities

We next consider adolescents' social representations or images of the social identities of smokers and non-smokers derived from their responses using the fourteen identity descriptors. Pupils rated a girl smoker, a girl non-smoker, a boy smoker and a boy non-smoker on each of the fourteen descriptors. Ratings for each of the four smoking identities were analysed separately. The social representations that adolescents hold of smoker and non-smoker identities have implications for future smoking status and for interventions. There were overall differences in the representations of smokers and non-smokers. These images also varied in terms of the gender of the smoker or non-smoker being described, the gender of the pupil making the rating, and smoking status of the rater.

Initial analyses suggested that a global evaluative dimension yielded the most salient perception of smokers and non-smokers. All descriptors, except *breaking rules*, were included in this general factor. Nonetheless, a more differentiated approach to the description of smoking and non-smoking identities was employed. It used the three identity scales developed in the self-perception and ideal self analyses. These were:

- a positive versus negative evaluation scale
- a fun-loving scale
- a conforming–nonconforming scale.

Scores on the three identity scales were derived for each pupil for each of the four smoking identities. These more complex analyses revealed more substantial effects than those obtained using the general positive–negative evaluations.

Analyses with these twelve scales were carried out on the autumn and longitudinal data. The four smoking identities were:

- girl smoker
- boy smoker
- girl non-smoker
- boy non-smoker.

These were considered in relation to the gender and the smoking status of the pupils producing the ratings. Results are presented separately for each scale but only the most salient findings are shown.

Autumn term results

Figure 8.5 shows the overall ratings for the four smoking identities on the three identity scales.

1 Positive–negative scale. Smokers were viewed more negatively than non-smokers and this result held whether the smoker being rated

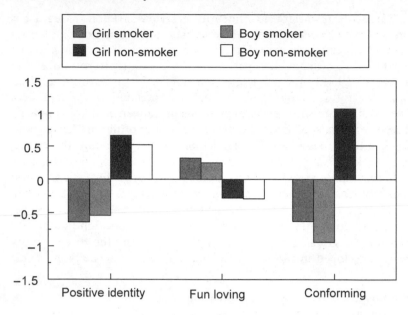

Figure 8.5 Overall ratings of the four smoking identities on the positive–negative, fun-loving and conforming–nonconforming scales

was a boy or a girl. The effect was substantial, accounting for over 25 per cent of the variability in ratings on the positive identity scale. In addition, the girl non-smoker identity was rated more favourably than the boy non-smoker identity, but a girl smoker was rated less favourably than a boy smoker.

2 Fun-loving scale. Smokers were viewed as being more fun loving than non-smokers. This effect was large, and applied to the smoker identities of boys and girls alike.

3 Conforming scale. Smokers were rated as less conforming than non-smokers. This effect was very large and accounted for over 55 per cent of the variability in the ratings on the four identities on the conforming scale. However, girls were rated more conforming.

These results confirm the first two hypotheses:

- Smokers will be evaluated less favourably than non-smokers.
- Smokers will be viewed as less conforming/more rule breaking.

In addition, the Sussex data revealed an important gender difference:

- The identities of both the girl smoker and the girl non-smoker were seen as more conforming than the boy smoker and the boy non-smoker identities.

Own smoking status and ratings of smoking identities

The smoking status of adolescents will moderate these evaluations so that smokers provide more favourable evaluations of adolescents who smoke.

Figure 8.6 indicates that adolescents' perceptions of smoking identities were influenced by their membership in one of the three smoking status groups. The Sussex data offer a more complex picture as they include the fun-loving and conforming scales as well as an overall evaluative dimension.

1 Positive–negative scale. The smoker identities were rated less positively than non-smoker identities (less *clever, popular, healthy*, etc.) overall. This finding was modified by the smoking status of raters.

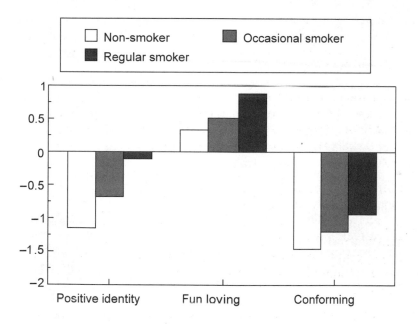

Figure 8.6 Never-smokers', occasional smokers' and regular smokers' perceptions of smoking identities on the positive–negative, fun-loving and conforming–nonconforming scales

The difference between smokers and non-smokers was greatest when non-smokers rated the four identities, less pronounced in the ratings of occasional smokers and only marginal when ratings were made by regular smokers.

2 Fun-loving scale. Although the smoker identities were rated more fun loving than the non-smoker identities overall, the magnitude of the difference varied according to the smoking status of the rater. Regular smokers were most likely and non-smokers least likely to perceive differences between smoker and non-smoker identities.

3 Conforming–nonconforming scale. The smoker identities were seen as less conforming than non-smoker identities overall. The effect is greater among raters who are themselves non-smokers than among adolescents who are smokers.

Smoker identities and smoking status

Ratings of the four smoker identities were used to predict smoking uptake over the school year, in terms of (1) changes in smoking status from never having smoked to having tried cigarettes, and (2) changes in smoking status from occasional to regular smoking. Although the results of this longitudinal analysis were less striking than the results for the autumn term data there was evidence that differing perceptions of smoker and non-smoker identities play a part in adolescents' decisions to begin or increase their smoking. These results are shown in Figure 8.7 and address the fourth hypothesis proposed in the first section of this chapter, namely that increases in smoking behaviour will be less likely among adolescents who evaluate smokers more negatively relative to non-smokers.

1 Positive–negative scale. The smoker identities tended to be viewed more negatively, and this trend was most pronounced among adolescents who did not smoke. The longitudinal analysis added evidence that among pupils who were initially non-smokers, a more negative view of smokers was associated with a decreased probability of trying cigarettes later in the school year. Similarly, among occasional smokers, having a more negative image of the young smoker appeared to inhibit progression to regular smoking.

2 Fun-loving scale. Results showed that the smoking identities were viewed as more fun loving. This applied to non-smokers, occasional smokers and regular smokers alike. The group differences were less coherent. Pupils who began smoking during the school year were *less* likely than those remaining never-smokers to view the smoking

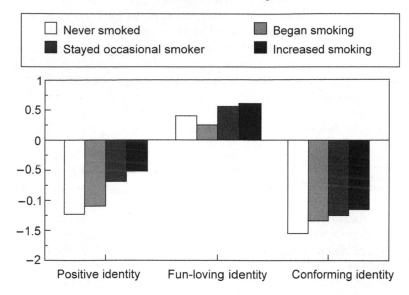

Figure 8.7 Smoking uptake and perceptions of smoking identities on the positive–negative, fun-loving and conforming–nonconforming scales

identity as fun loving. There was no significant difference between pupils who remained occasional smokers and those who became regular smokers. The group differences were small, and should not obscure the main conclusion that the smoking identities were viewed as more fun loving.

3 Conforming–nonconforming scale. The smoker identities were described as less conforming than non-smoker identities. This view was more typical of pupils who remained non-smokers throughout the school year than those who began smoking. Figure 8.7 shows that as levels of smoking increased, the tendency to view the smoking identity as nonconforming became less pronounced. However, even among those who had increased their smoking, the smoker identity was viewed as substantially less conforming than the non-smoker identity.

An ambivalence in adolescents' social representations of smoker identities is suggested from the questionnaire data and echoes that described in the London focus group image data. The smoking identities were perceived quite negatively. Socially desirable traits were less likely to be attributed to smokers than to non-smokers, particularly by adolescents who were themselves non-smokers. By contrast, there was evidence that smokers are perceived as being more fun loving and less conforming. These are characteristics that have appeal to many adolescents. Nonconformity is probably linked to a search for self-identity and differentiation from parents, while being fun loving seems closely related to sexual development.

Summary of Sussex questionnaire findings

- Ratings of perceived self yielded three identity scales: a positive versus negative self-evaluation scale, a fun-loving scale and a conforming–nonconforming scale. Ratings of ideal self provided three similar scales.
- Both the autumn term and longitudinal analyses of the perceived self identity data showed that regular smokers and occasional smokers about to become regular smokers described themselves as more fun loving and less conforming than their non-smoking peers. The ideal self identity ratings for both the autumn term and the longitudinal data yielded similar results in relation to smoking status but the relationships were weaker.
- The smoker identities were seen less favourably.
- The smoker identities were rated more fun loving and less conforming/more rule breaking.
- The identities of both the girl smoker and the girl non-smoker were seen as more conforming than the boy smoker and the boy non-smoker identities.
- Adolescents' perceptions of smoking identities were influenced by their membership in one of the three smoking status groups.

VIEWS OF SOCIAL IDENTITIES DERIVED FROM QUALITATIVE DATA

Qualitative data were collected in the Sussex study only from girls in Years 7 and 9 and only from those in four of the original schools, namely Country 1, Town 1, Town 3 and Town 4. Participants volunteered as intact friendship groups. An impression formation task preceded each focus group.

The impression formation task

Stimuli for the impression formation task were two videotapes of an actor, either as a non-smoker or as a smoker. She was shown talking about her weekend spent with her friends. Each group of girls was shown only one of the videos. From notes taken during the focus group discussions the smoking status of participants was identified. Because there were so few occasional and regular smokers in the groups, analyses of the video materials were based upon a dichotomous distinction between girls who had never smoked and those who had.

Girls rated the actor on the fourteen descriptors that comprised the identity items in the autumn term questionnaire. These fourteen descriptors were analysed individually taking account of the smoking status of the actor, that of the participants themselves and whether they were in Year 7 or 9. The smoking experience of the participants influenced their perception of the actor on nine of these descriptors. When the actor was portrayed as a smoker she was seen as more likely to:

- break rules
- like partying
- be popular.

On the other hand, when the actor portrayed a non-smoker she was seen as more likely to:

- make up her own mind
- be cool
- be grown up
- be healthy
- be clever
- care about the environment.

As a smoker, the actor was perceived as a fun loving, attractive and risk-taking girl. Although the non-smoker was described in a positive manner, she was also perceived to be sensible and attuned to adult values. These results echo those of the questionnaire study. The smoking identity was rated more negatively overall but was seen as more fun loving.

In summary, the impression formation task showed that:

- The young adolescent girl smoker in the impression formation task was rated by girls, whether non-smokers or smokers, as fun loving, attractive and risk taking.
- The non-smoker was also seen in a positive manner, but she was perceived to be sensible and attuned to adult values.

Focus group discussions

The analyses reported here derive from thirty-three focus group sessions. They centre around three themes:

- onset of smoking
- social identities, smoking onset and resistance
- changing images of the 'hard' identity.

The third, the 'hard' identity, is a view of adolescent identities that emerged during focus group discussions. It was salient for these girls and much discussed as an aspect of smoking.

The self-reported smoking behaviour of the group members provides a meaningful description of social characteristics of the group since the girls volunteered as ongoing friendship groups. Three types of group were identified in terms of the smoking status of group members but not all the groups that participated were classifiable. The three definable groups were:

- never-smoked: none of the members had tried smoking;
- occasional/situational smokers: all members had tried smoking, but none were a regular smokers;
- regular smokers: all members were regular smokers.

Age was strongly related to membership in different smoking status groups. Nine of the 'never-smoked' groups were from Year 7 and one was from Year 9 girls. There was one Year 7 and one Year 9 'occasional smokers' group, and the only 'regular smokers' group was in Year 9.

Onset of smoking: the views of members of three smoking status groups

The dynamics of the onset of smoking (imagined, observed or remembered) are reported in terms of girls' membership in one of three smoking-status groups. Consideration of the impact of smoking on the perceived identities of individuals and groups is then described.

All the girls appeared to be aware of the serious health risks of smoking, and they were generally somewhat afraid of it and of people who smoked. Smokers demonstrated fearlessness in this respect. The never-smoked groups claimed they had good sense about smoking and accused smokers of foolhardiness rather than fearlessness; that is, of being 'stupid'. In discussions about adult smoking, particularly that of their parents, girls stated that adults started smoking because they had not known it was bad for them: either the detrimental effects were not known at the time or these adults had not been told about them.

Never-smoked groups' views about the onset of smoking

Girls who belonged to never-smoked groups construed the onset of smoking largely in terms of *group* identity and behaviour. Their understanding of their present and future resistance to smoking was both *group*-oriented and *individual*-oriented:

Never-smoked groups' views of smokers and the onset of smoking Never-smoked group members easily identified groups of smokers. The smokers were described as *active, predatory* and *demanding conformity to their smoking behaviour*. These attributes were seen as leading to the onset of smoking in erstwhile non-smokers.

1 Activity of smoking groups. Smoking groups were seen as 'active-in-the-world', 'doing-things-going-places' groups. Three observations in particular contributed to this perception:

- Their smoking occurs in places and at times outside the remit of the major regulators of the girls' lives – for example, on the way to school, or near youth clubs – because young smokers are not allowed to smoke at school or in the home.
- Attracting boys is seen as high on the agenda of smoking groups, and is believed to be one of the reasons for their smoking. Attracting boys often involves other behaviours unlikely to be approved of by authority figures, and so takes place largely away from them.
- The first experience of smoking (observed by non-smokers) is likely to involve going somewhere out of doors specifically to smoke (see discussion of the 'hard' identity starting p. 155).

By contrast, in the never-smoked groups girls often talked of themselves as sensible and quiet, preferring to stay in, as this discussion illustrates:

v: Erm, I don't think F's really the type [laughs] to start smoking though if she did, erm, I would tell her not to.
INTERVIEWER: Can you tell me why she's not the type to smoke?
v: I think she's too sensible.
INTERVIEWER: Too sensible. Does that mean people who smoke are stupid, then?
v: Yeah. [Laughs.]
INTERVIEWER: Okay. So F's sensible. What else about her?
L: She's quite quiet as well.
INTERVIEWER: Can you not be quiet and smoke?
v: And she doesn't try to impress people and things like that.
INTERVIEWER: Is F the type to drink?
v: [Laughs] No.

INTERVIEWER: No. Is she the type to go clubbing? Sorry F, we're asking all these questions about you. You can disagree with them if you like.

V: I don't think so.

INTERVIEWER: No? Why would she not go clubbing?

V: I think 'cos she's a bit like me, would rather just stay home watch the telly or [laughs] do something like that.

2 Predatory nature of smoking groups. Members of the never-smoked groups described smoking groups as predatory; that is, as seeking to adopt new members on the groups' terms. Among these terms is the necessity to smoke:

> 'These other people are quite wimps and they [smokers] actually get them and like [say]: "Oh come on, come and join us", and you can try it [smoking] and all that and they make you like it.'

Aggressive behaviour (described below in tactics to ensure conformity) also contributed to a predatory image.

3 Tactics employed by smoking group members to ensure conformity. Girls in the never-smoked groups believed that smoking groups did not tolerate non-smoking members for long, even when they initially accepted them as new members. Smoking groups were reputed to adopt three methods to encourage eventual compliance among potential and new members:

- Persuasion: there was some belief that good friends would not try to encourage one to smoke, but there was rather more reporting of strong and deceitful persuasion. Smokers were reported to deny the addictive potential of cigarettes when offering them to non-smokers (although the regular smoking group freely admitted that they were addicted).
- Physical intimidation: the never-smoked groups told of friends who said they were in fear of future beatings for not smoking:

> 'There's one girl, she hangs round with one of my friends, and she's in another form, and my friend doesn't smoke but she says she doesn't actually like being with the others that smoke because she feels that one day she's going to actually start smoking. And she also says, "What if I don't smoke? I'm going to get beaten up when I'm older."'

- Social ostracism: continual non-smoking is seen as likely to lead to being removed from the smoking friendship group:

'I think they'd be really sly about it and they would get you thinking that you're their friend and if you don't smoke later on they'll chuck you out their group.'

Never-smokers' descriptions of these tactics suggested that they viewed smoking groups as uncompromising in their attachment to the smoking aspect of their group identity. The sole regular smoking group denied, however, that such relentless conformity formed a part of their friendships. The apparent necessity for the never-smoked groups to differentiate themselves radically from smokers is discussed further later.

Never-smoked groups' views of the effects of the onset of smoking on never-smoked groups   Never-smoked group members made efforts to differentiate themselves clearly from smoking groups. In this context smoking groups were reported as aggressive and predatory and never-smoked groups adopted a highly defensive stance towards them. Girls frequently used the descriptor 'sensible' to characterise themselves as non-smokers, and the descriptor 'stupid' for anyone who smoked.

In addition, smoking was seen as analogous to a highly contagious social disease that challenged loyalty to friends and group identity. The 'contagion' model is evident in the following description of the aetiology of a smoking outbreak:

'It was then they started, in Year 8 I think, that they started going to [night-clubs] and then more girls started. Just recently, a couple of weeks ago, more girls started smoking 'cos a big group of them go down to [leisure centre], and then one started smoking who came to this school just recently, and then they all started smoking.'

The dynamics of group 'infection' and resistance were linked, and contributed to the images that the never-smoked groups had of smoking groups. Two routes to 'infection' were described by the never-smoked groups. The first involved an experimental episode, resulting from one or two children acting on their curiosity and love of lighting matches (etc.). The second and more likely route was seen as predation by a smoking group. (These two routes were recalled by the regular smokers in their stories of their first experience of smoking; see below). The methods of 'infection' were believed to include the tactics described above, but also an effect associated with passive smoking:

'My friends smoke and they're in Year 7, they're in [school name], and I went round to their house and she goes, "Do you want a cigarette?" and I go, "No". And they were all smoking and then all their friends came and they were all smoking, but I just went home early because then I didn't want to get hooked on it or anything.'

The group dynamics of resistance to smoking challenged loyalty to friends. The never-smoked groups reported that they would react very unfavourably to a group member starting to smoke. Most girls said that they would initially stay friends with the new smoker, at least to try to persuade her not to smoke. Eventually some social ostracism would be likely, either partial:

'I think I'd be their friend during school because they wouldn't be allowed to smoke, but after school, you know, at clubs and that we go to, I think I'd be where she doesn't, where you're not allowed to smoke.'

or complete:

'And if it ruined a friendship I wouldn't really mind, because I know that smoking is bad and that, but losing your friend, you can always get another friend, so losing a friendship isn't as bad as cigarettes.'

Many reasons are given by the never-smoked groups for the necessity of avoiding smokers, although all are understood in terms of the smoker having 'gone bad', and that this 'badness' becomes a threat to a never-smoked group identity and to the individual group members:

'I would stay away from her... because she would have bad breath all the time, and I don't really like people that smoke.... Just every time you say something that they don't like they just lash out at you all the time.'

'Well because I don't like smoking, I think it ruins the person that they are. 'Cos people judge by what they do, like smoking, and so some people would just say just 'cos they smoke they're not as good as everyone else. And I feel they're wasting themselves.'

INTERVIEWER: You'd be prepared to say, 'Right I'm not going to hang around with you any more'. Why would you be saying that to them?

H: Just so they would give up... 'cos it's bad for them... and because we might start smoking.

The discussions in this context frequently involved efforts to mark off the new smoking part of a friend from the rest, in order to banish smoking behaviour from the group, while not losing a friend and group member. Thus, some girls said they would remain friends with new smokers if they did not smoke around them, or if they did not offer cigarettes to the non-smoker. When a never-smoker took up smoking, friendship and group membership became unstable.

Never-smoked individuals and the onset of smoking   Despite strong evidence of a group-oriented understanding of the consequences of smoking status and group membership there was consistent affirmation of the individual's freedom of choice or right to make a decision. Personal choice was always invoked in the context of a new smoker deciding to ignore her friends' advice and to continue to smoke. The never-smoked friends would affirm the right of the new smoker to make her choice, but this affirmation served as a boundary point in several senses:

- as the point in time at which the new smoker ceased to be a concern of the never-smoked friendship group;
- as the boundary in social space between the friendship group and its environment;
- as a marker within the friendship group, delimiting acceptable behaviours and marking off the unacceptable.

The demand for conformity the never-smoked groups attributed to smoking groups was also a feature of their own groups. The role played by the affirmation of personal choice in their groups was in practice a demand for conformity to their never-smoked status. An understanding of the dangers to their group identity of the change in smoking status of their group members probably led them to demand this conformity.

Occasional smokers' groups' views about the onset of smoking

Compared with never-smoked group members, occasional smokers had qualitatively different views about the onset of smoking. Their descriptions were based in part on memories of their own experiences as well as on observation and imagination. From their perspective, the clear distinction between smoking and non-smoking friendship groups offered by the never-smoked groups was less stable, although it was still present, and sometimes important. The affirmation of individual choice that had formed a key element in the self-definition of the never-smoked groups was much less obvious among occasional smokers.

Occasional smokers' views of the first instance of smoking   Three common elements appeared in the occasional smokers' accounts of their first experience of smoking.

- an instigator
- a sense of place
- smokers' claims about harmlessness and pleasure.

The role of the *instigator*, often an older person, was always filled by a person who was known to the new smoker, but this person was not always among the new smokers' closest existing friends. The instigator claimed, or was known, to have smoked previously, although the context of this smoking is not clear. (The equivalent of the instigator role within the never-smoked groups' aetiology of smoking is that of a 'germ' or 'carrier'.)

A *sense of place* was always associated with the first experience of smoking. The instigator usually accompanied one or two people to an outside location for the specific purpose of smoking, although in one case they were both in a night-club. (The sense of going somewhere to smoke fits with the never-smoked groups' description of smoking groups as active in the world; see above.) This sense of place, and the presence of an acknowledged instigator gave the event some of the attributes of ritual or initiation, especially since the first cigarette was often passed around a number of girls. In this context cigarettes may have a symbolic significance, indicating daring (access to cigarettes for girls of this age usually requires some nerve) or fearlessness (in the face of a known killer).

The insistence by any smokers present that smoking just one cigarette would not hurt, and that the new smoker would not get addicted, and (if necessary) that the smoking experience was pleasant once you got used to it, was the third common element. In the context in which the girls found themselves, there appeared to be few legitimate responses to these half-truths.

Occasional smokers' group issues arising from the first instance of smoking   The outcome of girls' first experiences of smoking in terms of the reaction within their friendship groups was similar to that described in hypothetical terms by the never-smoked groups. Non-smoking friends put pressure on the new smoker not to continue smoking, especially as smoking represented a threat to the integrity of non-smoking friendship groups. The form of this pressure was first to offer reasons for not smoking that were oriented towards the short term, and then to suggest that the new smoker would no longer be wholly within her old friendship group. This suggestion might be implied in the affirmation of an individual's right to choose.

> [To new smoker] ''Cos I said that you'll be stupid; "Even though other people are doing it doesn't mean that you have to. You're not going to be any different. You'll still be my friend if you try it, but", I said, "it's just for you that I'm telling you. So it's up to you. But", I said, "I wouldn't if I was you, but it's up to you."'

However, the instigator continued to offer cigarettes, and the new smoker found herself in a position of having to choose friendship groups. All the participants within the occasional smokers' groups claimed to have chosen to remain within their non-smoking friendship groups. The choice, and the decision to try smoking cigarettes, raised the question of loyalty to the groups' non-smoking identities, which could no longer be taken for granted.

Regular smokers' group members' views about the onset of smoking

Some of the members of the regular smoking group recalled being very anti-smoking before they began smoking regularly. One of these girls recalled being close to a relative who suffered and died of lung cancer.

Regular smokers' group's view of the three phases of smoking   The regular smokers described three phases in their careers as regular smokers:

- the first experience
- hesitant smoking
- regular smoking

Regular smokers confirmed never-smoked groups' suspicions that there are two routes to the first instance of smoking. Some described a curiosity-based experiment (involving either just themselves, or a small group of non-smokers). Others described being pressured into smoking by a friendship group of smokers. The role of the instigator was given less emphasis in their accounts than in the reports by occasional smokers. The sense of place was strong for regular smokers, as it had been for occasional smokers. The first smoking experience was not always described as unpleasant.

There were various descriptions of the hesitant phase. One girl emphasised the difficulty in saying 'no' after she had been seen smoking. Others noted the desire to be active and out in the world with

their friends rather than being bored. Smoking gave them an opportunity to go off to the woods and 'have a laugh'. Finally, one girl said
that the second cigarette had been less unpleasant than she remembered the first one to have been, and this lent credence to smokers'
claims that smoking is pleasant once you get used to it.

Most of the girls said they just continued to smoke 'hesitantly', until
one day they realised they smoked regularly and were addicted. However, one girl, pressured into smoking by her friendship group,
reported that she suddenly realised she would be a smoker:

> 'Before I went round with you lot [smoking friendship group] I
> never smoked, and everyone's going, "You're going to smoke in a
> year, I bet you next year you're going to be smoking." And I
> never ... And then after that I thought, "I'm going to smoke", like
> something happened, I can't remember what.'

Apart from the above, there was no mention in this context of exclusion from non-smoking friendship groups, or of any reaction from
non-smoking (ex)-friends (see below). There was little mention of
boys, except to say that one reason younger girls smoked more than
boys might be that at this age, boys were not yet in a position to take
part in 'adult' pursuits, such as smoking and relationships:

> 'You do it for a laugh with your friends. It's something to do 'cos it
> like gets boring after a while. Before you've actually been intro-
> duced to boys and stuff, you know, like, started going out with
> them, not serious like, you just go out with them for a joke. But I
> mean when you've got something to do like smoke you just go out
> into the woods or something and have a fag.'

Social identities, smoking onset and resistance

The practice of, and resistance to, smoking formed major parts of the
social representations that constituted the specific social identities of
friendship groups. The views of the groups, defined by smoking status,
reflect this.

Views of the never-smoked groups

One of the girls who had never smoked noticed that a change of
schools was related to previously non-smoking girls taking up smoking for the first time: 'She ... seems to have gone that one step further
now we're at secondary school.' A change of schools is recognised by

girls as an opportunity to choose new behaviours, new friends and possibly a new social identity. It is also likely to have disrupted friendship groups established during primary/other school, and to have placed the identities of such groups in a new and challenging environment.

Most girls from the never-smoked groups agreed that if a girl from a non-smoking group took up smoking, she would almost inevitably leave their group to join other smokers. Smoking or non-smoking were perceived as primary factors in girls' friendship groups' identities. Girls who had never smoked recognised that if an individual from a non-smoking group started smoking she had to change groups. The group and its identity would not change to accommodate her new behaviour.

The girls from the never-smoked groups acknowledged that they tended to reject members in their group who took up smoking. They explained this rejection as being a consequence of the girl's unacceptable behaviour within the group, behaviour that was not part of the social identity of the group and thus could not be tolerated:

'No, they try and hang round with us but we don't really like them.'

The never-smoking groups talked about instances when they had tried to persuade a group member who started smoking to stay with them, but only on the condition that she gave up smoking:

'We said to Carole that we liked her a lot more before.'

If a group member tried smoking only once and concluded, independently, that she did not like smoking nor want to continue, then her group membership with the 'never-smoked' group was not threatened:

'We're best friends, but she has tried smoking, but it hasn't really changed her 'cos I think she's only done it once.'

Views of the occasional smokers' groups

The reasons that the occasional smokers' groups gave for taking up smoking (that they acknowledged more comfortably than the desire to seem 'hard') were the pressures to be 'one of the crowd'. Being 'one of the crowd' was recognised elsewhere by occasional smokers as a weakness of personality, and alternatively constituted a reason for quitting. Other reasons for giving up smoking were:

- the active persuasion of non-smoking friends;
- fear of losing their non-smoking friends, and group membership;

- long-term health risks as recounted by one girl who had smoked occasionally:

> 'My auntie's dad died from it and I saw it . . . and how he suffered from it . . . and . . . and my dad's ill so . . . so I gave it up, and I didn't touch them again.'

Groups of occasional smokers all reported that although they had tried smoking, they no longer smoked. It is not possible to judge whether this is a truthful report or an account representing pressures in the setting; that is, the presence of adults and the school. In both occasional smokers' friendship groups it also seemed that the presence of a dominant personality with a strong conviction against smoking may have persuaded the rest of the group to reject smoking. This is consistent with the idea that smoking is a primary defining factor among girls' friendship groups; groups either smoke on a regular basis or do not. The identification of an 'occasional smokers' group' may only be useful for analytic purposes.

Views of the regular smokers' group

Some members of the regular smokers' group were quite angry with the attitude of some of their old (non-smoking) friends when they started smoking:

> 'I mean I don't smoke 'cos I think its hard – she goes, "Oh you think you're so hard", and the things she says get on my nerves . . . and I feel like saying, "Oh shut up."'

Regular smokers described themselves as being misunderstood and asserted that they had not changed as people because they smoked cigarettes. The group mentioned instead social pressures to smoke as the reasons why they had started smoking. They saw these as a family background of smokers who accepted their onset of smoking as inevitable, and pressures from their friendship groups:

> '. . . but she's very persistent and she goes, "Oh ELLEN [name changed], have one"; I went, "No", and she went, "Have one! Go on!", and I went, "Oh, all right."'

Finally, in defence of the occasional smokers' belief that people start smoking in groups and not as individuals, one regular smoker stated that her group had started smoking as a group 'for a laugh really'. It is worth noting that non-smokers were recorded as laughing during the interviews only once, occasional smokers four times, and regular smokers six times in total. The regular smoker group was outnumbered 2 to 1 by occasional smokers' groups and 10 times by never-smoked groups. Nonetheless, laughter may occur among smokers not only as an aspect of their fun-loving natures but to release tension in the presence of adults. The interviewer may have been perceived as disapproving of their smoking.

Changing images of the 'hard' identity

An important source of information about adolescent identities arose from girls' spontaneous discussion of the 'hard' identity. Perceptions and valuations of the 'hard' identity vary between girls who are non-smokers and those who are smokers. Girls who described themselves as occasional and regular smokers were older than never-smokers.

Never-smoked groups' views of the 'hard' identity

Once again we observe that smokers are evaluated negatively and that the strength of this negative evaluation is a function of an individual's own smoking group membership. The never-smoked groups perceived smokers' groups negatively, describing them as being 'aggressive', 'hard', 'not nice', always 'in trouble at school', and always 'trying to impress'. Individuals who had previously been never-smokers but who became smokers were viewed as being in 'the wrong crowd':

'I suppose her attitude became a bit worse, didn't it?'

'About two years ago she didn't smoke and she was really nice and now she's started to beat up people, shouting at them and all that.'

On the whole, girls who had never smoked believed that girls who took up smoking were consciously attempting to achieve a 'harder' image. They themselves regarded this hard image as negative but believed it was an attraction for others.

The never-smoking groups were highly critical of new smokers' attempts to emulate 'hard' group behaviour and described this change as a partial loss of the new smokers' individual identity:

'I suppose if you hang around with the wrong people then you tend to go with their flow and ways so then you change as well.'

'She copies L.'

'She's always trying to be hard and shouting at everyone, and saying the last word.'

'They've got to pretend like they're funny.'

The identity of the never-smoked group may be inferred from the group's negative comments about smokers, namely that they are (by comparison with smokers) nice people and a collection of individuals as well as part of a group: sensible, responsible, stronger personalities, friendly, genuine, reasonable and concerned about their education and future:

> 'Yeah, she used to be quite sort of, erm, [pause] all for you, you know, stuff like "it doesn't matter what you wear, what you look like, it's who you are" and all that lot.... But now she has to have the fashionable stuff, or [mimics] "It's so embarrassing, you know!" '

> 'They're probably more interested in going out with their friends than in their education.'

Occasional smokers' groups' views of the 'hard' identity

Occasional smokers, like the groups of girls who had never smoked, understood part of the attraction of smoking to be due to its association with a 'harder' identity. They viewed the attribution of 'hardness' more ambiguously than did girls who had never smoked. They also mentioned that the company of boys was more likely if a girl was a smoker.

> 'He sort of got to like B and E a bit more because they were smoking and he was talking to them more because they were smoking.'

However, occasional smokers' groups overwhelmingly distanced themselves from the desire to impress others, and to be 'hard', as the reasons they smoked. They viewed these as reasons that lead other people to smoke cigarettes:

> 'Actually a lot of *us* started out [smoking] recently...'

But later:

> 'It's the impression; *they* want to make an impression on other people. *They'll* think, "Oh I'm hard..." '

Regular smokers' views of the 'hard' identity

Some members of the group who identified themselves as regular smokers admitted that when they were younger (and non-smokers) they thought that the image of smoking was 'cool' and 'hard':

'When I didn't smoke I used to think, "Cor, look at her, she's smoking! wow!"'

'She's really hard, like.'

'You see them all smoking down town and you think, "cool", but then . . .'

Now regular smokers themselves, these girls denied that they had changed in an effort to become 'hard' themselves:

'But as you grow up you begin to think it's not cool.'

Despite regular smokers' denial of smoking only to gain a 'harder' reputation (the view held by never-smokers), one regular smoker admitted to there being some truth in this assertion. This girl counter-accused her cousin (who was urging her to stop smoking) of being a 'sad' person and lacking the courage to take up smoking herself:

'I think she wishes she could smoke but she just hasn't got the guts to go ahead with it.'

Summary

Data from the focus group discussions are summarised here in terms of smoking group membership or more clearly in terms of two smoking identities: those of a girl non-smoker and a girl smoker.

- Beliefs and opinions varied in focus group discussions according to smoking group membership. *Never-smokers* viewed their status as sensible and considered regular smokers to be stupid. Membership in their groups was threatened by smoking uptake though they claimed that an individual had the right to choose. Smokers were believed to have a more exciting life but were seen as predatory and willing to resort to underhanded tactics to recruit new members to their groups.
- *Regular smokers* reported feeling misunderstood by their non-smoking peers. They were hesitant in admitting that social pressure and a desire to appropriate a 'hard' identity had influenced their decision to smoke. They felt that they had 'slipped' into regular smoking.

- *Occasional smokers* conceptualised their smoking experiences in terms of an instigator, a place and sceptically received assurances that smoking was not really harmful. Occasional smoking appeared to be a *transient* identity.

GENDER IDENTITIES AND SMOKING BEHAVIOUR

Viewing adolescent identities from another research tradition, an American study reported that sex role identities influenced adolescent smoking frequency (Evans *et al.*, 1990). Bem (1974) had proposed that sex roles be measured by requiring individuals to place themselves on both masculine and feminine scales. 'Masculine' traits included being competitive, competent, self-confident and persistent. 'Feminine' traits included being kind, emotional, helpful, empathetic. Persons described as having a masculine identity rated themselves significantly higher on the masculine scale than on the feminine scale. A feminine identity was achieved by scoring significantly higher on the feminine scale than on the masculine scale. Masculine identities were more prevalent among men, and feminine identities among women. Individuals whose scores on the two scales were not significantly different were described by Bem as androgynous. Spence *et al.* (1975) later suggested that individuals who rated themselves as below average on masculine and feminine traits be viewed as 'undifferentiated' in terms of their sex role identities but that those who scored above average on both still be described as 'androgynous'. Evans *et al.* (1990) found that adolescents whose ratings allowed them to be classified by psychologists as 'androgynous' were less likely to smoke cigarettes than were adolescents with other gender identities.

Pupils in the Sussex questionnaire study described their gender identities by rating themselves on a 6-point scale on four masculine and four feminine dimensions. The masculine items were:

- competent (skilful)
- competitive (wants to win)
- self-confident (sure of self)
- persistent (doesn't give up easily).

The four feminine items were:

- emotional (has strong feelings)
- helpful to others
- empathetic (aware of others' feelings)
- kind.

Pupils were classified as having one of four gender identities on the basis of their ratings on these items. The four possible gender identities are:

- masculine identity
- feminine identity
- androgynous identity
- undifferentiated.

Boys were about three times more likely than girls to be assigned a masculine identity and girls about three times more likely than boys to be classified as having a feminine identity. Boys were somewhat more likely to be classified as androgynous and girls slightly more likely to be classed as undifferentiated. There was a strong association between sex and masculine and feminine identities but categorisation in terms of androgynous and undifferentiated identities was not predicted by sex (Table 8.1).

When the autumn term questionnaire results were analysed there was a small but statistically significant relationship between gender identities and smoking status (Table 8.2). Adolescents with an androgynous identity were most likely to be never-smokers. This finding is

Table 8.1 Proportion of boys and girls classified as masculine, feminine, androgynous and undifferentiated on the basis of their autumn self-reports

	Boys	Girls
Masculine	814 (33.6%)	210 (9.7%)
Feminine	258 (10.6%)	766 (35.5%)
Androgynous	594 (24.5%)	454 (21.0%)
Undifferentiated	760 (31.3%)	728 (33.7%)

Note: The chi-square statistic for the sex by gender identity contingency table was highly significant (chi-square = 614, 3 df, p < 0.000005)

Table 8.2 Masculine, feminine, androgynous and undifferentiated identities and smoking status

	Non-smoker	Occasional smoker	Regular smoker
Masculine	570 (55.7%)	318 (31.1%)	136 (13.3%)
Feminine	561 (54.7%)	309 (30.1%)	155 (15.1%)
Androgynous	617 (59.0%)	299 (28.6%)	130 (12.4%)
Undifferentiated	761 (51.2%)	489 (32.9%)	235 (15.8%)

Note: Chi-square = 17.1, 6 df, p = 0.009

consistent with the American study (Evans *et al.*, 1990), but it may be worth noting, first, that the American research was carried out in a single school year, and second, that for Sussex pupils androgyny decreased with age.

Given that adolescents are somewhat less likely to be classified as androgynous with increasing age, except for Year 11, and that smoking prevalence increases with age, the association between androgyny and smoking behaviour found in the autumn term data may be accounted for primarily by age. The autumn term classification of gender identities was used to predict smoking uptake. The four gender identities failed to predict changes from never smoking to occasional smoking, or progressions from occasional to regular smoking. Results using gender identities failed to explain smoking uptake among Sussex pupils.

The Sussex questionnaire data, however, showed that regular smokers described themselves as more fun loving and less conforming than their non-smoking peers. Although the ideal self identity ratings for both the autumn term and the longitudinal data yielded results in relation to smoking status that were similar to those for self-perception, the relationships were weaker.

Both the autumn term and longitudinal analyses of the perceived self identity data showed that regular smokers described themselves as more fun loving and less conforming.

9 Interventions

> We must distrust our instinct of intervention, for the desire to make one's own will prevail is often disguised under the mask of solicitude.
>
> Henri-Frédéric Amiel

> 'If everybody minded their own business,' the Duchess said in a hoarse growl, 'the world would go round a deal faster than it does.'
>
> Lewis Carroll

This chapter begins with a review of published studies reporting school-based interventions. The following sections use data from the Sussex and London studies to consider intervention strategies in the light of its findings. The first factor considered is smoking prevalence and adolescents' knowledge of the effects of smoking. Later sections examine the influence of families, friends, beliefs, attitudes towards the body, the effects of stress and coping, social identities and social settings on smoking behaviour. The contribution of the qualitative findings is considered in subsequent sections. Finally, developmentally based school interventions are proposed.

SCHOOL-BASED INTERVENTION STUDIES

Published reports about smoking prevention programmes in schools provide a starting-point for consideration of intervention strategies. Bruvold (1993) carried out a meta-analysis of school-based smoking prevention studies published in the 1970s and 1980s that contained sufficient data to allow quantification of the effectiveness of these interventions. Meta-analysis is a statistical technique that determines whether there is a difference between groups on a particular dimension and provides an estimate of the size of the effect. It was possible to employ this statistical technique since each of the studies selected for inclusion contained a control group that did not receive the prevention programme, as well as post-tests and follow-ups.

Earlier meta-analyses (Bruvold and Rundall, 1988; Bangert-Drowns, 1988) had already established that traditional, information-giving approaches produced larger changes in adolescents' knowledge about smoking than did newer approaches, but that the newer interventions had a greater effect upon attitudes and behaviour. Drawing upon earlier work by Battjes (1985), Bruvold developed a four-category system for classifying different approaches to interventions in schools. The traditional approach Bruvold labelled *rational*, and he described the three more recent approaches as *developmental, social norms* and *social reinforcement*. The aims of each approach and details of significant work by researchers who have made a major contribution to each are presented below:

- Rational approaches seek to provide information about cigarette smoking, its effects and consequences. The theories of Ajzen and Fishbein (1980) and Ajzen and Madden (1986) have been applied extensively to cigarette smoking, and have underpinned, either explicitly or tacitly, much health promotion activity. Such applications have been reviewed comprehensively by Sutton (1987).
- Developmental approaches offer affective education aimed at increasing self-esteem and self-reliance, reducing alienation and developing interpersonal and decision-making skills (Rosenberg, 1979).
- Social norms approaches seek to provide alternatives to smoking and also aim to increase self-esteem and reduce alienation and boredom (Jessor and Jessor, 1977).
- Social reinforcement approaches focus on social pressures with the aim of enabling the identification and resistance to such pressures (Bandura, 1988).

Specific procedures are usually associated with the differing perspectives of these four intervention approaches. Rational approaches are based on lectures and demonstration material such as pictures of tar-coated lungs. Such activities are generally backed up by worksheets and a question-and-answer period. Developmental approaches may also use didactic methods, but these are supplemented with discussions, group problem solving and, occasionally, with role play. By contrast, social norms-based interventions attempt to offer alternatives to cigarette smoking. They also tend to involve participation in community improvement projects, providing opportunities for recreational activities alongside vocational training and tutoring. Discussion, modelling behaviour, role play and practice form the basis of the social reinforcement approach. Public commitment not to smoke may also be employed.

In practice, intervention programmes often employ more than one of these approaches. It was necessary, therefore, for Bruvold to identify the major and subsidiary approaches in order to determine which were the more effective. To do this, he devised a coding system to identify the approaches used in the eighty-four reports that comprised his meta-analysis. This procedure yielded ninety-four separate, classifiable classroom interventions.

Two major dimensions were employed to structure the meta-analyses. The first was based around the four approaches described above. The second employed an assessment of the measures used to evaluate the effectiveness of a given intervention, concentrating on the *adequacy of the quantitative measures used* in making such assessment. It identified the more methodologically sound reports, and allowed for the weighting of results accordingly. The forty-eight studies that were classified as more methodologically adequate were analysed first. Next, the effect sizes were calculated for all ninety-four interventions. Both sets of studies were examined to determine the size changes in knowledge, attitude and behaviour in the post-test and later follow-ups. Results were presented separately for change in knowledge, attitude and behaviour.

All four intervention approaches were shown to have a sizeable effect upon *knowledge*. Bruvold suggests that this reflects the use of direct teaching procedures as a secondary element in interventions that were primarily classified as developmental, social norms or social reinforcement approaches. Changes in knowledge among groups that had taken part in the methodologically superior set of studies were similar to those in the total set of studies.

Changes in *attitudes*, however, were not as consistent nor as large as changes in knowledge. In this respect, the most successful interventions were those that employed a social reinforcement approach. The next most successful category of interventions in terms of changing attitudes was those using a developmental approach. Comparison of these two more successful types of intervention with those employing rational and social norms approaches was made difficult because of the limited use of attitude measures in post-tests and follow-ups.

The most complete picture emerged from analyses based upon behavioural measures. Most studies included such measures, and they were often reported for later follow-ups as well. These findings are valuable not just for the completeness of the statistical analyses, but also in terms of the *aims* of school intervention. It is, after all, changes in smoking *behaviour* that are the ultimate goal of all such programmes. *Both the social reinforcement and social norms approaches produced changes that were consistently positive and significant*. The changes reported from interventions including a developmental approach were generally positive and significant, but those resulting from interventions using a rational approach were neither significant nor consistently positive.

The abundance of behavioural measures of effectiveness allowed further analyses of these results. In seeking to explain changes in smoking behaviour, other measures were added to the meta-analyses. Earlier meta-analyses of adolescent smoking behaviour (Bangert-Drowns, 1986; Bruvold and Rundall, 1988) had already demonstrated the influence of numbers of sessions and of school year (or grade level) on the effectiveness of school-based smoking interventions. Evidence of a decline in the prevalence of adolescent smoking between the 1970s and 1980s (Glynn, 1989) prompted the use of publication date as a further variable. Bruvold therefore included the following in his subsequent analyses:

- number of sessions within an intervention programme;
- year level (grade level) of pupils participating in an intervention;
- year the report was published;
- subsidiary approaches.

These further analyses employed a method that is analogous to traditional analysis of variance as differences both *between* approaches and *within* approaches were compared. Although there were significant effects for all the additional variables, only school year (grade level) consistently reduced variability within a specific approach. Although effectiveness was greater at higher grade or year levels, the effects for the other variables, number of sessions and year of publication were not consistent. In some comparisons the higher year (grade) effects were associated with fewer sessions, earlier date of publication and the addition of fewer secondary approaches, but in others they were associated with more sessions, later date of publication and the addition of other approaches.

However, at the *same* grade or year levels, social reinforcement interventions produced changes in smoking behaviour that were larger than those of interventions based upon a rational approach. Developmental and social norm-based interventions also produced effect sizes larger than those of interventions based upon a rational approach at the same grade or year level. Finally, the average weighted behavioural effect sizes for social reinforcement, developmental and social norm approach-based interventions did not differ significantly when comparisons were made at the same grade or year level.

Bruvold (1993) concluded his report with a set of recommendations. His first was an endorsement for the use of the social reinforcement approach, as exemplified by the work of McAlister *et al.* (1980). In mass-media campaigns, without translating probability data into messages that may be interpreted as inevitability, which may be contrary to young people's experience and/or perceptions.

PREVALENCE AND KNOWLEDGE

When pupils first enter secondary school at age 11–12, smoking prevalence is very low. Around 8 out of 10 individuals will never have tried a cigarette, and less than 1 per cent will be smoking regularly (defined as one cigarette or more a week). By the end of the first year of secondary school, about 30 per cent will have tried a cigarette, but regular smoking rates remain below 4 per cent, and these rates are broadly similar for boys and girls.

Pupils have considerable knowledge about the deleterious effects of cigarette smoking by this age. The great majority of individuals are aware that tobacco causes diseases of the circulatory and respiratory systems, and nearly all believe smoking to be addictive. At this age, young people's attitudes and intentions are consistent with this knowledge; nearly all pupils at this age appear to believe that smoking is an undesirable activity and very few have any intention to take up smoking in the near future. It seems very probable, therefore, that these attitudes and intentions may have been at least partly formed as a result of the health education programmes conducted in primary schools up to and including Year 6.

Smoking behaviour at any given age from 11 to 16 years varies by physical maturity. For boys, the relationship is simple: boys who are physically mature are more likely to have tried a cigarette or to be regular smokers than are boys who are not yet physically mature. This relationship remains roughly constant at least up to the age of 16 years. For girls, the relationship is more complex. Like boys, post-pubescent girls are more likely to be smokers than are pre-pubescent girls of the same age. However, while the rate of increase in smoking prevalence remains roughly constant for post-pubescent girls, the rate for pre-pubescent girls rises sharply around the age of 13.5–14 years, somewhat later than the average age of menarche in the United Kingdom. Cigarette smoking appears to compensate for a lack of obvious physical maturity in late-developing girls. Such quantitative findings were confirmed verbally during focus group discussions. Smoking appears to be used as a 'badge' of maturity at a time when such outward signs are vitally important in securing an adult identity, and may well override beliefs about the negative effects of smoking that have been developed in earlier years.

addition, he supported the social norm approach as employed by Coe *et al.* (1982) and the developmental approach exemplified by Botvin *et al.* (1984). Bruvold concluded that traditional, information-giving rational approaches would require revision before being of greater value, despite being widely accepted and requiring little teacher training. (It is noteworthy here that such approaches still dominate mass-media campaigns aimed at reducing smoking among adults. Such campaigns have the advantage of being relatively cheap, and are politically useful in that they show that 'something is being done'.) The theory of reasoned action propounded by Ajzen and Fishbein (1980) represents an improvement on older rational approaches. However, as Bruvold points out, such interventions are dependent for their implementation on the modification of belief structures. This would require more individually based (and thus more expensive) interventions than have traditionally been employed in rational approaches.

A recent (1993) study has shown that a rational approach, giving information about the physical consequences of cigarette smoking, can be effective in reducing both smoking uptake and cigarette consumption. However, innovative features of the materials employed played an important part in that success (Sussman *et al.*, 1993). Over 6,000 seventh-grade (12- to 13-year-old) pupils took part in the study and completed self-report instruments assessing uptake and usage prior to and following the intervention, and again 1 year later. The authors noted that giving information about smoking-related diseases was almost as successful as social influences interventions, a finding which appeared to contradict earlier research. However, it should be noted that the intervention also included correcting myths about tobacco experimentation and addiction, the role-playing of various diseases, and describing probabilities of acquiring such diseases. The effort to present information *in a manner more personally relevant to adolescents*, rather than describing the long-term consequences of smoking in general, may have been an important factor in the intervention's success.

School-based interventions are not alone in being able to effect change in adolescents' cigarette smoking. American researchers (Johnson *et al.*, 1993) compared the effectiveness of school-, parental-, mass media- and community-based interventions delivered to 12- to 14-year-olds in eight schools. These interventions targeted drugs as well as cigarette smoking. Control schools received only mass media- and community-based interventions, while the targeted schools had all four components. The school interventions included ten sessions of resistance skills training, together with homework which focused on active interviews and role playing. The school-based intervention may be seen as including developmental, social norms and social reinforcement approaches according to Bruvold's categorisation described above. Three years later, it was found that schools receiving all four interventions had reduced levels of both cigarette and drug use. Moreover, individual differences in students' specific behavioural, social and demographic risks did not influence the effectiveness of the full programme. By contrast, the control group (which received only mass media and community interventions) showed only modest reductions in use. It may be concluded that although school interventions may not be *sufficient* to affect adolescent smoking, they are certainly *necessary* to bring about such changes.

EVIDENCE FROM THE SUSSEX STUDY

Current intervention approaches result in teenagers having an understanding of smoking that reflects a traditional medical viewpoint. The Sussex data showed clearly that adolescents accepted that there are long- and short-term risks involved in cigarette smoking, but that they also saw smoking as a passport to a sophisticated, sexually mature and socially aware identity. The social identity of the smoker was characterised by enjoying parties, being popular with (and attractive to) the opposite sex, and adopting a non-conformist outlook on life. These attributes compensated for the acknowledged effects on physical health, and helped to create a much-desired 'hard' identity.

The social identity of a non-smoker included acceptance of adult values, but was also seen as conventional and unexciting. Non-smokers themselves acknowledged this image but appeared to be content with it, as their social representations were consistent with its attributes. Individuals adopting this identity were unlikely to smoke in any case, irrespective of the content or nature of their school's health education programme. It is therefore our contention that health education programmes need to associate the identity of a non-smoker specifically with those desirable social representations that are usually associated with the social identity of smokers.

The need to maintain and develop those areas of antismoking interventions that emphasise assertiveness and refusal skills was highlighted by data from the behavioural study. Smokers were reported to use a number of tactics to persuade non-smokers to experiment with cigarettes. Such exchanges seem most likely to occur between Year 7 and Year 9, and the content of personal, social and health education teaching (PSHE sessions) needs to reflect these findings.

There is also a need to recognise that adolescents' family structures have particularly important effects on their smoking behaviour. *Living with both biological parents clearly militated against experimentation with cigarettes.* With an increasing proportion of children being raised within reconstituted families, there is need for integration of such issues into PSHE programmes. Despite the limited success of initiatives that have attempted to involve other family members (Nutbeam *et al.*, 1993), intervention programmes need to include the issue of parental smoking behaviour and the reasons for it. Specific efforts might be directed at reducing smoking among new parents. Such efforts need to address the effects of parental smoking on children in terms of smoking uptake in addition to those of passive smoking.

Non-smokers believed that their parents' smoking reflected an addiction to tobacco, and regular smokers claimed that they themselves were addicted. This latter observation supports Regis's (1990) assertion that an overemphasis on the addictive properties of cigarettes may be counterproductive: expected, as well as actual, addiction is used by adolescents and adults alike as a rationalisation for continuing to smoke. Indeed, even occasional smokers *expected* to become addicted. Despite their own relatively low levels of consumption, nicotine addiction was used by them to explain their smoking behaviour.

Interventions need to recognise that smoking is experienced by smokers as having definite positive effects. Regular smokers in this study believed that smoking would be both anxiolytic and an aid to concentration, both of which may well be subjectively true for the smoker. Health education programmes should not seek to deny the subjective experiences of smokers, but should attempt to promote alternative ways of achieving such effects.

Despite popular belief, there was no evidence to support the notion that smoking is used by girls aged 11 to 16 as a means of controlling weight. Such avenues do not seem likely to be productive in health education programmes where curricular time is limited.

Overstating the health risks involved in smoking may lead to a rejection of the messages given. While the traditional knowledge–attitude–behaviour formula assumes that risk is a deterrent, the possibility that young people view health at least ambivalently should also be considered. Regular smokers described lifelong smokers they knew who appeared to be healthy and well. These individuals were offered as an illustration of the discrepancy between the message, *as they saw it*, and their own experiences. In a target group whose opinions and attitudes tend to be polarised, it is important to strike a balance between producing messages simple enough to be appropriate for

FAMILIES AND SMOKING

The nature of the household in which children are raised profoundly affects their chances of becoming a smoker, and this effect is most marked for adolescents aged 13–15. Teenagers who are raised in lone-parent families and stepfamilies are much more likely to become smokers than are children who are raised by both biological parents. The effects of divorce and separation on the emotional well-being of adolescents is well known and documented. The increased rate of smoking uptake among children in such families may be interpreted as symptomatic. Issues such as self-esteem, self-worth and negative affect may be of greater influence on behaviour than the rationalism to which smoking education generally appeals.

The smoking behaviour of family members also has a direct effect on children's smoking. When family members are smokers, an adolescent is nearly twice as likely to have smoked compared to adolescents in households where all family members are non-smokers. This effect is particularly pronounced on the transition from having never smoked to experimenting with cigarettes.

FRIENDS AND SMOKING

The effect of having a best friend who smokes is roughly similar to that of having parents or older siblings who smoke. Overall, adolescents who have a best friend who is a smoker are about twice as likely to have tried cigarettes than are children who have a best friend who is a non-smoker. However, the effect of best friend's smoking is not constant with age. At 11–12 years, the increased probability of smoking is about threefold, but this effect decreases linearly until age 15–16, where best friend's smoking makes no difference at all. The reason for this is twofold: first, the pool of available never-smokers with whom to be best friends decreases with increasing age, and second, those adolescents who have reached the age of 15 or above without smoking are likely to be more entrenched in their views and more resistant to peer influences to smoke. It does not seem useful, therefore, to discuss the issue of best friend's smoking behaviour in interventions with older adolescents.

BELIEFS AND SMOKING

All young people possess considerable knowledge as well as arrays of beliefs and attitudes about the health and social consequences of smoking which contribute to forming their intentions to smoke, or not to smoke cigarettes. The desire to comply with what are perceived to be the norms for a desired group is also an important contributor to all young people's smoking decisions, and this influence is more pronounced in girls than in boys. While almost all adolescents hold appropriate beliefs about the deleterious physical effects of smoking, these kinds of beliefs contribute less to the formation of an intention to smoke than do beliefs about the positive psychological effects of cigarettes.

Not only smokers, but also adolescents who have never tried cigarettes hold positive beliefs about smoking. For example, the positive effect of nicotine on mood and concentration, commonly reported by smokers, appeared to be accepted as fact by most adolescents, irrespective of their personal experience of smoking. In addition, such beliefs were reinforced in smokers by their own subjective experiences. Evidence for this was found in the observation that a belief in the positive psychological effects of smoking was predictive of a transition to more regular use of cigarettes in occasional smokers. The (at least subjectively) real positive effects of smoking on psychological states cannot be ignored when discussing smoking issues, especially with older adolescents.

BODY IMAGE: THINNESS AND ATTRACTIVENESS

The dramatic bodily changes that occur during adolescence, together with the concurrent interest in personal relationships, have led to a general assumption that smoking is utilised as a means of controlling weight by teenagers wishing to stay (or become) slim. This commonly held belief has been reinforced by the popular assertion that a continual stream of media images of fashionably emaciated models contributes further to anxiety about body image and results in cigarette smoking, particularly among girls.

While girls were found to be more generally concerned about thinness than were boys, there was little evidence to link this concern with cigarette smoking in either the quantitative or the behavioural phases of the Sussex study. Although a relationship between smoking behaviour and concern with thinness was identified, the magnitude of that relationship was extremely small, accounting for less than 2 per cent of the variance in smoking behaviour. It is very likely that this relationship may be much more a function of a general personality trait such as neuroticism than of a specific concern with weight. Moreover, controlling for such factors reduced the association between smoking and concerns with body image in the Sussex sample to a negligible level.

It is, therefore, firmly concluded from this study that body image concerns are unlikely to be of any major importance in explaining the smoking behaviour of young adolescents. Individuals high in trait neuroticism have a greater tendency to experience negative emotional states, to have more life problems, to worry more, to be more dissatisfied with life and cope less well with stress. In adolescents, high neuroticism has been demonstrated to be related to low self-esteem.

STRESS AND COPING

In the Sussex sample, girls consistently reported experiencing more stress in their lives than did boys. However, further analyses have shown that the observed gender differences in smoking prevalence cannot be directly attributed to either perceived stress or coping styles. Nevertheless, negative affect is the most common reason given by adolescents for relapsing following a period of abstinence from smoking, and regular smokers reported experiencing more stress than did either never-smokers or occasional smokers.

Two points need to be made concerning the relationship of stress to smoking. First, smokers were significantly more likely to use cathartic mechanisms in order to cope with stress (for example screaming, slamming doors) than were non-smokers, who were more likely to employ problem-focused coping techniques. This observation is consistent with the suggestion that smoking may be linked to personality factors such as neuroticism. Second, smokers viewed smoking as a resource to deal with stress. Such a view is not simply an abstract attribution: smokers reported using cigarettes for their psychoactive effects, and such effects were subjectively real.

A general point emerges: in adolescents, smoking may in part be seen as a symptom of perceived stress and ineffective coping strategies, as well as a discrete behaviour in its own right. Focusing directly on a symptom is unlikely to bring about a change if the factors that are causing it are ignored.

SOCIAL IDENTITIES

Three dimensions of adolescent identities were highlighted by the Sussex study: a general positive–negative evaluation, a 'fun loving' dimension and a conforming–nonconforming dimension. For the adolescents in this study, 'fun loving' was characterised by a party-going individual, fond of, and attractive to, the opposite sex, with an active social life. Current smokers rated themselves as being more fun loving than did non-smokers.

More importantly, rating oneself as being more fun loving was predictive both of experimentation with cigarettes in individuals who had previously been never-smokers, and of increased frequency of smoking among experimental or occasional smokers. This finding should be viewed in tandem with those of other studies which have shown a larger discrepancy between ratings of current and ideal self in adolescent smokers when compared to non-smokers. Smoking was seen, particularly among older adolescents, as an accessory to a fun-loving, sociable and sexually aware identity, a short-term goal which was well worth the concomitant long-term risks to physical health.

Adolescents differentiated clearly between their images of smokers and non-smokers in terms of the social identities with which they are associated. Further, distinctions were drawn between girls and boys of the same smoking status. This distinction was further complicated by differences determined by the smoking status of the individual making the rating.

The social identity of an adolescent of either sex or of any given smoking status thus has a complex ontogeny. In general, smoker identities were seen less favourably, but they were also seen as more fun loving and less conforming. Girls were seen as more conforming than boys, irrespective of their smoking status. While smokers rated themselves as more mature than non-smokers, non-smokers saw themselves as more mature than smokers. This contradiction may be understood when the meanings of the term 'maturity' are clarified for the two groups. For non-smokers, maturity was identified with adopting adult values such as personal responsibility and an industrious attitude to academic work. For smokers, maturity was defined more in terms of an adult social life of which partying and popularity with the opposite sex are vital ingredients. *Moreover, while non-smokers considered themselves to be more 'sensible' than smokers, smokers willingly ascribed this characteristic to non-smokers as well; they simply did not find such a trait important for themselves.*

Taken in combination, these findings are consistent with the enduring popularity of the social identity of many adolescent role models. Across four decades of adolescent culture many, if not most, teenage heroes have been characterised by unhealthy, risk-taking behaviour. A fast, chaotic and risky lifestyle is very attractive to some teenagers, and it is the very negative effects which define their appeal. Interventions which attempt to portray non-smoking as a 'mature' or sensible, 'informed choice' are likely to have credence only with adolescents who are committed non-smokers already.

SOCIAL SETTINGS

Antismoking interventions in schools cannot be viewed in isolation from the characteristics of the individual schools in which they are conducted. Despite producing remarkably consistent public statements regarding their policies on smoking, the schools in the Sussex study showed considerable variation in how such rules were interpreted, monitored and enforced. In one school, a severely punitive stance was consistently adopted towards pupils caught smoking, while in another there was simple denial that smoking was a problem at the school, despite clear evidence to the contrary. In a third school, a pragmatic 'damage limitation' approach was adopted on school outings in which smoking and non-smoking areas were established.

Given that many state secondary schools use the same nationally available antismoking resources in PSHE time, the effect of these materials cannot fail to be modified by the ethos of the individual school in which they are employed. No particular difference was found between single-sex and coeducational schools in any aspect of smoking examined in this study. However, large differences in smoking behaviour were observed between state schools and a single-sex independent school after controlling for socio-economic factors. This finding suggests strongly that the specific culture of any given school may contribute to adolescent smoking behaviour in a manner over and above the individual social characteristics that the children bring into the school with them.

INDICATIONS FROM BEHAVIOURAL STUDIES

The finding that all young people appear to be well informed about the physical risks associated with smoking was confirmed in the behavioural phase of the Sussex study. Teenagers explained adult smoking in terms of the facts either not being known, or not being properly taught, when they were young. Adolescents who had never smoked identified their peers' smoking in terms of constructing a group identity which was distinct from that of non-smokers. This identity was seen as sociable, exciting and party-going, while non-smokers were seen as sensible and quiet. Never-smokers reported considerable pressure from smokers to begin smoking, and described smokers as predatory in their attempts to gain conformity from them. It was suggested that techniques of persuasion, physical intimidation and social ostracism were applied by smokers to non-smokers to achieve this end.

Individuals belonging to never-smoking groups were supportive of each other and developed methods of protecting themselves against such techniques. They adopted a highly defensive stance in which smokers were seen as 'stupid' while they identified themselves as sensible. The path to smoking was seen as analogous to 'infection', with the causal agent being either curiosity or (more usually) predation by smokers who were already 'infected'. Although the pressure to try cigarettes was strong and multi-faceted, there was opposing pressure from non-smokers to resist. The demand for conformity that never-smokers attributed to smokers was also a feature of their own groups. The result was often a strain on friendships, which would either break or be modified in such a way that the relationship existed only in settings in which smoking was prohibited, such as at school. Despite a general view that groups of smokers were seen by non-smokers as having 'gone bad', there was a consensus that friendships with previous never-smokers who had recently taken up smoking could be preserved in the safety of a non-smoking environment.

Adolescents who have smoked have qualitatively different views about the onset of smoking compared to those of never-smokers. Their perceptions are based not only on their attitudes, beliefs and observations, but also on their own subjective experience. This experience is generally associated with the memory of an instigator, and a sense of place as to where the event occurred. Regular smokers described a phase of hesitant, intermittent smoking. Having been seen smoking was reported as making it more difficult to refuse subsequent offers of cigarettes, and this phase continued until occasional smokers found themselves 'addicted'. During this transition, the unpleasant effects of smoking were reported to diminish, supporting the persuasive claims of instigators that smoking became more pleasurable after some persistence.

Going on to secondary school was seen by many adolescents as being an opportunity to choose new behaviours, new friends and possibly a new social identity. The social identities of many friendship groups were constructed in no small part from the social representations of the adoption or rejection of cigarette smoking. Indeed, smoking behaviour was a primary defining factor among friendship groups in adolescent girls. Taken in combination with the effects of experiencing smoking for the first time, attitudes and beliefs inculcated at primary school appear to be fundamentally modified during the early years of secondary education.

COMBINED FINDINGS

The popular notion that adolescents smoke in an attempt to appear more grown up was strongly disputed by both quantitative and behavioural studies, with less than 1 per cent of the pupils agreeing with this statement. Similarly low levels of agreement were recorded with regard to smoking making young people feel more grown up. Even allowing for some level of denial, it seems unlikely that looking or feeling more grown up is an important factor in determining smoking behaviour in adolescents. Similarly, few pupils associated smoking with anxiolytic effects, attributing such outcomes to be more salient to adults' (notably parents') smoking.

By contrast, a large majority of pupils believed smoking to be addictive, and addiction was seen as the real risk of smoking. Moreover, 'addiction' was included as part of social identity, by becoming an essential accessory to the image of the smoker.

Although the relationship between concerns with thinness and smoking becomes non-significant when factors such as age and trait neuroticism are controlled, there is a complex relationship between smoking, weight and perceptions of fitness. Many adolescents both smoke and take part in sports; while smoking may reduce their potential performance, in reality many adolescents' fitness appears adequate to undertake sporting activity *to the extent that they wish*. In this way, sports are seen to compensate for any reduction in fitness that may result from smoking. This trade-off enables the view to be formed that it is better to be a slim, fit smoker than an overweight, unfit non-smoker.

Both parts of the study showed clearly that adolescents have learned, and are able to recall, the effects of smoking on health. However, it was also clear that the recital of these medical outcomes has become ritualised for many teenagers. Moreover, regular smokers stated that they had come to 'switch off' from such messages, which they regarded as propaganda, preferring to trust their own knowledge of adult smokers who did not seem to be suffering from smoking-related disease. By contrast, teenagers' descriptions of the negative effects of smoking on appearance and social competence are more convincing. These effects were both more immediate than the threat of chronic diseases presented by medical 'authority', and more real because they were the result of the adolescent's own observations and experience.

The evidence that the social representations of smoking that girls adopt was linked to the social groups in which they situated themselves has implications for future smoking intervention programmes. Early school-based programmes highlighted the damage to health caused by smoking, but it is now appreciated widely that for the majority of adolescents the risk of developing smoking-related diseases in middle age is of little, if any, consequence. Two influential studies (Evans, 1976; Evans *et al.*, 1978) prompted a shift in the emphasis in intervention programmes towards withstanding social pressure. Subsequently a succession of programmes, employing various techniques, sought to equip adolescents with the social skills required to resist 'peer pressure' to smoke. However, such approaches neglect to consider the meanings of smoking for adolescents.

The combination of quantitative and behavioural procedures adopted in the Sussex study has identified several meanings of smoking for adolescent girls. The data demonstrate that there are different routes to achieving a desired social identity depending upon membership in a group of either non-smokers or smokers. The structures of the nonsmoking and smoking identities were very similar, but the meanings attached to their constituent representations depend upon an individual's group membership. Among adolescent girls who smoked, cigarettes were an important means to establishing a desirable identity.

In terms of preventing smoking uptake, adolescent girls have conventionally been viewed as a homogeneous group. Analyses in terms of membership of different groups and data from different smoking identities suggest that 'blanket' approaches to anti-smoking interventions, whether based upon messages of risk or upon developing refusal skills, are inappropriate. Indeed, two of the most commonly used programmes in the United Kingdom have been shown to be ineffective (Nutbeam *et al.*, 1993; Michell, 1994).

Simple interventions are likely to result in differing responses because membership of different groups results in adolescents' attaching different values to social representations of smoking. The data in the Sussex study demonstrated that non-smokers value health. Most interventions targeted at these non-smokers would be successful if they included health-related issues. Conversely, such interventions would have little impact on regular smokers, who value health at least ambivalently. While regular smokers consider non-smokers to be 'sensible', they do not actively desire such attributes for themselves,

The smoker identity places greater value on liking, and being attractive to, the opposite sex, and on having a successful social life. Appeals to being 'healthy', 'cool', 'grown-up' and 'independent of the crowd' are therefore likely to meet with the lack of success that has been already observed in current programmes. Future intervention programmes aimed at smokers might seek to enhance the desirability of the social representations associated with the non-smoker identity, or to reduce the perceived worth of those associated with the smoker identity, although neither of these is a simple task.

A greater understanding of the different meanings of smoking to adolescent girls, and their role in the construction of different social identities, may enable interventions to focus more effectively than has hitherto been the case. Never-smokers would probably respond well to most health-related interventions. By contrast, regular smokers pose the greatest challenge as they themselves view smoking as a useful means of developing an adult social identity, rather than as the deviant behaviour portrayed by current health education programmes. It is among occasional smokers, however, that there is the greatest scope for intervention. Analyses of smoking prevalence have demonstrated that the behaviour of occasional smokers is not as powerfully determined by fixed variables such as age, puberty or gender as is that of non-smokers and regular smokers. Occasional smokers may, therefore, be more susceptible to influence, if programmes can be devised that make the social representations of non-smokers more highly valued than those of regular smokers.

RECOMMENDATIONS FOR SCHOOL-BASED INTERVENTIONS

In designing anti-smoking interventions, the clear message that emerges from the Sussex and London studies is that there is a need to re-evaluate existing programmes from *within a developmental framework*. Adolescents are not a homogeneous group. Young people in their first year of secondary school aged 11–12 are very different in terms of their needs, images, social identities and social representations, and life experiences from those in their third year aged 14–15, and even more different from those leaving secondary school at age 16. The focus of smoking education must therefore shift throughout the school curriculum in ways that are salient to children and adolescents, and which reflect developmental changes in young people as they mature.

Primary education up to age 11

It is obvious that at the time that young people enter secondary school at the age of 11–12, they already have a more than adequate knowledge of the long-term effects of tobacco use. It seems very unlikely that further repetition or elaboration of these facts is likely to bring about any substantial reduction in the number of adolescents who take up smoking. Indeed, there is always a danger in adding to ever-increasing lists of 'things that smoking does to you'; the risk is that messages about relative risks of acquiring chronic diseases much later in life may become rejected in favour of anecdotal but concrete experience of long-term adult smokers who appear to be well. The preference of lay people to give credence to the experience of significant others, personally known to them, over arguments about relative risks has been described elsewhere, and this study suggests that such may also be the case for adolescents with regard to smoking.

Nevertheless, it remains true that the majority of children go on to become non-smoking adults, and the main reason given by adults for not smoking (and for the adolescents in this study) is the adverse health outcomes that smoking is known to cause. Further, the more polarised thinking of younger children would appear to be particularly receptive to simple messages about the effects of smoking. For these reasons, it is recommended that existing primary education about smoking should continue with an emphasis of how tobacco smoke affects the body. Such classroom activity should seek to embed facts about the effects of smoking within the teaching of basic human biology in order to emphasise the links between bodily structure and function, and how smoking causes disease. A number of nationally available resources achieve this integration and should continue to be utilised.

Secondary school

Secondary school smoking education programmes should comprise three distinct phases that reflect the changing interrelationship between knowledge, attitudes and social representations which characterise the development of the adolescent. These phases might be linked by a spiral curriculum in which there is an initial shift away from the specific focus on smoking recommended for primary school children in the lower age range of secondary school. The curriculum could then revisit specific aspects of smoking in the middle years. The upper years should be characterised by a closer focus on smoking, but should include different aspects of the behaviour that are appropriate to this age group. The school years and age ranges given below are not mutually exclusive in their categorisation. This is a reflection of the range of chronological ages found in school years and of the range of developmental maturity observed in young people of similar chronological ages. The timings of these phases are given as indicators rather than strict divisions. Age and developmental characteristics should be taken into account when planning activity for any given group.

Years 7–8 (age range 11–13)

During this stage of development, the findings of the Sussex study suggest that it may be most effective for PSHE programmes to turn away from a focus on smoking *per se*. Some of the most powerful determinants of smoking behaviour in this age group appear to be linked to a more general sense of self-esteem and concepts of self-worth. Moreover, living in a lone-parent family or stepfamily increases the risk of becoming a smoker in adolescents of all age groups, but the effect is most marked for pupils in Years 7 and 8. It follows that to concentrate on cigarette smoking in young people who are already well aware of the health risks of smoking is to concentrate on a symptom rather than the cause of the behaviour. This period of health education activity should be characterised by an emphasis on improving the self-esteem and assertiveness of those pupils in whom such qualities are most weak. This emphasis resembles the developmental approach to smoking described by Bruvold (1993). Examination of developmental interventions might well provide material for classroom use in this age group.

Cigarettes may also be used at this age to compensate for a real or imagined lack of physical maturity when compared to one's peers; this is especially true for girls. It is during this period that improving self-esteem, assertiveness training, developing refusal skills and learning to deal with peer pressures *in general* are likely to be most effective in preventing experimentation with cigarettes, rather than treating smoking as a 'special' activity in its own right.

Years 8–9 (age range 13–15)

Although having parents or older siblings who smoke increases the likelihood that any adolescent will take up smoking, the effect of parental and older sibling smoking status on adolescent smoking behaviour is most pronounced during Years 8 and 9. In the third year of secondary school there should therefore be a shift to examining and discussing the reasons why parents and other adults smoke. Such activity should also openly discuss the nature and effect of peer pressure to begin smoking, as well as the effect of an individual's smoking uptake on friendship groups, and of forming and maintaining relationships in general. Particular emphasis should be given to classroom discussion of the effects of having a best friend who becomes a smoker. The social reinforcement approaches that focus on the social pressures to begin smoking may also provide material for adaptation to classroom use.

Space should also continue to be given to more general mental health issues, particularly around how to deal with stress effectively. An emphasis should be placed on teaching problem-solving styles of coping as well as specific training in relaxation techniques. These issues are more typical of the social norms approaches described by Bruvold (1993).

Years 10–11 (age range 15–16)

By this age, the influence of peer pressure and of having a best friend who smokes becomes unimportant in determining an individual adolescent's smoking behaviour, and the emphasis in classroom work should shift away from these issues. Activities should now take account of the pupils' own subjective experience of smoking. These include reports of stress relief and enhanced performance on intellectual tasks.

Although such reports are subjective, there is a contemporary psychopharmacological literature which does indeed document the positive effects of nicotine on decision times for both complex and hard-to-attend-to tasks (Bates *et al.*, 1995), on the elementary information-processing correlates of IQ (Stough *et al.*, 1994), and in enhancing some of the physiological processes underlying intellectual performance (Stough *et al.*, 1995). In addition, Warburton and Arnall (1994) have demonstrated that such effects cannot be ascribed simply to the relief of withdrawal symptoms. At this age, beliefs about the positive psychological effects of smoking become stronger predictors of intention to smoke than beliefs about the social or health consequences, and such beliefs are predictive of a transition to regular smoking among occasional or experimental smokers. Consideration should now be given to how the perceived psychological benefits of smoking (improved concentration and study efficiency, relaxation, reduction in irritability and anxiety) can be obtained without using cigarettes. Discussion of these topics should recognise the reality of these reported effects for the smoker and should not attempt to dismiss them lightly. Drawing on the experience of individuals who have smoked in the past but who have stopped may be valuable in that they will have social representations that are more easily identified with by smokers compared to those of never-smokers.

We suggest that intervention programmes be adapted to take account of the existence of adolescent smoker identities that value smoking behaviour in different ways. There is no easy formula to developing more effective interventions, but if their creators are grounded in a thorough understanding of how young people themselves view smoking, repetition of some of the dead-ends of earlier programmes may be avoided.

IMPLICATIONS FOR SCHOOLS

The implications of a schools programme such as that outlined above are considerable. The Sussex study identified a commonly expressed concern of teachers that time for PSHE was increasingly under pressure from the demands of both the National Curriculum and schools management to improve GCSE results in the light of published 'league tables'. Both the Sussex and London studies and other published work (Digiusto, 1994) suggest that smoking cessation work in secondary schools is not likely to be effective. Other workers (Reid *et al.*, 1995) concur, and suggest that such activity is not an appropriate use of health department funding. We would support this assertion. However, some of the most effective programmes focus on social reinforcement, including specific refusal skills in relation to cigarettes (Bruvold, 1993). The difficulty is that such programmes require far more curricular time than is likely to be available in UK secondary schools to spend solely on smoking issues: Silvestri and Flay (1989) estimate that 6–7 hours is necessary in Year 7, with further sessions in later years.

By contrast, general programmes which focus on reducing alienation and increasing self-esteem without direct reference to cigarettes are also effective (Bruvold, 1993). For this reason, making part of the antismoking curriculum address more general issues should be doubly helpful. Such programmes not only would assist in reaching a workable compromise between effective delivery of an antismoking programme and restrictions on curricular time, but seem likely to have positive outcomes across a range of health behaviours. A recent review (Reid *et al.*, 1995) concluded that 'health departments should focus on support for comprehensive programmes...with its emphasis on self esteem, health promoting policies and family and community links'. The conclusions of this study lend empirical support to, and are wholly consistent with, such a recommendation. Such programmes would thus be cost-effective as well.

There is also a need for adequate training of teachers in order to deliver more sophisticated programmes effectively. This training need not be excessively costly: Rohrbach *et al.* (1993) demonstrated that intensive training does not necessarily achieve better behavioural results than does more brief training. Certainly, there is a clear indication that funding should be supplied by the health sector for providing such training.

Finally, there is a pressing need for health education to take a more prominent place in the English and Welsh National Curriculum. The pressure on schools to perform academically has resulted in the marginalisation of other, equally important activities. It is only by allocating adequate time for work in the classroom, and for the training of teachers to deliver it, that schools-based interventions will become more effective.

10 Breaking the mould

> After all, the ultimate goal of research is not objectivity, but truth.
>
> Helene Deutsch

What, then, after all these words, can be said about teenage cigarette smoking, images of smoking, and the social identities of adolescents? Can the mass of data points, focus group transcriptions and review of current social psychological theory offer better insights into what it is like to be neither a child nor an adult in the 1990s? In this final chapter, we attempt to draw together the threads of those preceding in order to provide a more complete picture of an adolescent's view of his or her own health.

First, it is clear that health professionals and educators can no longer view adolescent cigarette smoking as a feckless, deviant behaviour. Despite the undoubted co-occurrence of cigarette smoking with other health-threatening behaviours, which has led to the compelling notion of a syndrome of 'problem behaviours', it is obvious that some of these activities are nevertheless a part of normal adult society. Drinking alcohol and engaging in sexual intercourse are seen as 'problematic' only when they occur precociously. Cigarette smoking may well result in very serious health consequences, but it remains an activity undertaken by a substantial proportion of the adult population. It is difficult to defend, therefore, a perspective which views smoking among teenagers as 'unnatural'. In fact, it could be argued that by experimenting with cigarettes, teenagers are simply 'testing out' one of the most common social representations of adults. Adults use tobacco openly, legally and to the background of fabulously expensive and sophisticated advertising and promotion. It is conceivable that adolescent smokers are acting in a manner which is entirely logical and psychologically 'healthy' in developmental terms. They are simply experiencing a very common aspect of adulthood for themselves.

Moreover, it must be appreciated that 'adolescents' are not a homogeneous group of whom all aspire to the same aspects of adulthood, nor do they all define 'adult' behaviour in the same terms. While some teenagers express their transition to adulthood in officially sanctioned ways (such as participation in sport and academic engagement), others choose to express their approach to adulthood through behaviours which adults see as threatening (such as smoking and drinking).

In the Sussex study, there were clear differences in the ways in which smokers and non-smokers defined maturity. While non-smokers tended to associate maturity with adult *values*, such as academic success and responsibility, smokers tended to identify maturity with participation in the *behaviours* engaged in by adults, such as smoking, drinking and having parties. A strong motivation to pursue fun was an important predictor of smoking uptake. Smoking may be seen as a quite logical, developmental outcome for such adolescents which results from their adoption of what they perceive to be adult behaviour. Interventions and campaigns that assume a homogeneous 'youth culture' (often as defined by adults) are thus fundamentally flawed.

The contagion model is also problematic. Cigarette smoking in adolescence cannot be seen as a kind of 'behavioural disease' which spreads from one individual to another through some all-encompassing, yet poorly defined, process conveniently (if loosely) labelled 'peer pressure'. This view of it is, we believe, a result of attempts (largely perpetrated by medical practitioners) to describe human behaviour in medicalised terms. Such attempts are, in our opinion, as outmoded as they are mechanistic. This is not to state that peer influence is not a contributory factor in adolescent smoking: our findings are consistent with those of many other researchers. Having a best friend who smokes is a significant risk factor for taking up cigarettes, and for increasing cigarette consumption in existing smokers. It must, nonetheless, be better appreciated that the effect of having friends who smoke is only one of a range of much wider influences on teenage smoking behaviour.

Second, it must be recognised that there is a complex interplay between risk and protective factors for engagement in adolescent problem behaviours in general, and cigarette smoking in particular. Although such factors have been recognised for many years, the reciprocity of their relationship is much less widely appreciated. Moreover, it must be acknowledged that many of these factors are:

- difficult to influence by conventional, mass-media interventions (for example, poor parenting styles);
- the result of factors over which adolescents have little or no control (for example, family breakdown and divorce); or

- a result of influences beyond the personal or familial (for example, the lack of a coherent sense of community or communal identity).

This latter observation is manifest in the consistently observed differences in smoking rates between adolescents of different cultural backgrounds.

Next, the complexity of the decision-making process concerning the adoption of health-related behaviours must not be underestimated. Much health promotion activity has been predicated on somewhat simplistic interpretations of influential social-psychological models, in which such decisions are interpreted as logical and straightforward. An individual's motivation for engaging in a given behaviour is not simply the opposite pole of his or her motivation for avoiding that behaviour. Motivations for and against engagement are commonly very *different* psychological structures, both carrying with them constellations of associated outcomes which are embedded in an individual's social world, aspects over which many people have little or no direct personal influence. It is also important, for the successful modification of beliefs, that the risks should not be exaggerated for the sake of emphasis, nor be excessively oversimplified. The consequence of such exaggeration may be a reduction in credibility of future messages brought about by a perceived discrepancy between health messages and people's own experiences. In any programme or intervention, it is essential to be aware of the importance of striking a balance between producing information that is direct enough to be appropriate to the medium used, without translating probability data into messages that may be interpreted as implying inevitability and which may be contrary to most people's experience.

A further problem with the traditional knowledge–attitude–behaviour formula so often employed in health promotion is that it assumes that a risk to physical health is necessarily a deterrent. Despite the familiar suggestion that reducing risk in one area may result in people increasing risks in another (the example of wearing seat belts in cars resulting in faster 'driving is perhaps one of the best known), the possibility that young people view health at least ambivalently should also be considered. From the 1950s' James Dean to the 1960s' Jimi Hendrix, from the 1970s' Sid Vicious through to the 1990s' Kurt Cobain and beyond, teenage heroes have been characterised by 'unhealthy', risk-taking behaviour. There is an undeniable appeal in the image of the artist, actor or musician whose lifestyle is fast, chaotic and exciting. Across nearly five decades of teenage culture, appearing 'fashionably wrecked' by such behaviour has only served to heighten charisma and desirability. The ideas of 'dying young' and 'not growing old' have a certain fascination.

LESSONS FROM EMPIRICAL RESEARCH

Health promotion programmes for young people must be theory driven and also based on research that uses adequate, representative samples which are capable of rigorous objective analysis. The inadequacy of strategies based on myth and popular opinion has been illustrated by the failure of many intervention programmes to date. Moreover, a danger exists whereby the adoption and promulgation of such myths by health professionals results in their being accepted as fact and threaten to produce a self-fulfilling prophecy.

For example, it has been widely assumed that all teenage girls are profoundly influenced and encouraged to smoke by media images of an emaciated ideal body shape, and that smoking provides an effective means of staying slim. Contrary to our expectations, while we found that girls in the Sussex study were much more concerned with thinness and weight than were boys, this concern with body image was not predictive of smoking uptake for girls. Instead, they identified smoking as a means of appearing tough or 'hard'. The belief that adult women smoke to stay thin may be supported by empirical evidence, but girls aged 11 to 16 years do not yet find it necessary to use cigarettes in this way.

A further example, quite unrelated to adolescence, also demonstrates this principle. Some writers have argued that women's smoking is often a result of difficulties in relationships with intransigent (male) partners. However, the evidence offered to support this belief is typically presented in the form of anecdotes. It might be argued that an a priori selection of respondents is likely to provide the evidence required. In one much-quoted study, based upon a dozen or so interviews, one of the respondents presented is a 57-year-old working-class woman who had undergone cardiac surgery, had six children, and was separated from her alcoholic husband, who paid her no maintenance but occasionally returned to assault her, causing her serious injuries. Although smoking is likely to be an important coping strategy for some women in such intolerable circumstances, it is questionable whether it is appropriate to extrapolate to women's smoking in general. Nonetheless, this research is well known to health promotion workers and remains highly influential to this day. It is essential that interventions in health promotion be guided by sound, testable hypotheses and reliable and valid data.

Sound research may sometimes yield uncomfortable truths. Such truth is the accumulating evidence that many smokers *enjoy* smoking. While this may seem an obvious truism, it is a fact which, in our experience, many professionals choose to ignore or dismiss as unimportant. There an increasing body of pharmacological evidence for the positive psychological effects which smoking may have on the smoker. In addition, we found anecdotal evidence that smokers derive pleasure from the physical act of smoking. For these people, smoking provides a ready-made set of 'meaningful rituals' which punctuate and orientate their waking hours. When considering smoking maintenance and cessation processes it is unwise wilfully to dismiss such psychopharmacological effects and the comfort provided by smoking as trivial.

There is now, we believe, compelling evidence to support the view that the quality of an adolescent's home environment will impact on his or her health-related behaviour, including the likelihood of taking up cigarettes. By 'quality of home environment' we do *not* mean material wealth. We use this term to indicate the presence or absence of basic skills in the business of what has become known as 'parenting', and the stability of the family as a unit. We would argue that poor parenting fails to provide the consistency and stability of environment that is conducive to the healthy development of adolescent social identities. There is now clear, sound and methodologically sophisticated evidence that it is in such difficult circumstances that the occurrence of 'problem behaviours', including cigarette smoking, becomes much more likely. It is a lamentable fact that (in the United Kingdom at least) the curriculum of parenting education is, for the vast majority of people, restricted to the basic physical care of the newborn infant. As a result, most parents adopt styles of parenting from the only role models they have: their own parents. For many, such models were far from ideal, and in this way inadequate or inappropriate practices are transmitted from one generation to the next.

No matter how well informed are efforts to prevent or reduce adolescent smoking, the sad truth is that the vastly increased rate of family break-up and subsequent reconstitution in many Western countries militates against the formation of stable social identities. Adolescents who are caught up in the process have an increased likelihood of engaging in a range of potentially harmful behaviours, which include cigarette smoking. The authors recognise that this observation could potentially be expropriated by the unscrupulously reactionary, and used as a means to castigate any individual who is raising a child outside a traditional (married) family unit. This is not our intention: we seek only to emphasise the obvious need of children and adolescents for stability in their home environments, irrespective of how that environment is constructed, and to present the increasing body of evidence that family breakdown and reconstruction are major risk factors in terms of health-related behaviour.

School and peer culture are also important factors in adolescent development. Our evidence highlights the significance of individual school cultures. They have a profound effect upon the values and social representations which children and teenagers choose to adopt. It seems that this culture is quite independent of whether the school has a single- or mixed-sex intake, and is not entirely predicated by the social background of the pupils attending it. It is clear from the Sussex study that each school contributes its own culture to its pupils' social identities over and above what they bring to school with them. The contribution of school culture to health-related values and behaviour cannot be underestimated and needs to be systematically addressed by education authorities.

One aspect of adolescent culture is revealed by the images of smokers and non-smokers held by teenagers. They are many, varied and often contradictory and internally inconsistent. Adolescents' images of smokers encompass an individual's physical appearance, psychological factors and social standing. Smoking is seen to be both an individual act or statement, and a symbol of group membership and belonging. Just as images of smokers tended to be negative, so too were descriptions of smoker identities.

POINTERS FOR INTERVENTIONS

The pressure to provide specific interventions dealing with adolescent smoking may blunt us to the need to address the wider issues which shape adolescent psychological well-being. It is a mixture of risk and protective factors that contribute to the occurrence or absence of problem behaviours, which include cigarette smoking.

It is necessary for those developing school intervention programmes to have the courage to resist pressures to 'do something about the smoking problem'. Such motivation is often imposed by well-meaning and concerned parents, headteachers and governors. However, it is our contention that in order to make significant inroads on the task of reducing smoking prevalence in pupils, it is critical that a wider perspective be adopted. This has two major dimensions: one is an appreciation of smoking as a symptom of adolescent unhappiness and the other is an awareness of developmental constraints. The former is evidenced by the co-occurrence of a range of problem behaviours and the latter by the meaninglessness of smoking as an appetite suppressant among *young* teenage girls.

Progress will be made in reducing smoking prevalence in secondary schools only as the result of a fundamental rethinking of the role of education not only as a vehicle leading to academic qualifications but as an opportunity to promote self-esteem, to instil a sense of purpose, to develop positive relationships with adults and to foster an appreciation in both adolescents and adults of pupils' developmental potentials and limitations.

References

Aaro, L. F., Hauknes, A. and Berglund, E. L. (1981) 'Smoking among Norwegian school children 1975–1980: II. The influence of the social environment'. *Scandinavian Journal of Psychology*, 22, 297–309.

Aitken, P. P. (1980) 'Peer group pressures, parental controls and cigarette smoking among 10 to 14 year olds'. *British Journal of Social and Clinical Psychology*, 19, 141–146.

Ajzen, I. and Fishbein, M. (1980) *Understanding Attitudes and Predicting Social Behaviour*. Englewood Cliffs, NJ: Prentice-Hall.

Ajzen, I. and Madden, T. J. (1986) 'Prediction of goal-directed behavior: Attitudes, intentions and perceived behavioral control'. *Journal of Experimental Social Psychology*, 23, 453–474.

Allbutt, H., Amos, A. and Cunningham-Burley, S. (1995) 'The social image of smoking among young people in Scotland'. *Health Education Research*, 10, 443–454.

Allen, O. and Page, R. M. (1994) 'Variance in substance use between rural Black and White Mississippi high school students'. *Adolescence*, 29, 401–404.

Allen, O., Page-Randy, M., Moore, L. and Hewitt, C. (1994) 'Gender differences in selected psychosocial characteristics of adolescent smokers and non-smokers'. *Health Values: The Journal of Health Behavior, Education and Promotion*, 18, 34–39.

Allen, S. and Hiebert, B. (1991) 'Stress and coping in adolescents'. *Canadian Journal of Counselling*, 25, 19–32.

Allgood-Merton, B., Lewinsohn, P. M. and Hops, H. (1990) 'Sex differences and adolescent depression'. *Journal of Abnormal Psychology*, 99, 55–63.

Allison, K. R. (1992) 'Academic stream and tobacco, alcohol and cannabis use among Ontario high school students'. *International Journal of the Addictions*, 27, 561–570.

Aloise-Young, P. A., Graham, J. W. and Hansen, W. B. (1994) 'Peer influences on smoking initiation during early adolescence: A comparison of group members and group outsiders'. *Journal of Applied Psychology*, 79, 281–289.

Andreski, P. and Breslau, N. (1993) 'Smoking and nicotine dependence in young adults: Differences between Blacks and Whites'. *Drug and Alcohol Dependence*, 32, 119–125.

Ashby, J. S. (1995) 'Impact of contextual variables on adolescent situational expectation of substance use'. *Journal of Drug Education*, 25, 11–22.

Axelrod, R. (1976) *Structure of a decision*. Princeton, NJ: Princeton University Press.

Bachman, J. G., Johnston, L. D. and O'Malley, P. M. (1981) 'Smoking, drinking and drug use among American high school students: Correlates and trends 1975–1979'. *American Journal of Public Health*, 71, 549–569.

Bachman, J. G., Wallace, J. M., O'Malley, P. M., Johnston, L. D., Kurth, C. L. and Neighbors, H. W. (1991) 'Racial/ethnic differences in smoking, drinking and illicit drug use among American high school seniors'. *American Journal of Public Health*, 81, 372–377.

Bailey, S. L., Ennett, S. T. and Ringwalt, C. L. (1993) 'Potential mediators, moderators, or independent effects in the relationship between parents' former and current cigarette use and their children's cigarette use'. *Addictive Behaviors*, 18, 601–621.

Balding, J. (1995) *Young people in 1994: The health related behaviour questionnaire results for 48,297 pupils between the ages of 11 and 16*. School Health Education Unit, University of Exeter.

Bandura, A. (1988) *Social foundations of thought and action*. Englewood Cliffs, NJ: Prentice-Hall.

Bangert-Drowns, R. L. (1986) 'Review of developments in meta-analytic method'. *Psychological Bulletin*, 99, 388–399.

Bangert-Drowns, R. L. (1988) 'The effects of school-based substance abuse education: A meta-analysis'. *Journal of Drug Education*, 18, 243–264.

Barone, C., Weissberg, R. P., Kasprow, J. and Voyce, C. K. (1995) 'Involvement in multiple problem behaviors of young urban adolescents'. *Journal of Primary Prevention*, 15, 261–283.

Barton, J., Chassin, L., Presson, C. C. and Sherman, S. J. (1982) 'Social image factors as motivators of smoking initiation in early and middle adolescence'. *Child Development*, 53, 1499–1511.

Bates, T., Mangan, G., Stough, C. and Corballis, P. (1995) 'Smoking, processing speed and attention in a choice reaction time task'. *Psychopharmacology*, 120, 209–212.

Battjes, R. J. (1985) 'Prevention of adolescent drug abuse'. *International Journal of Addiction*, 85, 1113–1134.

Bauman, K. E. and Ennett, S. T. (1994) 'Tobacco use by Black and White adolescents: The validity of self-reports'. *American Journal of Public Health*, 84, 394–398.

Bauman, K. E., Botvin, G. J., Botvin, E. M. and Baker, E. (1992) 'Normative expectations and the behaviour of significant others: An investigation of traditions in research on adolescents' cigarette smoking'. *Psychological Reports*, 71, 568–570.

Belgrave, F. Z., Johnson, R. S. and Carey, C. (1985) 'Attributional style and its relationship to self-esteem and academic performance in Black students'. *Journal of Black Psychology*, 11, 49–56.

Bell, D. S. and Champion, R. A. (1979) 'Deviancy, delinquency and drug use'. *British Journal of Psychiatry*, 134, 269–276.

Bem, S. L. (1974) 'The measurement of psychological androgyny'. *Journal of Consulting and Clinical Psychology*, 42, 155–162.

Bettes, B. A., Duserbury, L., Kerner, J., James-Ortiz, S. *et al.* (1990) 'Ethnicity and psychosocial factors in alcohol and tobacco use in adolescence'. *Child Development*, 61, 557–565

Bewley, B. R. and Bland, M. (1978) 'The child's image of a young smoker'. *Health Education Journal*, 37, 236–241.

Bewley, B. R., Bland, J. M. and Harris, R. (1974) 'Factors associated with the start of cigarette smoking by primary school children'. *British Journal of Preventive and Social Medicine*, 28, 37–44.

Beyth-Marom, R., Austin, L., Fischoff, B. and Palgren, C. (1993) 'Perceived consequences of risky behaviours: Adults and adolescents'. *Developmental Psychology*, 29, 549–563.

Bhaskar, R. (1986) *Scientific realism and human emancipation*. London: Verso.

Biafora, F. A., Warheit, G. J., Vega, W. A. and Gil, A. G. (1994) 'Stressful life events and changes in substance use among a multiracial/ethnic sample of adolescent boys'. *Journal of Community Psychology*, 22, 296–311.

Biglan, A., Meltzer, C. W., Wirt, R., Ary, D., Noell, J., Ochs, L., French, C. and Hood, D. (1990) 'Social and behavioral factors associated with high-risk sexual behavior among adolescents'. *Journal of Behavioral Medicine*, 13, 245–261.

Biglan, A., Duncan, T. E., Ary, D. V. and Smolkowski, K. (1995) 'Peer and parental influences on adolescent tobacco use'. *Journal of Behavioural Medicine*, 18, 315–330.

Blaikie, N. (1996) *Approaches to social inquiry*. Cambridge: Polity Press.

Bland, M., Bewley, B. R. and Day, I. (1975) 'Primary schoolboy: Image of self and smokers'. *British Journal of Preventive Medicine*, 29, 262–266.

Block, J. H., Block, J. and Gjerde, P. F. (1986) 'The personality of children prior to divorce: A prospective study'. *Child Development*, 57, 827–840.

Bonney, M. E. (1971) 'Assessments of efforts to aid socially isolated elementary school pupils'. *Journal of Educational Research*, 64, 345–364.

Boomsa, D. I., Koopmans, J. R., Van Doornen, L. J. P. and Orlebeke, J. F. (1994) 'Genetic and social influences on starting to smoke: A study of Dutch adolescent twins and their parents'. *Addiction*, 89, 219–226.

Borland, B. L. and Rudolf, J. P. (1975) 'Relative effects of low socio-economic status, parental smoking and poor scholastic performance on smoking among high school students'. *Social Science and Medicine*, 9, 27–30.

Botvin, G. J., Baker, E., Resnick, N. L., Filazzola, A. D. and Botkin, E. M. (1984) 'A cognitive–behavioural approach to substance abuse prevention'. *Addictive Behaviour*, 9, 137–147.

Botvin, G. J., Dusenbury, L., Baker, E. and James-Ortiz, S. (1992) 'Smoking prevention among urban minority youth: Assessing effects on outcome and mediating variables'. *Health Psychology*, 11, 290–299.

Bowen, D. J., Dahl, K., Mann, S. L. and Peterson, A. V. (1991) 'Descriptions of early triers'. *Addictive Behaviors*, 16, 95–101.

Brannen, J., Dodd, K., Oakley, A. and Storey, P. (1994) *Young people, health and family life*. Milton Keynes: Open University Press.

Breslau, N., Kilbey, M. M. and Andreski, P. (1993) 'Vulnerability to psychopathology in nicotine-dependent smokers: An epidemiologic study of young adults'. *American Journal of Psychiatry*, 150, 941–946.

Brook, J. S., Nomura, C. and Cohen, P. (1989) 'Prenatal, perinatal and early childhood risk factors and drug involvement in adolescence'. *Genetic, Social and General Psychology Monographs*, no. 116.

Bruns, C. and Geist, C. S. (1984) 'Stressful life events and drug use among adolescents'. *Journal of Human Stress*, 10, 135–139.

Bruvold, W. H. (1993) 'A meta-analysis of adolescent smoking prevention programs'. *American Journal of Public Health*, 83, 872–880.

Bruvold, W. H. and Rundall, T. G. (1988) 'A meta-analysis and theoretical review of school based tobacco and alcohol intervention programs'. *Psychology and Health*, 2, 53–78.

Burke, R. H. and Weir, T. (1978) 'Sex differences in adolescent life stress, social support and well being'. *Journal of Psychology*, 98, 277–288.

Burton, D., Sussman, S., Hansen, W. B., Johnson, C. A. and Flay, B. R. (1989) 'Image attributions and smoking intentions among seventh grade students'. *Journal of Applied Social Psychology*, 19, 656–664.

Buswell, M. M. (1953) 'The relationship between social structure of the classroom and the academic successes of the pupils'. *Journal of Experimental Education*, 22, 37–52.

Byrne, D. G., Byrne, A. E. and Reinhart, M. I. (1995) 'Personality, stress and the decision to commence smoking in adolescence'. *Journal of Psychosomatic Research*, 39, 53–62.

Camp, D. E., Klesges, R. C. and Relyea, G. (1993) 'The relationship between body weight concerns and adolescent smoking'. *Health Psychology*, 12, 24–32.

Carver, C. S., Sheier, M. F. and Weintraub, J. K. (1989) 'Assessing coping strategies: A theoretically based approach'. *Journal of Personality and Social Psychology*, 56, 267–283.

Castro, F. G., Maddahian, E., Newcom, M. D. and Bentler, P. M. (1987) 'A multivariate model of the determinants of cigarette smoking among adolescents'. *Journal of Health and Social Behavior*, 28, 273–289.

Charlton, A. (1986) 'Evaluation of a family linked smoking programme'. *Health Education Journal*, 45, 140–149.

Charlton, A. and Blair, V. (1989) 'Predicting the onset of smoking in boys and girls'. *Social Science and Medicine*, 29, 813–818.

Charlton, A., Gillies, P. and Ledwith, F. (1985) 'Variations between schools and regions in smoking prevalence among British schoolchildren: Implications for health education'. *Public Health*, 99, 243–249.

Chassin, L., Presson, C. C., Sherman, S. J., Corty, E. and Olshavsky, R. W. (1981) 'Self-images and cigarette smoking in adolescence'. *Personality and Social Psychology Bulletin*, 7, 670–676.

Chassin, L., Presson, C. C., Sherman, S. J., Corty, E. and Olshavsky, R. W. (1984) 'Predicting the onset of cigarette smoking in adolescents: A longitudinal study'. *Journal of Applied Social Psychology*, 14, 224–243.

Chassin, L., Presson, C. C., Sherman, S. J., Montello, D. and McGrew, J. (1986) 'Changes in peer and parent influence during adolescence: Longitudinal versus cross-sectional perspectives on smoking initiation'. *Developmental Psychology*, 22, 327–334.

Chassin, L., Presson, C. C., Sherman, S. J. and Edwards, D. A. (1992) 'Parental educational attainment and adolescent cigarette smoking'. *Journal of Substance Abuse*, 4, 219–234.

Chisick, M. C., Lee, S., Raker, T. and Williams, T. R. (1992) 'A profile of tobacco use among teenage dependents'. *Military Medicine*, 157, 354–357.

Choquet, M. and Manfredi, R. (1992) 'Sexual intercourse, contraception and risk-taking behaviour among unselected French adolescents aged 11–20 years'. *Journal of Adolescent Health*, 13, 623–630.

Coe, R. M., Crouse, E., Cohen, J. D.and Fisher, E. B. (1982) 'Patterns of change in adolescent smoking behavior and results of a one year follow-up of a smoking intervention program'. *Journal of School Health*, 52, 348–353.

Compas, B. E., Orosan, P. G. and Grant, K. E. (1993) 'Adolescent stress and coping: implications for psychopathology during adolescence'. *Journal of Adolescence*, 16, 331–349.

Cooreman, J. and Perdrizet, S. (1980) 'Smoking in teenagers: Some psychological aspects'. *Adolescence*, 15, 581–588.

Copeland, E. P. and Hess, R. S. (1995) 'Differences in young adolescents' coping strategies based on gender and ethnicity'. *Journal of Early Adolescence*, 15, 203–219.

Costa, P. T. and McCrae, R. R. (1981) Stress, smoking motives, and psychological well-being: The illusory benefits of smoking. *Advances in Behaviour Research and Therapy*, 3, 125–150.

Cowen, E. L., Pederson, A., Babigian, M., Izzo, L. D. and Trost, M. A. (1973) 'Long-term follow-up of early detected vulnerable children'. *Journal of Consulting and Clinical Psychology*, 41, 438–446.

Cummings, E. M. (1994) 'Marital conflict and children's functioning'. *Social Development*, 3, 16–36.

DeCourville, N. H. (1995) 'Testing the applicability of problem behavior theory to substance use in a longitudinal study'. *Psychology of Addictive Behaviors*, 9, 53–66.

Dent, C. W., Sussman, S. and Flay, B. R. (1993) 'The use of archival data to select and assign schools in a drug prevention trial'. *Evaluation Review*, 17(2), 159–181.

Deosaransingh, K., Mareno, C., Woodruff, S. I., Sallis, J. F. *et al.* (1995) 'Acculturation and smoking in Latino youth'. *Health Values: The Journal of Health Behavior, Education and Promotion*, 19, 43–52.

DeVries, H. (1995) 'Socio-economic differences in smoking: Dutch adolescents' beliefs and behaviour'. *Social Science and Medicine*, 41, 419–424.

Diamond, A. and Goddard, E. (1995) *Smoking among secondary school children in 1994*. London: OPCS/HMSO.

Digiusto, E. (1994) 'Pros and cons of cessation interventions for adolescent smokers at school'. In R. Richmond (ed.) *Interventions for smokers: An international perspective*. Baltimore: Williams and Wilkins.

Dinh, K. T., Sarason, I. G., Peterson, A. V. and Onstad, L. E. (1995) 'Children's perceptions of smokers and non-smokers: A longitudinal study'. *Health Psychology*, 14, 32–40.

Dise-Lewis (1988) 'Life events and coping inventory: An assessment of stress'. *Psychosomatic Medicine*, 50, 484–499.

Dishion, T. J., Capaldi, D., Spracklen, K. M. and Li, F. (1995) 'Peer ecology of male adolescent drug use'. Special issue: Developmental processes in peer relations and psychopathology. *Development and Psychopathology*, 7, 803–824.

Doherty, W. J. and Allen, W. (1994) 'Family functioning and parental smoking as predictors of adolescent cigarette use: A six-year prospective study'. *Journal of Family Psychology*, 8, 347–353.

DuBois, D. L., Felner, R. D., Meares, H. and Krier, M. (1994) 'Prospective investigation of the effects of socioeconomic disadvantage, life stress, and social support on early adolescent adjustment'. *Journal of Abnormal Psychology*, 103, 511–522.

Duncan, T. E., Tildesley, E., Duncan, S. C. and Hops, H. (1995) 'The consistency of family and peer influences on the development of substance use in adolescence'. *Addiction*, 90, 1647–1660.

Dusenbury, L., Kerner, J. F., Baker, E. and Botvin, G. J. *et al.* (1992) 'Predictors of smoking prevalence among New York Latino youth'. *American Journal of Public Health*, 82, 55–58.

Duveen, G. and Lloyd, B. (1986) 'The significance of social identities'. *British Journal of Social Psychology*, 25, 219–230.

Duveen, G. and Lloyd, B. (1990) Introduction to G. Duveen and B. Lloyd (eds) *Social representations and the development of knowledge*. Cambridge: Cambridge University Press.

Eckert, P. (1983) 'Beyond the statistics of adolescent smoking'. *American Journal of Public Health*, 73, 439–441.

Eiser, J. R., Morgan, M., Gammage, P., Brooks, N. and Kirby, R. (1991) 'Adolescent health behaviour and similarity-attraction: Friends share smoking habits (really), but much else besides'. *British Journal of Social Psychology*, 30, 339–348.

Ennett, S. T., Bauman, K. E. and Koch, G. G. (1994) 'Variability in cigarette smoking within and between adolescent friendship cliques'. *Addictive Behaviors*, 19, 295–305.

Erickson, E. (1946) 'Ego development and historical change'. *Psychoanalytic Study of the Child*, 2, 359–396.

Erickson, E. (1950) *Childhood and society*. New York: Norton.

Escobedo, L. G., Anda, R. F., Smith, P. F., Remington, P. L. and Mast, E. E. (1990) 'Sociodemographic characteristics of cigarette smoking initiation in the United States'. *Journal of the American Medical Association*, 261, 49–55.

Evans, R. I. (1976) 'Smoking in children: Developing a social psychological strategy of deterrence'. *Preventive Medicine*, 5, 122–127.

Evans, R. I., Rozelle, R. M., Mittelmark, M. B., Hansen, W. B., Bane, A. L. and Havis, J. (1978) 'Determining the onset of smoking in children: Knowledge of immediate physiological effects and coping with peer pressure, media pressure and parent modelling'. *Journal of Applied Social Psychology*, 8, 126–135.

Evans, R. R., Turner, S. H., Ghee, K. L. and Getz, J. G. (1990) 'Is androgynous sex-role related to cigarette smoking in adolescents?' *Journal of Applied Social Psychology*, 20, 494–505.

Farrell, A. D., Danish, S. J. and Howard, C. W. (1992) 'Relationship between drug use and other problem behaviors in urban adolescents'. *Journal of Consulting and Clinical Psychology*, 60, 705–712.

Feigelman, W. and Lee, J. A. (1995) 'Patterns of cigarette use among Black and White adolescents'. *American Journal on Addictions*, 4, 215–225.

Feij, J. A. and van Zuilen, R. W. (1984) *SBL Handleiding: Spanningsbehoeftiligst*. Lisse, Netherlands: Swets & Zeitlinger.

Fergusson, D. M. and Horwood, L. J. (1995) 'Transitions to cigarette smoking during adolescence'. *Addictive Behaviours*, 20, 627–642.

Fergusson, D. M., Lynskey, M. T. and Horwood, L. J. (1995) 'The role of peer affiliations, social, family and individual factors in continuities in cigarette smoking between childhood and adolescence'. *Addiction*, 90, 647–659.

Fidler, E. E., Michell, L., Raab, G. and Charlton, A. (1992) 'Smoking: A special need?' *British Journal of Addiction*, 87, 1583–1591.

Flay, B. R., Hu, F. B., Siddiqui, O., Day, L. E., Hedeker, D., Petraitis, J., Richardson, J. and Sussman, S. (1994) 'Differential influence of parental smoking and friends' smoking on adolescent initiation and escalation of smoking'. *Journal of Health and Social Behavior*, 35, 248–265.

Fletcher, A. C., Darling, N. E., Dornbusch, S. M. and Steinberg, L. (1995) 'The company they keep: Relation of adolescents' adjustment and behavior to their friends' perceptions of authoritative parenting in the social network'. *Developmental Psychology*, 31, 300–310.

Folkman, S. and Lazarus, R. S. (1985) 'If it changes it must be a process: Study of emotion and coping during three stages of a college examination'. *Journal of Personality and Social Psychology*, 48, 150–170.

Forgays, D. G., Bonaiuto, P. and Wrzesniewski, K (1993) 'Personality and cigarette smoking in Italy, Poland and the United States'. *International Journal of the Addictions*, 28, 399–413.

Foxcroft, D. R. and Lowe, G. (1991) 'Adolescent drinking behavior and family socialization factors: A meta-analysis'. *Journal of Adolescence*, 14, 255–273.

Franzkowiak, P. (1987) 'Risk taking and adolescent development: The functions of smoking and alcohol consumption in adolescence and its consequences for prevention'. *Health Promotion*, 2, 51–61.

Frydenberg, E. and Lewis, R. (1990) 'How adolescents cope with different concerns: The development of the Adolescent Coping Checklist (ACC)'. *Psychological Test Bulletin*, 3, 63–73.

Frydenberg, E. and Lewis, R. (1991) 'Adolescent coping in the Australian context'. *Australian Educational Researcher*, 18, 65–82.

Frydenberg, E. and Lewis, R. (1993) 'Boys play sport and girls turn to others: Age, gender and ethnicity as determinants of coping'. *Journal of Adolescence*, 16, 253–266.

Furby, L. and Beyth-Marom, R. (1992) 'Risk taking in adolescence: A decision-making perspective'. *Developmental Review*, 12, 1–44.

Galan, F. J. (1988) 'Alcoholism prevention and Hispanic youth'. *Journal of Drug Issues*, 18, 49–68.

Garmezy, N. (1985) 'Stress resistant children: The search for protective factors'. In J. E. Stevenson (ed.) *Recent research in developmental psychopathology. Journal of Child Psychology and Psychiatry, Book Supplement*, Vol. 4. Oxford: Pergamon Press.

Ge, X., Lorenz, F. O., Conger, R. D., Elder, G. H. *et al.* (1994) 'Trajectories of stressful life events and depressive symptoms during adolescence'. *Developmental Psychology*, 30, 467–483.

Gerber, R. W. and Newman, I. M. (1989) 'Predicting future smoking of adolescent experimental smokers'. *Journal of Youth and Adolescence*, 18, 191–201.

Glendinning, A., Shucksmith, J. and Hendry, L. (1994) 'Social class and adolescent smoking behaviour'. *Social Science and Medicine*, 38, 1449–1460.

Glynn, T. J. (1989) 'Essential elements of school based smoking prevention programs'. *Journal of School Health*, 59, 181–188.

Goddard, E. (1990) *Why children start smoking: An enquiry carried out by the Social Survey Division of OPCS on behalf of the Department of Health.* London: HMSO.

Goddard, E. (1992) 'Why children start smoking'. *British Journal of Addiction*, 87, 17–18.

Golding, J. F., Harpur, T. and Brent-Smith, H. (1983) 'Personality, drinking and drug-taking correlates of cigarette- smoking'. *Personality and Individual Differences*, 4, 703–706.

Golombok, S. and Fivush, R. (1994) *Gender development.* Cambridge: Cambridge University Press.

Gordon, N. P. (1986) 'Never smokers, triers and current smokers: Three distinct target groups for school-based antismoking programs'. *Health Education Quarterly*, 13, 163–179.

Gottlieb, N. H. and Green, L. W. (1984) 'Life events, social networks, lifestyle and health: An analysis of the 1979 national survey of personal health practices and consequence'. *Health Education Quarterly*, 11, 91–105.

Graham, H. (1993) *When life's a drag: Women's smoking and disadvantage.* London: HMSO.

Green, G., Macintyre, S., West, P. and Ecob, R. (1990) 'Do children of lone parents smoke more because their mothers do?' *British Journal of Addiction*, 85, 1497–1500.

Green, G., Macintyre, S., West, P. and Ecob, R. (1991) 'Like parent like child? Associations between drinking and smoking behaviour of parents and their children'. *British Journal of Addiction*, 86, 745–758.

Gritz, E. R. (1986) 'Gender and the teenage smoker'. *National Institute on Drug Abuse Research Monograph Series*, Monograph No. 65, 70–79.

Gurin, P. and Marcus, H. (1990) 'Cognitive consequences of gender identity'. In S. Skeffington and D. Baker (eds) *The social identity of women.* London: Sage.

Hahn, L. P., Folsom, A. R., Sprafka, J. M. and Norsted, S. W. (1990) 'Cigarette smoking and cessation behaviors among urban Blacks and Whites'. *Public Health Reports*, 105, 290–295.

Harré, R. (1986) *Varieties of realism: A rationale for the natural sciences.* Oxford: Blackwell.

Harré, R. and Secord, P. F. (1972) *The explanation of social behaviour.* Oxford: Blackwell.

Hawkins, J. D., Catalano, R. F. and Miller, J. Y. (1992) 'Risk and protective factors for alcohol and other drug problems in adolescence and early adulthood: Implications for substance abuse prevention'. *Psychological Bulletin*, 112, 64–105.

Headen, S. W., Bauman, K. E., Deane, G. D. and Koch, G. G. (1991) 'Are the correlates of cigarette smoking initiation different for Black and White adolescents?' *American Journal of Public Health*, 81, 854–858.

Henry, B., Feehan, M., McGee, R., Stanton, W. *et al.* (1993) 'The importance of conduct problems and depressive symptoms in predicting adolescent substance abuse'. *Journal of Abnormal Child Psychology*, 21, 369–380.

Henwood, K. L. and Pidgeon, N. F. (1992) 'Qualitative research and psychological theorising'. *British Journal of Psychology*, 83, 97–111.

Hetherington, E. M. (1988) 'Parents, children and siblings: Six years after divorce'. In R. A. Hinde and J. Stevenson-Hinde (eds) *Relationships within the family*. Oxford: Clarendon Press.

Hetherington, E. M., Cox, M. and Cox, R. (1979) 'Play and social interaction in children following divorce'. *Journal of Social Issues*, 35, 26–49.

Hoffman, J. P. (1993) 'Exploring the direct and indirect effects on adolescent drug use'. *Journal of Drug Issues*, 23, 535–557.

Holland, J., McGrellis, S. and Arnold, S. (1996a) *Protective factors in adolescent smoking*. Report commissioned for the Department of Health. Institute of Education, London.

Holland, J., Mauthner, M. and Sharp, S. (1996b) *Family matters: communicating health messages in the family*. London: Health Education Authority.

Hundleby, J. D. (1987) 'Adolescent drug use in a behavioral matrix: A confirmation and comparison of the sexes'. *Addictive Behaviors*, 12, 103–112.

Hundleby, J. D. and Mercer, G. W. (1987) 'Family and friends as social environments and their relationship to young adolescents' use of alcohol, tobacco, and marijuana'. *Journal of Marriage and the Family*, 49, 151–164.

Isohanni, M., Moilanen, I. and Rantakallio, P. (1991) 'Determinants of teenage smoking, with special reference to non-standard family background'. *British Journal of Addiction*, 86, 391–398.

Jackson, C., Bee-Gates, D. J. and Henriksen, L. (1994) 'Authoritative parenting, child competencies, and initiation of cigarette smoking'. *Health Education Quarterly*, 21, 103–116.

Jacob, T., Krahn, G. L. and Leonard, K. (1991) 'Parent–child interactions in families with alcoholic fathers'. *Journal of Consulting and Clinical Psychology*, 59, 176–181.

Jacobs, G. A., Jerome, A., Sayers, S., Spielberger, C. D. *et al.* (1988) 'Family smoking patterns and smoking among eighth and tenth grade students'. *Applied Psychology: An International Review*, 37, 289–299.

Jessor, R. and Jessor, S. L. (1977) *Problem behaviour and psychosocial development: A longitudinal study of youth*. New York: Academic Press.

Jessor, R., Van Den Bos, J., Vanderryn, J. and Costa, M. (1995) 'Protective factors in adolescent problem behavior: Moderator effects and developmental change'. *Developmental Psychology*, 31, 923–933.

Johnson, C. A., Pentz, M. A., Weber, M. D., Dwyer, J. H., Baer, N., MacKinnon, D. P. Hansen, W. B. and Flay, B. R. (1993) 'Relative effectiveness of comprehensive community programming for drug abuse prevention with high-risk and low-risk adolescents'. *Journal of Clinical and Consulting Psychology*, 58, 447–456.

Johnston, L. D., O'Malley, E. M. and Bachman, J. G. (1984) *Drugs and American high school students: 1975–1983*. Washington, DC: National Institute on Drug Abuse Department of Health and Human Services.

Juon, H. S., Shin, Y. and Nam, J. J. (1995) 'Cigarette smoking among Korean adolescents: Prevalence and correlates'. *Adolescence*, 30, 631–642.

Kandel, D. B. and Wu, P. (1995) 'The contributions of mothers and fathers to the intergenerational transmission of cigarette smoking in adolescence'. *Journal of Research on Adolescence*, 5, 225–252.

Kannas, L. (1985) 'The image of the smoking and the non-smoking young person'. *Health Education Journal*, 44, 26–30.

Kearney, C. A., Drabman, R. S. and Beasley, J. F. (1993) 'The trials of childhood: The development, reliability, and validity of the Daily Life Stressors Scale'. *Journal of Child and Family Studies*, 2, 371–388.

Kelder, S. H., Perry, C. L., Klepp, K. I. and Lytle, L. L. (1994) 'Longitudinal tracking of adolescent smoking: physical activity and food choice behavior'. *American Journal of Public Health*, 84, 1121–1126.

Klesges, R. C., Meyers, A. W., Klesges, L. M. and La Vasque, M. E. (1989) 'Smoking, body weight and their effect on smoking behaviour: A comprehensive review of the literature'. *Psychological Bulletin*, 106, 204–230.

Konrad, K. M., Flay, B. R. and Hill, D. (1992) 'Why children start smoking cigarettes: Predictors of onset'. *British Journal of Addiction*, 87, 1711–1724.

Krause, N. (1990) 'Stress measurement'. *Stress Medicine*, 6, 201–208.

Kroger, J. (1996) *Identity in adolescence: The balance between self and other*. London and New York: Routledge.

Krosnick, J. A. and Judd, C. M. (1982) 'Transitions in social influence at adolescence: Who induces cigarette smoking?' *Developmental Psychology*, 18, 359–368.

Krueger, R. A. (1994) *Focus groups: A practical guide for applied research*. Beverly Hills, CA: Sage Publications.

Kupersmidt, J. B. and Coie, J. D. (1990) 'Preadolescent peer status, aggression and school adjustment as predictors of externalizing problems in adolescence'. *Child Development*, 61, 1350–1362.

Lamb, M. E. (1978) 'Qualitative aspects of mother-and father-attachments'. *Infant Behavior and Development*, 1, 265–275.

Landrine, H., Richardson, J. L., Klonoff, E. A. and Flay, B. R. (1994) 'Cultural diversity in the predictors of adolescent cigarette smoking: The relative influence of peers'. *Journal of Behavioral Medicine*, 17, 331–346.

Lavery, B. and Siegel, A. (1993) 'Adolescent risk-taking: An analysis of problem behaviors in problem children'. *Journal of Experimental Child Psychology*, 55, 277–294.

Lazarus, R. S. and Folkman, S. (1984) *Stress, appraisal and coping*. New York: Springer.

Lerner, R. M. and Spanier, G. B. (1978) 'A dynamic interactional view of child and family development'. In R. M. Lerner and G. B. Spanier (eds) *Child influences on marital and family interaction: A lifespan perspective*. San Francisco: Academic Press.

Leventhal, H. and Cleary, P. (1980) 'The smoking problem: A review of the research and theory in behavioral risk modification'. *Psychological Bulletin*, 88, 370–405.

Levitt, M. Z. and Selman, R. L. (1996) 'The personal meaning of risk behavior: A developmental perspective on friendship and fighting in early adolescence', in G. G. Noam and K. W. Fisher (eds) *Development and vulnerability in close relationships*. Mahwah, NJ: Lawrence Erlbaum.

Lloyd, B. and Lucas, K. (1996) *Why do young girls smoke? A quantitative/behavioural study*. Report commissioned by the Department of Health (United Kingdom).

Lotecka, L. and Lassleben, M. (1981) 'The high school "smoker": A field study of cigarette related cognitions and social perceptions'. *Adolescence*, 16, 513–526.

Lucas, K. C. (1994) 'The relationship between beliefs, attitudes, negative affect and changes in smoking behaviour during pregnancy'. PhD thesis, University of Sussex, UK.

McAlister, A., Perry, C., Killen, J., Slinkard, L. A. and Maccoby, N. (1980) 'Pilot study for smoking, drinking and drug abuse prevention'. *American Journal of Public Health*, 70, 719–721.

McCalister, A. L., Krosnick, J. A. and Milburn, M. A. (1984) 'Causes of adolescent smoking: Tests of a structural equation model'. *Social Psychology Quarterly*, 47, 24–36.

McCrae, R. R. (1990) 'Controlling neuroticism in the measurement of stress'. *Stress Medicine*, 6, 237–241.

McCrae, R. R. and Costa, P. T. (1990) *Personality in adulthood*. New York: Guilford Press.

McKennell, A. and Bynner, J. (1969) 'Self images and smoking behaviour among school boys'. *British Journal of Educational Psychology*, 39, 27–39.

McNeill, A. D., Jarvis, M. J., Stapleton, J. A., Russell, M. A. H., Eiser, J. R., Gammage, P. and Gray, E. M. (1988) 'Prospective study of factors predicting uptake of smoking in adolescents'. *Journal of Epidemiology and Community Health*, 43, 72–78.

Marcos, A. C. and Bahe, S. J. (1995) 'Drug progression model: A social control test'. *International Journal of the Addictions*, 30, 1383–1405.

Melby, J. N., Conger, R. D., Conger, K. J. and Lorenz, F. O. (1993) 'Effects of parental behavior on tobacco use by young male adolescents'. *Journal of Marriage and the Family*, 55, 439–454.

Metzler, C. W., Noell, J., Biglan, A. and Ary, D. (1994) 'The social context for risky behavior among adolescents'. *Journal of Behavioral Medicine*, 17, 419–438.

Michell, L. (1994) *Smoking prevention programmes for adolescents: A literature review*. Anglia and Oxford Regional Health Authority.

Millar, W. J. and Hunter, L. (1990) 'Relationship between socioeconomic status and household smoking patterns in Canada'. *American Journal of Health Promotion*, 5, 36–43.

Miller, T. Q. (1994) 'A test of alternative explanations for the stage-like progression of adolescent substance use in four national samples'. *Addictive Behaviors*, 19, 287–291.

Mitic, W. R., McGuire, D. P. and Neumann, B. (1985) 'Perceived stress and adolescents' cigarette use'. *Psychological Reports*, 57, 1043–1048.

Mittelmark, M. B., Murray, D. M., Luepker, R. V., Pechacek, T. F., Pirie, P. L. and Pallonen, U. E. (1987) 'Predicting experimentation with cigarettes: The childhood antecedents of smoking study (CASS)'. *American Journal of Public Health*, 77, 206–208.

Morgan, H. (1995) 'Drug use in high school: Race and gender issues'. *Journal of Educational Research*, 88, 301–308.

Moscovici, S. (1973) 'Foreword to C. Herzlich, *Health and illness*. London: Academic Press.

Moscovici, S. (1976) *La Psychanalyse, son image et son public*. Paris: Presses Universitaires de France.

Moscovici, S. (1981) 'On social representations'. In J. Forgas (ed.) *Social cognition*. London: Academic Press.

Moscovici, S. (1984) 'The phenomenon of social representations'. In R. Farr and S. Moscovici (eds) *Social representations*. Cambridge: Cambridge University Press.

Moscovici, S. (1988) 'Notes towards a description of social representations'. *European Journal of Social Psychology*, 18, 211–250.

Murray, M., Swan, A. V., Johnson, M. R. and Bewley, B. R. (1983) 'Some factors associated with increased risk of smoking by children'. *Journal of Child Psychology and Psychiatry and Allied Disciplines*, 24, 223–232.

Newcomb, M. D. and Felix-Ortiz, M. (1992) 'Multiple protective and risk factors for drug use and abuse: Cross-sectional and prospective findings'. *Journal of Personality and Social Psychology*, 63, 280–296.

Newcomb, M. D., McCarthy, W. J. and Bentler, P. M. (1989) 'Cigarette smoking, academic lifestyle and social impact efficacy: An eight year study from early adolescence to young adulthood'. *Journal of Applied Social Psychology*, 19, 251–281.

Noller, P. and Bagi, S. (1985) 'Parent–adolescent communication'. *Journal of Adolescence*, 8, 125–144.

NUD*IST: Q. S. R. NUD*IST 3.0 for Windows, Power Version, Education Edition. © 1985–1994. Qualitative Solutions and Research Pty Ltd, Melbourne, Australia.

Nutbeam, D. and Aaro, L. E. (1991) 'Smoking and pupil attitudes toward school: The implications for health education with young people'. *Health Education Research*, 6, 415–421.

Nutbeam, D., Macaskill, P., Smith, C., Simpson, J. M. and Catford, J. (1993) 'Evaluation of two school education programmes under normal classroom conditions'. *British Medical Journal*, 306, 102–107.

Oechsli, F. W. and Seltzer, C. C. (1984) 'Teenage smoking and antecedent parental characteristics: A prospective study'. *Public Health*, 98, 103–108.

Oei, T. P., Egan, A. M. and Silva, P. A. (1986) 'Factors associated with the initiation of "smoking" in nine year old children'. *Advances in Alcohol and Substance Abuse*, 5, 79–89.

Office of Population Censuses and Surveys (1994) *General household survey 1992*. London: HMSO.

Oygard, L., Klepp, K., Tell, G. and Vellar, O. (1995) 'Parental and peer influences on smoking among young adults: Ten-year follow-up of the Oslo youth study participants'. *Addiction*, 90, 561–569.

Parker, K. D., Weaver, G. and Calhoun, T. (1995) 'Predictors of alcohol and drug use: A multi-ethnic comparison'. *Journal of Social Psychology*, 135, 581–590.

Patterson, J. M. and McCubbin, H. I. (1987) 'Adolescent coping style and behaviors: Conceptualization and measurement'. *Journal of Adolescence*, 10, 163–186.

Patterson, G. R., DeBaryshe, B. D. and Ramsay, E. (1989) 'A developmental perspective on antisocial behavior'. *American Psychologist*, 44, 329–335.

Pederson, W., Clausen, S. E. and Lavik, N. J. (1989) 'Patterns of drug use and sensation seeking among adolescents in Norway'. *Acta Psychiatrica Scandinavica*, 79, 386–390.

Perry, C. L., Murray, D. M. and Klepp, K. I. (1987) 'Predictors of adolescent smoking and implications for prevention'. *Morbidity and Mortality Weekly Report*, 36, 415–455.

Pfeffer, J. (1993) 'An exploratory study of decision making as related to the tobacco and alcohol use of eighth graders'. *Journal of Alcohol and Drug Education*, 39, 111–122.

Piaget, J. (1971) *Biology and knowledge*. Edinburgh: Edinburgh University Press.

Pierce, J. P., Fiore, M. C., Novotny, T. E., Hatziandreau, E. J. and Davis, R. M. (1989) 'Trends in cigarette smoking in the United States: Educational differences are increasing'. *Journal of the American Medical Association*, 261, 56–60.

Presti, D. E., Ary, D. V. and Lichtenstein, E. (1992) 'The context of smoking initiation and maintenance: Findings with interviews with youths'. *Journal of Substance Abuse*, 4, 35–45.

Rantakallio, P. (1983) 'Family background to, and personal characteristics underlying teenage smoking'. *Scandinavian Journal of Social Medicine*, 11, 17–21.

Rauste von Wright, M. (1989) 'Body satisfaction in adolescent girls and boys'. *Journal of Youth and Adolescence*, 18, 71–83.

Regis, D. (1990) 'Is health education hooked on addiction?' *Education and Health*, 8, September/October.

Reid, D. J., McNeill, A. D. and Glyn, T. J. (1995) 'Reducing the prevalence of smoking in youth in Western countries: An international review'. *Tobacco Control*, 4, 266–277.

Rice, K. G., Herman, M. A. and Petersen, A. C. (1993) 'Coping with challenge in adolescence: A conceptual model and psycho-educational intervention'. *Journal of Adolescence*, 16, 235–251.

Roff, M., Sells, S. B. and Golden, M. M. (1972) *Social adjustment and personality development in children*. Minneapolis: University of Minnesota Press.

Rohrbach, L. A., Graham, B. W. and Hansen, W. B. (1993) 'Diffusion of a school-based substance abuse prevention program: Predictors of program implementation'. *Preventive Medicine*, 22, 237–260.

Rosenberg, M. (1979) *Conceiving the self*. New York: Basic Books.

Rowe, D. C., Chassin, L., Presson, C. and Sherman, S. J. (1996) 'Parental smoking and the "epidemic" spread of cigarette smoking'. *Journal of Applied Social Psychology*, 26, 437–454.

Sameroff, A. J. (1975) 'Early influences on development: Fact or fancy?' *Merrill-Palmer Quarterly*, 21, 267–294.

Santi, S., Best, J. A., Brown, K. S. and Cargo, M. (1990) 'Social environment and smoking initiation'. Special issue: Environmental factors in substance misuse and its treatment. *International Journal of the Addictions*, 25, 881–903.

Schaffer, H. R. (1990) *Making decisions about children: Psychological questions and answers*. Oxford: Blackwell.

Schaffer, H. R. (1996) *Social development*. Oxford: Blackwell.

Schultz, A. (1963) 'Concept and theory formation in the social sciences'. In M. A. Natanson (ed.) *Philosophy of the social sciences*. New York: Random House.

Seiffge-Krenke, I. (1989) 'Bewältigung alltäglicker Problemsituationen: Ein Coping-Fragebogen für Jugendliche'. *Zeitschrift für Differtielle und diagnostische Psychologie*, 10, 201–220.

Seiffge-Krenke, I. (1993a) Introduction to special issue on 'Stress and coping in adolescence'. *Journal of Adolescence*, 16, 227–233.

Seiffge-Krenke, I. (1993b) 'Coping behavior in normal and clinical samples: More similarities than differences?', *Journal of Adolescence*, 16, 285–303.

Selman, R. L. (1980) *The growth of interpersonal understanding*. New York: Academic Press.

Shulman, S. (1993) 'Close relationships and coping behavior in adolescence'. *Journal of Adolescence*, 16, 267–283.

Siegal, J. M. and Brown, J. D. (1988) 'A prospective study of stressful circumstances, illness symptoms, and depressed mood among adolescents'. *Developmental Psychology*, 24, 715–721.

Silvestri, B. and Flay, B. R. (1989) 'Smoking education: Comparison of practice and state-of-the-art'. *Preventive Medicine*, 18, 257–266.

Simon, T. R., Sussman, S., Dent, C. W., Burton, D. *et al.* (1995) 'Prospective correlates of exclusive or combined adolescent use of cigarettes and smokeless tobacco: A replication–extension'. *Addictive Behaviors*, 20, 517–524.

Skinner, W. F., Massey, J. L., Krohn, M. D. and Lauer, R. M. (1985) 'Social influences and constraints in the initiation and cessation of adolescent tobacco use'. *Journal of Behavioral Medicine*, 8, 353–376.

Spence, J. T., Helmreich, R. and Stapp, J. (1975) 'Ratings of self and peers on sex-role attributes and their relation to self-esteem and concepts of masculinity and femininity'. *Journal of Personality and Social Psychology*, 32, 29–39.

Stanton, W. R. and Silva, P. A. (1992) 'Children's exposure to smoking'. *International Journal of Epidemiology*, 20, 933–937.

Stice, E. and Barrera, M. (1995) 'A longitudinal examination of the reciprocal relations between perceived parenting and adolescents' substance use and externalizing behaviors'. *Developmental Psychology*, 31, 322–334.

Stough, C., Mangan, G., Bates, T. and Pellet, O. (1994) 'Smoking and Raven IQ'. *Psychopharmacology*, 116, 382–384.

Stough, C., Mangan, G., Bates, T., Frank, N., Kerkin, P. and Pettett, O. (1995) 'Effects of nicotine on perceptual speed'. *Psychopharmacology*, 119, 305–310.

Sussman, S., Dent, C. W., Stacy, A. W., Sun, P., Craig, S., Simon, T. R., Burton, D. and Flay, B. R. (1993) 'Project towards no tobacco use: 1-year behaviour outcomes'. *American Journal of Public Health*, 83, 1245–1250.

Sutton, S. R. (1987) 'Social-psychological approaches to understanding addictive behaviours: Attitude–behaviour and decision-making models'. *British Journal of Addiction*, 82, 355–370.

Swan, A. V., Cresser, R. and Murray, M. (1990) 'When and why children first start to smoke'. *International Journal of Epidemiology*, 19, 323–330.

Swan, A. V., Murray, M. and Jarrett, L. (1991) *Smoking behaviour from preadolescence to young adulthood*. Aldershot: Avebury.

Sweeting, H. and West, P. (1985) 'Family life and health in adolescence: A role for culture in the health inequalities debate?' *Social Science and Medicine*, 40, 163–175.

Tajfel, H. (1981) *Human groups and social categories: Studies in social categories*. Cambridge: Cambridge University Press.

Tajfel, H. (ed) (1982) *Social identity and intergroup relations*. Cambridge: Cambridge University Press.

Teichman, M., Barnea, Z. and Rahav, G. (1989) 'Sensation seeking, state and trait anxiety, and depressive mood in adolescent substance users'. *International Journal of Addictions*, 24, 87–89.

Terre, L., Ghiselli, W., Taloney, L. and DeSouza, E. (1992) 'Demographics, affect, and adolescents' health behaviors'. *Adolescence*, 27, 13–24.

Tildesley, E. A., Hops, H., Ary, D. and Andres, J. A. (1995) 'Multitrait–multimethod model of adolescent deviance, drug use, academic and sexual behaviors'. *Journal of Psychopathology and Behavioral Assessment*, 17, 185–215.

Tucker, A. L. (1985) 'Physical, psychological, social, and lifestyle differences among adolescents classified according to cigarette smoking intentions'. *Journal of School Health*, 55, 127–131.

Ullman, C. A. (1957) 'Teachers, peers and tests as predictors of adjustment'. *Journal of Educational Psychology*, 48, 257–267.

Urberg, K. A. (1992) 'Locus of peer influence: Social crowd and best friend'. *Journal of Youth and Adolescence*, 21, 439–450.

Urberg, K. A., Shyu, Shiang jeou and Liang, J. (1990) 'Peer influence in adolescent cigarette smoking'. *Addictive Behaviors*, 15, 247–255.

Van Roosmalen, E. H. and McDaniel, S. A. (1989) 'Peer group influence as a factor in smoking behaviour in adolescents'. *Adolescence*, 24, 801–816.

Vilhjalmsson, R. and Thorlindsson, T. (1992) 'The integrative and physiological effects of sport participation: a study of adolescents'. *Sociological Quarterly*, 33, 637–647.

Waldron, I. and Lye, D. (1990) 'Relationships of teenage smoking to educational aspirations and parents' education'. *Journal of Substance Abuse*, 2, 201–215.

Waldron, I., Lye, D. and Brandon, A. (1991) 'Gender differences in teenage smoking'. *Women and Health*, 17, 65–90.

Wallace, J. M. and Bachman, J. G. (1991) 'Explaining racial/ethnic differences in adolescent drug use: The impact of background and lifestyle'. *Social Problems*, 38, 333–357.

Wallerstein, J. S., Colbin, S. B. and Lewis, J. M. (1988) 'Children of divorce: A 10-year study'. In E. M. Hetherington and J. D. Arasteh (eds) *Impact of divorce, single parentship and step-parentship in children*. Hillsdale, NJ: Lawrence Erlbaum.

Wang, M. Q., Fitzhugh, E. C., Westerfield, C. and Eddy, J. M. (1995) 'Family and peer influences on smoking behavior among American adolescents: An age trend'. *Journal of Adolescent Health*, 16, 200–203.

Warburton, D. M. and Arnall, C. (1994) 'Improvements in performance without nicotine withdrawal'. *Psychopharmacology*, 115, 539–542.

Warheit, G. J., Biafora, F. A., Zimmerman, R. S. and Gil, A. G. (1995) 'Self-rejection/derogation, peer factors, and alcohol, drug, and cigarette use among a sample of Hispanic, African-American, and White non-Hispanic adolescents'. *International Journal of the Addictions*, 30, 97–116.

Webster, R. A., Hunter, M. and Keats, J. A. (1994) 'Personality and socio-demographic influences on adolescents' substance use: A path analysis'. *International Journal of the Addictions*, 29, 941–956.

Wells, L. E. and Rankin, J. H. (1991) 'Families and delinquency: A meta-analysis of the impact of broken homes'. *Social Problems*, 38, 71–93.

Welte, J. W. and Barnes, G. M. (1987) 'Youthful smoking: Patterns and relationships to alcohol and other drug use'. *Journal of Adolescence*, 10, 327–340.

Young, E. W., Jensen, L. C., Olsen, J. A. and Cundick, B. P. (1991) 'The effects of family structure on the sexual behavior of adolescents'. *Adolescence*, 26, 977–986.

Zuckerman, M. (1979) 'Sensation seeking and risk taking'. In C. E. Izard (ed.) *Emotions in Personality and Psychopathology*. New York: Plenum.

Zuckerman, M. (1988) 'Sensation seeking, risk taking and health'. In M. P. Janisse (ed.) *Individual differences, stress and health*. New York: Springer-Verlag.

Zuckerman, M. (1994) *Behavioral expressions and biosocial bases of sensation seeking*. Cambridge: Cambridge University Press.

Zuckerman, M. and Neeb, M. (1980) 'Demographic influences in sensation seeking and expressions of sensation seeking in religion, smoking and driving habits'. *Personality and Individual Differences*, 1, 197–206.

Zuckerman, M., Bone, R. M., Neary, R., Mangelsdorf, D. and Brustman, B. (1972) 'What is the sensation seeker? Personality trait and experience correlates of the Sensation Seeking Scale'. *Journal of Consulting and Clinical Psychology*, 39, 308–321.

Author Index

Subject Index